The Gwangju Uprising

The Pivotal Democratic Movement
That Changed the History
of Modern Korea

Communication

US gov ⟷ civilians
Korean gov ⟷ civilians
Troops ⟷ Civilians
Civilians ⟷ civilians
Civilians → country

The Gwangju Uprising

The Pivotal Democratic Movement
That Changed the History
of Modern Korea

Choi Jungwoon

Translated by Yu Young-nan

HOMA & SEKEY BOOKS
Paramus, New Jersey

FIRST AMERICAN EDITION

This book is published with the support of the Korea Literature Translation Institute in commemoration of Korea being the Guest of Honor at the Frankfurt Book Fair 2005.

Library of Congress Cataloging-in-Publication Data

Ch'oe, Chŏng-un, 1953-
    [Owŏl ŭi sahoe kwahak. English]
The Gwangju uprising : the pivotal democratic movement that changed the history of modern Korea / by Choi Jungwoon; translated by Yu Young-nan
—1st ed.   p. cm.
Includes bibliographical references and index.
ISBN 1-931907-29-3 (hardcover)—ISBN 1-931907-36-6 (pbk.)
1. Kwangju uprising, Kwangju-si, Korea, 1980. 2. Korea (South)—Politics and government—1960-1988. I. Title.
DS922.445.C49 2006
951.9504'3—dc22   2005019689

Homa & Sekey Books
3rd Floor, North Tower
Mack-Cali Center III
140 E. Ridgewood Ave.
Paramus, NJ 07652

Tel: 800-870-HOMA, 201-261-8810
Fax: 201-261-8890, 201-384-6055
Email: info@homabooks.com
Website: www.homabooks.com

Edited by Hal Piper
Printed in U.S.A.
1 3 5 7 9 10 8 6 4 2

CONTENTS

Foreword

It is my great pleasure that the translation of *Sociology of the Gwangju Uprising* has been made available for English readers in time for the 2005 Frankfurt Book Fair as *The Gwangju Uprising: The Pivotal Democratic Movement That Changed the History of Modern Korea*.

The character and meaning of the Gwangju uprising—the event of 10 days, from May 18 to 27, 1980, which took place in Gwangju, South Jeolla Province of the Republic of Korea—have yet to be fully defined. It was an event that is hard to describe with words. Numerous theories and conjectures have been put forth, but it is impossible to determine the truth of the incident. The event can be summed up as the clash and destruction of bodies. The objective facts, including the number of the dead, have not been fully revealed, and subsequently, the core of the event can never be defined with only words or photographs.

The essence of the incident is the experience shared by Gwangju citizens at the time. They went through a gamut of feelings—fear of death, humiliation, relief, sympathy, frustration, hatred, love, courage, gladness, elation, hope, pain, disgust and disillusionment—as they moved from life to death and braced themselves against rapids of emotions. The uprising has gained deep significance in Korean history partly because it exposed the cruelty of the military dictatorship, which resulted in a large number of civilian casualties; also, it revealed the people's yearning for democratization. The ramifications of the event, however, are more widespread, for the incident was like a disturbance at the end of one world and, at the same time, chaos at the beginning of a new world. We can say that South Korean history was rewritten in the wake of this event. All political and sociological ideologies came alive, in the temporal and spatial sense, in an area completely isolated from the outside world.

The incident began on May 18, 1980 with the military authorities' dispatch of two Special Warfare Command brigades to the heart of Gwangju to quell a university students' demonstration calling for democratization. The paratroopers brutalized all citizens, regardless of age and sex. As trained, they exerted all possible force on the demonstrators, short of opening fire. However, the citizens' resistance, unexpectedly, was not subdued. The next day, an additional brigade was sent in, then another brigade the following day, but the citizens' protest grew stronger. On the afternoon of May 21, paratroopers opened intensive fire in front of the Provincial Hall, which triggered citizens to wrest arms from various armories, including those of the reserve forces, and to start battling in the streets. The paratroopers withdrew from Gwangju on the evening of May 21, leaving the city "liberated." It wasn't until the re-entry of martial law troops at dawn on May 27 after several days of surrounding the city that some citizens attempted to negotiate with military authorities. They also worked to disarm their fellow citizens. With the re-appearance of the martial law troops, hundreds of youths who resisted at the Provincial Hall and other places were killed or arrested. This is the outline of the uprising accepted by everyone, regardless of their political leaning.

Despite the military authorities' relentless persecution, the Gwangju uprising was not buried in history, but instead ended up as a victory for the Gwangju citizens and Korean public. This is in part because the resistance continued after the incident. Yet the more fundamental reason lies in the Gwangju citizens' unprecedented fight against the paratroopers. In the face of the paratroopers' atrocities, they overcame the fear of death and humiliation and managed to take to the streets to recover their dignity. During the street battles, they found each other's greatness, and their appreciation of this characteristic bound them into an absolute community. They experienced one communal life, in which there were no private properties or individual lives. In liberated Gwangju, the absolute community showed cracks and ultimately disintegrated when citizens returned to their daily lives. Yet those who experienced the fervent hope of life could never forget the experience. This feeling was a driving force that changed contemporary Korean history. For those who went through the uprising in 1980, it was almost a religious experience, and as a social scientist, I feel honored to have studied this historical spectacle.

Choi Jungwoon
Department of International Relations
Seoul National University

Translator's Note

The Gwangju Uprising was an unprecedented incident in contemporary South Korean history in that the country's elite paratroopers cracked down on demonstrators and innocent bystanders in broad daylight. This prompted the Gwangju citizens to put up a brave fight, which resulted in hundreds of civilian casualties over the course of 10 days in May 1980. During and after the uprising, the military regime circulated rumors that North Korean spies and unsavory elements were responsible for the rebellion, misleading the public about the nature of the incident and casting the Gwangju citizens in an ominous light. On the other hand, anti-government activists glorified the incident as they tried to come to terms with the tragedy. When Professor Choi Jungwoon published *Sociology of the Gwangju Uprising* in 1999, it was touted as groundbreaking because there had yet to be any academic attempt to look at the event with such a balanced point of view.

The book originated from a paper the author wrote in 1997 for an academic seminar. Some Gwangju City Hall officials had attended a Korean Political Science Association executives' meeting, where Professor Choi was present, and offered to sponsor a seminar on the uprising. The attendants all agreed that it was due time to study the event; most Korean people, with the exception of those from the southwestern Jeolla region, had generally avoided the topic until then. A consensus was formed that those who were unfamiliar with the uprising should become involved in the project. One of the scholars suggested that Professor Choi be one of the presenters at the seminar. Professor Choi had not written anything about Korean politics and he was a complete outsider when it came to the Gwangju issue, both in terms of hometown and academic focus. A graduate of the Seoul National University Department of International Relations, he had obtained his doctorate in political science from the University of Chicago in 1989 with a

x

dissertation entitled "The Rise of the Knowledge State: the Establishment of Labor States in England, France, and the U.S.A."

At first Professor Choi was reluctant to take on the unexpected request that he deliver a paper on the uprising for the May 1997 seminar, but he began studying the discourses of the uprising with the eye of an outsider. During the seminar, he was struck by the intense interest of his audience, which was comprised of people from all walks of life. Soon he found himself almost obsessed with the so-called "Gwangju syndrome." The more he learned about the uprising, the more impressed he was by the ardent wish shared by many Gwangju citizens to uncover the truth about the event. He was affected by the range of feelings they had gone through, from fear to exaltation, as they moved from life and death during the uprising against the paratroopers' brutality. Confronted by frequent comments expressing incredulity and hostility about his research on the uprising, he experienced firsthand the prejudices and misunderstandings about the incident and vowed to present a fair view of this seminal event in Korea's democratization.

In *The Gwangju Uprising: The Pivotal Democratic Movement That Changed the History of Modern Korea*, the author analyzes the event in detail from different angles. To explain the magnitude of the uprising, he starts by delving into various discourses employed by different groups, from the military authorities to the media to the democracy fighters. Next, he describes how an absolute community—though fleetingly brief—was formed among the Gwangju citizens between May 18 and May 21, after paratroopers opened fire and demonstrators fought back by seizing arms from the armories throughout the city. He presents various sociological theories as to what prompted citizens to put up such a brave fight, although they were fully aware that they did not have a chance in defeating the paratroopers. The author goes on to examine the cracks that soon appeared in the citizens' absolute community, describing how the citizens coped in "liberated Gwangju," from the paratroopers' withdrawal on May 21 to their return on May 27. He attempts to explain the meaning of the final resistance by civilian militiamen and the death of young hard-line citizens. Professor Choi then analyzes the character of the Gwangju uprising in the context of contemporary Korean history and describes the aftermath of the event that forever changed the landscape of Korean politics.

Yu Young-nan
Seoul, Korea
May 30, 2005

Chronology of the Gwangju Uprising

May 17

21:40—An urgent government cabinet meeting is convened, where a resolution is passed to extend emergency martial law throughout the nation.

23:00—Some democracy fighters and student activists are rounded up nationally in a preliminary measure.

23:40—The Minister of Culture and Information announces that emergency martial law will be extended nationwide as of 24:00.

May 18

00:05—Some prominent democracy fighters in Gwangju are arrested.

01:00—The 33rd and 35th battalions of the 7th Brigade of the Special Warfare Command are sent to Chonnam National University.

10:20—Approximately 500 university students clash with paratroopers in front of Chonnam National University and advance toward the Provincial Hall.

11:00—Approximately 500 Chonnam National University students stage a sit-in in front of the Catholic Center on Geumnam 3-ga.

13:00—Paratroopers are dispatched downtown.

14:42—1,500 university students demonstrate all over Geumnam Avenue; police fail to quell the action.

15:40—The 33rd battalion of the 7th Airborne Unit launches an operation in front of the Catholic Center.

15:50—The 35th battalion of the 7th Airborne Unit starts an operation at Chungjang Avenue.

16:00—Demonstrators throw stones and set fire to police substations in Gwangju.

18:00—Paratroopers are sent to a rally site near Gwangju High School.

May 19

00:05-05:00—The 11th Special Warfare Brigade arrives in Gwangju, and the forces for clampdown are reorganized.

09:00—Crowds begin to gather on Geumnam Avenue.

09:50—The 33rd battalion is sent to quell demonstrators.

11:00—Armored vehicles and tanks are mobilized to suppress demonstrators.

13:40—Paratroopers and demonstrators clash in front of the Catholic Center.

14:50—The demonstration spreads the length of Geumnam Avenue. A fierce battle ensues, fires are set, and flamethrowers are used.

16:00—High school students join the demonstrators.

16:50—Gunshots are fired for the first time from a broken-down armored vehicle, seriously wounding four people.

19:40—Demonstrators set fire to the large arch in front of the Express Bus Terminal, and paratroopers confront them behind barricades.

20:00—Demonstrators set fire to police substations throughout the city.

23:08—The 3rd Special Warfare Brigade is dispatched to Gwangju.

May 20

0400—An appeal is posted downtown, urging citizens to rise up.

07:20—The corpse of Kim Haeng-bu is found in the empty lot of Jeonnam Brewery.

11:30—Three Special Warfare Command brigades are sent to Gwangju to stand guard.

14:20—The demonstration resumes. Paratroopers use flamethrowers at Seobang Rotary.

15:55—Thousands of citizens gather at Geumnam 4-ga, followed by a violent demonstration and police crackdown.

18:00—Some 200 taxi drivers gather at Mudeung Gymnasium and pass a resolution to participate in the demonstration.

19:20—Vehicles, headed by buses and trucks, advance toward the Provincial Hall as an act of protest.

21:13—Approximately 70,000 demonstrators gather around Geumnam Avenue.

21:30—Demonstrators lay siege to the Gwangju train station.

21:40—The Munhwa Broadcasting Company station is burned down.

22:30—A fierce battle takes place in front of the Gwangju train station, followed by sporadic gunshots.

23:00—Sporadic gunshots ring out in front of the Provincial Hall.

May 21

00:45—Demonstrators set fire to the Gwangju Tax Office.

02:13—Long-distance phone service is halted. The dailies *Jeonnam Maeil Ilbo* and the *Jeonnam Maeil Sinmun* stop their publication.

04:00—Martial law troops withdraw from the Gwangju train station.

05:00—The Korean Broadcasting System station is torched.

06:00—Demonstrators begin to race through the streets in seized vehicles.

09:49—Demonstrators attempt to attack the Provincial Hall with an armored vehicle seized at Asia Motors.

09:50—Citizens' representatives sit down with the governor to negotiate.

10:30—Martial law troops prepare to withdraw from the Provincial Hall, and the martial law commander issues a statement.

11:00—Demonstrators congregate in front of the Provincial Hall.

12:30—Demonstrating vehicles arrive from the neighboring cities and exhort citizens to participate in demonstrations.

12:58—Paratroopers open intensive fire on an armored vehicle racing toward the Provincial Hall.

13:00—Citizens begin to seize arms.

16:00—Trucks laden with arms arrive in Gwangju and weapons are distributed.

16:30—Paratroopers receive and follow an order to pull out .

20:00—Armed demonstrators and martial law troops stand in confrontation in many parts of the city.

May 22

04:55—Reinforced martial law troops continue to arrive on the outskirts of Gwangju.

08:10—High-ranking Provincial Hall officials discuss measures to settle the situation.

10:50—Citizens await the prime minister's arrival while preparing for a rally in front of the Provincial Hall.

12:00—50,000 citizens hold a rally in front of the Provincial Hall. The settlement committee members visit the Martial Law Command for a negotiation, which continues until 15:00.

18:00—The Student Settlement Committee is organized in the Provincial Hall.

19:00—The Martial Law Command issues a statement on the Gwangju situation.

22:00—Conflict appears among the citizens over weapons collection.

May 23

06:00—Stability is restored in Gwangju.

09:00—Professors and students gather at the Nokdu Bookstore to hold a protest.

11:20—The settlement committee members tour the outskirts of the city and begin to collect weapons.

13:00—The settlement committee members return 200 guns, and 34 students are released in return.

14:00—Paratroopers kill 18 innocent people of the Junam Village, near Gwangju.

May 24

08:00—Necessities of life are not available in Gwangju.

09:00—The martial law troops begin to deploy units for a crackdown operation.

14:05—Two martial law units mistake each other for civilian militia and exchange fire, resulting in civilian casualties.

15:00—The second citizen-wide rally to defend democracy is held in front of the Provincial Hall.

May 25

08:00—Two men in the civilian army in the Provincial Hall collapse, claiming they have been hit by poisoned needles (the poisoned-needle incident).

14:00—The Nam-dong Catholic Church Settlement Committee joins the Provincial Hall.

15:00—The third citizen-wide rally to defend democracy is held.

22:00—The Democratic Citizens' Struggle Committee is organized.

May 26

14:00-06:00—Martial law troops enter Gwangju.

04:30—Seventeen settlement committee members walk out of the Provincial Hall in protest of the martial law troops' entry, an act dubbed the "parade of death."

09:00—The settlement committee members visit the Martial Law Command Substation to hold dialogue.

11:30—The fourth citizen-wide rally to defend democracy is held.

12:00—The civilian militia organizes the mobile strike unit.

15:00—The fifth citizen-wide rally to defend democracy is held.

16:00—Catholic priest Kim Seong-yong escapes Gwangju to publicize the Gwangju situation.

May 27

00:00—The crackdown operation begins.

03:00—Fire is exchanged in front of Gyerim Elementary School.

04:30—A battle is waged in the Provincial Hall, which falls at 06:30.

05:00—The head of the Martial Law Command Substation issues a statement.

The Gwangju Uprising

Chapter One

Violence and the Politics of Language: Political Sociology for Discourse of the Gwangju Uprising

1. History of Silence

The Gwangju uprising was a rare incident in world history. One, it witnessed an immense scale of cruelty against citizens in broad daylight; and two, the residents of a city of 800,000 fought against 3,000 elite paratroopers from three brigades of the ROK Army's Special Warfare Command and held them at bay for several days in May 1980.[1] In terms of casualties, the incident was a massacre,[2] but it gave rise to a community in which all citizens were united as one with blood and tears and triumphant applause, however briefly. More than anything else, it produced numerous "citizens of Calais" who rose to the occasion and opted for death for the sake of their region and values. Both by its magnitude and by the depth of experience felt by everyone who was in Gwangju, the uprising was the biggest event in contemporary South Korean history after the Korean War. Its aftermath and meaning, as felt by Koreans today, are immeasurably heavy.

Despite this historical importance, silence has long shrouded discourse on the Gwangju uprising. Its immensity overwhelmed and prevented us from attempting to talk or write about it with our incompetent tongues and unreliable pens. Silence was imposed by different sources. From the outbreak of the uprising, the military regime controlled news coverage. Even after the media were allowed to report on the incident, silence, coerced by various methods, was broken only by official announcements. The military regime defined the uprising in its own way in June 1980 and kept mum for a long time thereafter; it repressed organizations and people related to the uprising in a bid to keep them quiet. Discussion began only after the legislative elections in 1985, which brought about a change in the political atmosphere. Also, openness followed in the aftermath of the student activists' seizure of the United States Information Service in May of the same year. Part of the truth was made public only during National Assembly hearings in 1988 and 1989, in the wake of a nationwide protest in June 1987 calling for democratization. Few people believe, however, that the truth about the Gwangju uprising has been fully exposed.

In other regions, a more complicated silence prevailed. In the beginning, the military regime's control over the uprising made it impossible to pursue information other than what was released, and this monopolistic discourse had a considerable impact on the silence. With the passage of time, the truth, relayed from person to person, sounded farfetched to those in other regions, and the details were so outrageous that it was difficult to recount them to friends and family members. For a long time, the Gwangju uprising was a topic the government dubbed "malevolent rumors." When people's actual experiences were made public through National Assembly hearings, most expressed outrage over the paratroopers' atrocities. The wide circulation of tales about the uprising coincided with the growing movement of radical dissident students and labor activists. This suggested that the uprising would be the cause solely of the activists. It was not that the middle class outside Gwangju supported the military regime. Rather, they may have harbored a vague fear that discussion of the uprising might radicalize the listeners and shake social stability, since they too were outraged upon hearing the details. Further, the moments of victory during the uprising that were broadcast on TV, such as the spectacle

2

of vehicle demonstrations and the Munhwa Broadcasting Company in flames, engendered anxiety and disbelief. The "minjung" (the masses or grass roots) were an object of new fear. The power of the minjung must have come as a surprise to the middle class; although the minjung had been expected to cause trouble from time to time, during the Gwangju uprising they armed themselves and held off the airborne unit, the cream of the ROK Army.

The Western middle class has a fear of a "mob" in its own way, which has worked as a motive for democratization and social reform. Even though Gwangju citizens have a homogenous ethnic community, people in other regions of Korea began to regard the same ethnic Koreans in Gwangju as foreign. In reality, fear of the minjung played an important role in the 1987 nationwide democratization campaign. In this sense, Korea's contemporary democracy has been realized at the expense of the bloodshed in Gwangju. Although people from other regions agreed with the battle cries of the uprising, supported its call for democratization, and sympathized with Gwangju citizens, they regarded both the minjung and Honam (Southwestern) residents with unease. In current South Korean politics, fear and awe of Honam people may eclipse that of the minjung. Residents of other regions have secretly felt threatened by the Honam people's consistent lopsided voting records since the Gwangju uprising and half-jokingly talked in private about the "Republic of Jeolla Province" and the "Republic of South Jeolla." It is hard to deny that people in other regions are conflicted over the Gwangju uprising.

Silence does not merely belong to those who suppressed or, conversely, aided the events in Gwangju. The oppression of the military regime aside, most participants and spectators have experienced linguistic frustrations. At the sight of what was happening before their eyes, the Gwangju citizens embraced each other, shuddered together, and cried out in despair, as if in a nightmare. Some might have begun to discuss their experience, but frustrated by the inadequacy of their words, they may have decided not to bring up the subject again. Many bravely stepped forward to give testimony, but may have found their words insufficient to describe what they had gone through. The reality of talking about Gwangju is that either words fail the speakers or that the experience of the uprising gets distorted by intemperate, even violent language. Isolation and silence still veil Gwangju and its uprising.

The hours between May 18 and May 27 were different from those before and after, both for the military and the Gwangju citizens. Various terms referring to this period have been introduced, which are controversial even today. That is why most Korean scholars refer to the days during this period merely as "May 18." This neutral name is not recent. The first official organization created after paratroopers withdrew from Gwangju on May 22, 1980 was the May 18 Settlement Measures Committee. Most of the committee members believed that what had happened after May 18 was accidental and could be wrapped up as if nothing had happened if the guns were collected and surrendered to martial law troops. Giving a neutral name to an incident means taking a stance in its own way. Other popular terms include the "Gwangju incident," the "Gwangju citizens' righteous resistance," the "Gwangju minjung uprising," the "Gwangju massacre," the "Gwangju minjung revolution," the "May 18 democratization movement," and the "May 18 minjung uprising," each defining the particular period in its own stubborn, unique way.

Since the Committee for Democracy and Reconciliation started its activities in February 1988, the government's official name has been the "May 18 democratization movement." Those who do not follow the government's view favor "minjung uprising." The former implies a political stance; the government since the Roh Tae-woo regime is the legitimate inheritor of the Gwangju uprising, and the event must be fitted into the existing governing ideology. The latter may be seen as descriptive of the reality of the times. The word "minjung," first introduced in the 1980s, connotes both a force that was allied with the democratization movement and the class-oriented character of the fighters in the uprising. The "Gwangju incident" has been the most widespread term in everyday conversation outside the Honam region since it was first used in the evening newspaper *Donga Ilbo* on May 21, 1980. The conflict over the various terms reveals the complexity of the experience, compared with the 1960 student uprising and the 1961 military coup d'état. It was impossible to define the event in a word or two. The 10 days in May 1980 were far from a short span of time for everyone concerned.

The diversity of interpretations failed to break down the wall of silence surrounding the uprising. Even today, the uprising is not an easy topic for everyone to discuss. Although many contradictions exist in the various interpretations, few debates have taken place. On the one hand, the interpretation of the event was not something that could be settled with a debate; it could be only resolved with violence or government power. On the other hand, those who disagreed with the military's position avoided debate, holding that the uprising contributed to democratization. The purpose of this chapter is to analyze several discourses about the Gwangju uprising and shed light on how they were constructed. Then, by revealing the limitations of these discourses against the backdrop of the depth of the uprising itself, I intend to open an arena of discussion regarding the uprising.

For the uprising to reveal its real spirit, it is time to send the dead to heaven. Rather than bickering stubbornly among the living, we need to tell the dead why they died and why they need to depart to the other world. The living must speak only from their own viewpoint, instead of killing the dead again by speaking on their behalf. There is no difference between scholarship and a shamanistic ritual when it comes to drawing a line between accounts of the living and the dead and helping the two sides to carry on a dialogue. The years after the event are too short to be recorded as history, and it may be too early to expect scientific rigor in researching the Gwangju uprising. I believe, however, that we must start while the memories are still fresh to ensure that true academic research can be conducted in the future. As far as the Gwangju uprising is concerned, the passage of time has not been a curing balm.

2. Frontline of Violence / Language

Students held daily rallies from May 14 to 16 in Gwangju and issued a series of statements, in lucid language, calling for democratization. Starting on May 18, however, paratroopers were sent to the front gate of Chonnam National University, and then to the intra-city bus terminal and Geumnam Avenue. They started slaughtering people, and students and citizens fought back, resulting in immense casualties. This extreme violence changed language a great deal.

1) Language of Violence and Struggle: from May 18 to 21

At the outset, the military authorities controlled the press to make sure that it would not report what had happened since May 18, and the dailies in the Gwangju area were forced to suspend publication on May 20. The first official mention came only in the Gwangju area from the National Police Headquarters. The first announcement by the Martial Law Command came on the afternoon of May 20; this was reported on the 7 o'clock evening news in Gwangju and its environs, but the media in Seoul kept quiet. According to this statement, light losses occurred due to disturbances on May 18 and 19, and all of the 176 arrested were released. Furious over the attitude of the broadcasting companies, the Gwangju citizens attempted to set fire to the buildings of the Munhwa Broadcasting Company and Korean Broadcasting Station that evening.[3]

The Martial Law Command issued its first nationwide announcement at 10:30 on the morning of May 21. This came when soldiers at the Provincial Hall were already being prepared to evacuate via helicopter and after live ammunition had been distributed.[4] This announcement, reported in the evening editions of May 21 and morning editions of May 22 in all of the Seoul dailies on their front pages in columns 1-3, had it that one civilian and five military and police personnel had died, that the "authorities are seeking measures," and that the incident had begun because "disgruntled elements, such as hooligans and Seoul students who had played a leading role in school disturbances, went to Gwangju in droves and spread malevolent rumors." This Martial Law Command statement viewed the Gwangju incident as an extension of previous student demonstrations. Then it put emphasis on the fact that the event developed in a different manner from previous student demonstrations, fingering "disgruntled elements, such as hooligans" as the core group in question. The key to this discourse was the theory of "malevolent rumors" and eight examples were provided.

The Martial Law Command seemed to have two goals in blaming the rumors. One was to preemptively deny the paratroopers' atrocities and transfer responsibility to another group. Many influential Gwangju citizens from all walks of life lodged complaints about the paratroopers' outrageous actions on May 18 and 19. It appears that blaming rampant rumors for escalating the incident was intended to stem the citizens' complaints.[5] It was one thing that rumors circulated among Gwangju citizens at the time, but it was another that these rumors were suggested as the cause of the incident. Going a step further, the theory of malevolent rumors linked political conspiracy with regional sentiment. The Martial Law Command's statement implied this: Remarks such as, "Gyeongsang Province soldiers came to annihilate the seed of Jeolla Province people," were intentionally concocted by a certain group, but they carried enormous power because Gwangju citizens already harbored regional animosities. As if shocked by the power of words, which seemed to have as much strength as violence, the military authorities put forth the theory of "malevolent rumors," but they themselves did not believe in the power of language.[6]

Following this statement, another announcement was issued in the afternoon of the same day in the name of the martial law commander, and it was reported on the front pages of the morning and evening papers. This was released after the troops opened fire on the crowd gathered in front of the Provincial Hall. The statement referred to the case as the "Gwangju incident" and suggested a different cause from the one offered in the morning.

The peaceful demonstration staged by hundreds of university students on May 18 developed into this current terrible situation because with the goal of driving it to extremity, a considerable number of impure personalities and fixed [North Korean] spies from other areas infiltrated into your region, agitated and provoked regional sentiment on purpose, and instigated riots by spreading farfetched malicious rumors, destroying and setting fire to public facilities, and looting equipment and assets.

Most of these people are impure elements who hope to worsen the current situation and the sympathizing hooligans and hoodlums who aligned with them, and they even went to the lengths of [attacking] a police armory. . . . Their ultimate goal is all too evident and it is crystal-clear that the worsening situation will lead to a catastrophic result for the state and the nation.

This press release, a revision of the morning statement, sounded as if the uprising were in a different league from student demonstrations. In addition, the "disgruntled elements" were removed, while "impure personalities and fixed spies" made an appearance for the first time as a major conspiring group. The statement went on to threaten that arms might be used. The announcement warned that "[the authorities] possess the authority to take

8

the necessary measures for inevitable self-defense," that "the rioters are few in number," and even cautioned the citizens to be "prudent and self-loving to prevent your region from being reduced to ashes, which will result in the destruction of your workplaces and homes." This statement was issued after firearms were opened on a crowd in front of the Provincial Hall. By the time it was printed in the dailies, all-level military units in the region had been officially instructed to exercise their self-defense rights and Gwangju had been completely cut off from the rest of Korea. Published on the same page of the newspapers was the "announcement of Kim Dae-jung's mid-term investigation results." Although this particular news release did not directly implicate Kim Dae-jung in the Gwangju disturbance, it strongly hinted at the possibility of his hand in it, by stating that he was alleged to have pulled strings behind the students.

The major feature of the military authorities' initial discourse was that there existed a conspiring group that had deliberately instigated the incident, and that members of this group intentionally provoked Gwangju citizens with malicious rumors. This theory was a device to conceal the real face of the uprising and suppress truth-telling attempts by government power. At the same time, it blamed the Gwangju citizens' regional sentiment as an underlying motive that fueled the incident. The intention of the conspiring group that took advantage of regional sentiment was purported to be against the state, but the identity of the group members was still blurry. Although certain parts of the discourse shifted depending on the situation, the basic direction and structure were consistent.

For the Gwangju citizens, the sickening violence from May 18 to 21 was a dominant reality, and their language was extremely emotional, far from systematic: it was almost a series of battle cries and exclamation marks. The refined words of the past, such as "democracy," were forgotten. The slogans most frequently shouted by demonstrators were "Down with Chun Doohwan!" and "Release Kim Dae-jung!" When the fight intensified, the cries grew violent: "Tear the limbs off Chun Doo-hwan and kill him!" and "Beat paratroopers to death!" This was not simply a matter of heightened vehemence. Whereas the usual rally slogan, "Down with . . ." was intended for the ears of Chun Doo-hwan and the general public, "Tear off his limbs and kill him" was not for the benefit of Chun's ears; rather, it was to appeal to the fury of fellow citizens. The language limited the range of the audience, i.e. the partners of linguistic exchange, and the target of "being torn off and getting killed" was excluded as a conversation partner with whom agreement could be sought. From May 20, the slogans turned desperate, such as "Let's die together!" and "Bring my dead son back to life!"

From May 19, various types of printed matter were distributed to the citizens. The representative example was *Fighters' Bulletin* penned by the Field Fire Night School Team led by Yun Sang-won, the leader of young Gwangju activists at the time. Before its appearance, there were a number of other leaflets, including the "plea" and the "declaration." Their language was similar.[7] All the fliers began by revealing the paratroopers' atrocious acts. They defined "Chun Doo-hwan and his gang" as their enemies in light of the paratroopers' brutality, the expansion of martial law, and the arrest of Kim Dae-jung. Simply put, they were the enemies because the paratroopers' atrocities were "no different from those of communists" and they were crueler than "the communists or the Japanese police."[8] The leaflets called for participation in a battle against these enemies, without exception, and appealed to the Gwangju citizens' "patriotism." In a considerable number of them, blatant abusive remarks and curses were used to convey hostility.[9]

On the morning of May 21, Yun Sang-won merged the leaflets published in various names as *Fighters' Bulletin* (JSRI 1991, 254-257). This bulletin would become the symbol of many leaflets during the uprising.[10]

Yun Sang-won's acute sense of reality encouraged him to delete the ideological term "democracy" from the title, turning it into the shorter *Fighters' Bulletin*, which successfully moved the hearts and minds of the citizens fighting in the street. The song most widely sung by the demonstrators was the "Song of Fighters." New lyrics replaced the sad song in a minor key that originally starts with the words, "Crossing over the bodies of our comrades-in-arms again and again." The song, by an unknown composer, was created during the Naktong battle[11] and has been widely sung by the ROK Army since then. Yun Sang-won could have come upon the name *Fighters' Bulletin* from the "Song of Fighters." The Gwangju citizens' mental and physical attitudes toward their uprising indicate that they identified more with the Naktong battle than with the 1961 Student uprising.

From May 21, *Fighters' Bulletin* not only encouraged the struggle by giving confidence with the impression of a systematic operation, including the continuous numbering of its issues, but also "hoped to become the citizens' eyes and ears." The information printed in this bulletin generally fell into two types. The first was about the movement of military troops, and the second had to do with the unfolding struggle. The latter was mostly exaggerated, such as that the struggle had spread to South Jeolla Province or throughout the nation. This was of course to encourage the resistance, but it was probably tolerated because citizens were primarily motivated by the existence of their enemies and their fury at them; they did not have time to reflect on what they wanted themselves. The enemy—those brutal beasts, demons, and evil spirits—had attacked, and for all Gwangju citizens it was their reasonable duty and "patriotism" to defend their hometown and family members.

People overcame the walls of fear surrounding them and joined ranks with their fellow citizens. In so doing, they recovered their dignity as human beings and obtained freedom, and they melded into a perfect community. This community of infinite affection felt like the "Korean nation" to them. Those who took up arms naturally became the "civilian militia." Gwangju citizens saw the image of "our country" while fighting paratroopers to defend their hometown. They sang the national anthem and "Our Wish Is Reunification" and waved the national flag. From time to time, the demonstrators shouted a somewhat incongruous slogan, "Kim Il Sung, do not misjudge," making it clear that with "our country," what they were envisioning was far different from North Korea, though it was not a country where military authorities and paratroopers ruled. The end of all this bloody protest was symbolized as a "torn flag."

The dominant reality of the uprising was a kind of situation in which people's blood surged to their heads and rendered them speechless, gasping for breath. The characteristic of the Gwangju citizens' discourse is that they shared the sensations they felt, rather than understanding and explaining the situation with logical language. They communicated with symbolic words, asserting that the paratroopers "beat up the citizens as if they were dogs," that they "dragged them as if they were dogs," that citizens were in danger of "being killed like dogs," and later that the paratroopers "should get paid for the price of blood." It is difficult to explain these words logically. These were expressions describing fragments of a concrete experience that could not be conveyed in ordinary language.[12] The act of writing, however, was a means to guide the struggle in a particular direction by imposing meaning on it. Yi Gwang-yong, a monk who returned from Naju to Gwangju on the morning of May 21, recalled his feelings as follows:

> Citizens—men, women, young, and old—all took to the streets, clapping and applauding. The atmosphere was almost like a festival. I began to think as I walked. Something seemed to be missing. There seemed to be no order, and everything seemed to be handled impromptu with a total lack of system; there seemed to be no leading force. I thought that someone had to play the leader. It appeared that a certain power was necessary to bind together the elated people, who were being swept up by the atmosphere. There, I felt the necessity of fliers. Making them was rather complicated, so I thought I could begin with

a placard to hang up and began to work on it (ICKHD 1990a, 5043:1017).

Unlike the slogans shouted by citizens in the street at the time, writing was created on the fringes of the struggle, rather than at the center. Writing—no matter how simple it is—was what intellectuals would come up with and put into practice. Their articles encouraging the struggle were a political action trying to impose meaning on the struggle and to lead the people's movement in a particular direction.[13]

2) Adhesion and Justification: From May 22 to 27

At the dawn of liberation, the whiff of revolution was strong in Gwangju. Its citizens saw in their struggle a community of the Korean nation and "our country," which was a "democratic country," or the "spirit of the national democracy" that had to be defended with patriotism. The picture of "our country" became more realistic with the retreat of martial law troops on May 21. Logically speaking, "our country" had no choice but to be the "country in opposition," another homeland, while "true patriotism" was an armed struggle against the ROK armed forces. Citizens of liberated Gwangju[14] discovered for themselves that they were at the crossroads between revolution and treason.

At about 8 a.m. on May 22, top officials of the provincial government convened a meeting, presided over by the deputy mayor (ICKHD 1990a, 81). Shortly thereafter, the deputy mayor held a series of meetings with influential local figures, followed by the formation around noon of the "May 18 Settlement Measures Committee," composed of 15 regional heavyweights. The committee members visited the Combat Training and Doctrine Command in the afternoon, and during the negotiation they forayed into the politics of discourse. In return for surrendering weapons, they demanded that "the airborne unit admit its extreme suppression." The deputy commander of the Combat Training and Doctrine Command admitted that "after hearing an on-site explanation of what happened I realize that excessive suppression had taken place." The committee requested a ban on the use of provocative terms (for example, "rioters") and got a reply from the Martial Law Command: "Innocent citizens have not been referred to as rioters; rather, the rioters are those who make ill use of their power. We have appealed to the higher quarters that gentle terms be used."[15] It appears that the committee members hoped to get concessions from the soldiers while exercising caution in order not to provoke them by using the mild expression "extreme suppression" for the airborne unit's brutality, the primary motive of the uprising, while the Martial Law Command seemed to have taken a step back by further neutralizing the reality with the use of "excessive suppression." In addition, the protest about the term "rioters," the term used in government fliers and frequent bullhorn warnings from helicopters, came from a third-party position that it would not do to provoke the citizens. From the fact that the committee members made a distinction between the paratroopers' atrocities and the use of "rioters" and took issue with them separately, it is also clear that the committee members tried to keep a distance from the position of the citizens involved in the struggle.

Soon after the settlement committee was organized under the auspices of the deputy mayor, it held talks with the Martial Law Sub-Station. Although the martial law authorities pressured the committee members to have the weapons returned, the martial law authorities supported the members' position to a certain extent so that they could be accepted by the citizens as their representatives. Most committee members favored "erasing" the incident; to dispel the revolutionary mood, they called for the collection and return of weapons. This stance, perceived by the citizens as "surrender," soon faced strong protest in a rally. While there are few records of the civilian militia's position, it was strongly against the committee's action. In particular, the militants clashed sharply with the student settlement committee, which was organized toward the evening. The civilian militia argued that the university students, who had backed off in the final stage of the struggle although they had initiated the resistance, no longer had a role to play. Amid this confusion, the issue of collecting weapons was kept alive for various reasons and justifications; in particular, the conservatives were conscious of the argument that the uprising might encourage North Korea to flex its muscle. The "poison needle scare"[16] on the morning of May 25 can be understood as the Martial Law Command's operation to undermine the elements clamoring for a continued struggle and to strengthen the argument for collecting and returning weapons.[17]

On the other hand, those who actively sought meaning and justification in the struggle mostly favored a continued fight. At 3 o'clock on the afternoon of May 23, a citizens' rally took place in the square in front of the Provincial Hall, led by Yun Sangwon, who had been fighting from the YWCA building. Kim Taejong, who presided over the meeting, received enthusiastic applause for his statement: "Democracy in this country is not just given. It is to be won with bloodshed and struggle" (ICKHD 1990a, 97; 4007:876). This remark, citing democracy as a justification of the Gwangju uprising, officially linked the two remote themes—armed struggle and democracy. After this statement, a number of essays and poems yearning for democratization were read aloud near the fountain in front of the Provincial Hall. The "democratization" slogan was never absent from the *Fighters' Bulletin* after its fifth issue, published on May 23.

Aside from the demand for democratization, the exposure of the paratroopers' atrocities and cruelty continued to occupy the largest part of the public discourse by the citizens of liberated Gwangju. The exposure of brutality was the primary reason for citizens' struggle, but it was also in response to the Martial Law Command's insistence that "malevolent rumors" and "rioters" fueled the incident. The stance revealed in "Our Opinion Regarding the Cause of the Gwangju Incident," released on May 25 in the name of the Gwangju Incident Settlement Measures Committee, an organization consisting of Gwangju citizens, was: "The brutality of the Airborne Special Warfare Command's slaughters infuriated 800,000 citizens, which sparked the citizens' uprising (righteous rebellion) as self-defense" (Gwangju City 1997 II, 64).[18] What we must note here is that the jump from fury to self-defense is not a natural course of logic. While fury expresses a strong emotional state, self-defense is a legal concept, an offensive defense carried out with a cool head. Kim Hyeon-chae relays the mood of the city on May 23 as follows:

> Citizens continued to clean up the streets. They were sweeping and repairing war wounds and damage strewn about. Revealed in the faces of all citizens cleaning up the streets was a firm belief. They exuded eerie calm; despite the profusion of bloodshed, they were neither stained with tears nor swept by extreme fury (Young Comrades Society of May 18 Gwangju Righteous Rebellion 1987, 107).

The struggle turned into self-defense after it was established that paratroopers and military authorities were the Gwangju citizens' enemies, objects to be fought with a cool head. Soon after the May 21 retreat of the martial law troops, citizens struggled to defend their region with their own hands, and the assertion that they should continue to defend their region and young people was naturally voiced. The expressions that smacked of the Martial Law Command—"Let us regain our reason" and "Let us return to our daily lives"—were suggested in this context, together with the declaration that they would keep fighting.[19] It appears that "democracy won through struggle," proposed by the resistance faction, was also understood in a similar context.

The word "democracy," as put forth after May 23, cannot be perceived as having the same meaning as it did before May

16

18. Democracy prior to the event was forgotten in the midst of blood, tears, and gun smoke. The lofty justification of protecting the region from enemies, which originated from the rhetoric of struggle, gave birth to the civilian militia, while democracy, discovered afresh, was the picture of their region that had been protected with blood from the enemies. "Defending our hometown with our own hands" and "democracy" were two justifications of the struggle during the uprising. The latter, despite its logical genesis from the former, seemed to be posited first in view of keeping consistent with the student demonstrations for democratization prior to May 18, and in consideration of the fact that democracy was the dominant political ideology of South Korean society at the time. Mixed in the Gwangju uprising discourse are democracy won by struggle and democracy as the universal political idea in South Korean society.

With the passage of time, the voices of the people who insisted on fighting until their demands were met gained the upper hand over the views of the citizens' settlement committee and the people gathered in the Provincial Hall calling for the surrender of weapons. The voice insisting on a continued fight became official with the formation of the "revolt leadership" on the evening of May 25. Its members argued that it was unacceptable to "sell the blood" of the Gwangju citizens and that the due "price of blood" had to be collected. This "price of blood, not to be paid on credit" meant the recovery of honor for the citizens. To be concrete, regaining honor meant receiving the government's official apology about the incident and compensation for damage. In principle, the "price of blood" was to secure the Gwangju citizens' ethical superiority over the regime in power. This demand, in turn, included the call for democracy as a yardstick of this ethical superiority.[20] Gwangju citizens finally found the discourse of community, starting from the discourse of struggle and by way of the discourse of state and war. They officially expressed their intention to secure their ethical superiority over the incumbent government, military authorities, and paratroopers as the condition of laying down weapons, giving up participation in a war, and returning to the rule of the existing state. Generally, it would be natural for the state to recognize a civic community's ethical superiority. For the sake of its own survival, however, it was impossible for the new military junta to accept the exposure of the airborne unit's actions.[21] This was because its behavior toward the general public was not merely a matter of its lower ethical standing; it was a crime against humanity. The Gwangju citizens could not put down their weapons and return to the state's rule without collecting their "price of blood." The reason, more than anything else, was that they could not permanently remain "rioters" after having been treated as less than animals by the airborne unit.

Gwangju was in total isolation. To the young people who were determined to resist, their last pronouncement was to "defend Gwangju to the death." They knew that in the face of martial law troops' military strength, they could not defend Gwangju, protect the Provincial Hall, obtain apologies, or achieve democratization. They understood, however, that some of them had to die for the "price of blood" that was not on credit, for the sake of the recovery of honor and rebirth of the Gwangju citizens. They did not opt for death for a war or a revolution; they did so for the morality and honor of the Gwangju community and the Korean nation. The cross to be borne by the survivors materialized itself, not because they were unable to fight bravely, but because they could be human only after dedicating those young people to the altar of sacrifice.

As can be seen by the fact that the Martial Law Sub-Station refrained from using the word "rioters" and partially admitted that "excessive suppression" had taken place, during this period the Martial Law Command focused on creating the conditions in which its forces could re-enter the city in a short period of time, by quelling the fervor of struggle without provoking the Gwangju citizens. After the "Gwangju incident" had been reported in the media, the Martial Law Command made sure that news companies wrote articles and editorials under its strict control, and official announcements and statements were released by the government, not by the Martial Law Command. The first statement was issued by the newly appointed Acting Prime Minister Bak Chung-hun on May 22. He did not enter Gwangju; he released his statement after being briefed at Songjeong-ri in the outskirts of the city. He distinguished innocent citizens from "rioters," pointed out that these "rioters" were not students, and emphasized that the military had restrained itself and that Gwangju at the time was in a "security vacuum." He supported the Martial Law Command's stance and attempted not to provoke the citizens, but citizens grew more rankled by his repeated references to "rioters."

During this period, the national media generally supported the innocent citizens' efforts to cope with the situation and restore the calm in the city, but they kept showing pictures of destroyed streets and dark smoke billowing out from burning vehicles. They made it clear that the government and the media were concerned about citizens, singling out a minority of "rioters." On May 22, newspapers printed a summary of daily events from May 18 amounting to the chronicle of a riot, in which paratroopers were not mentioned. Of the details, only the *Donga Ilbo* provided a glimpse into the incident between the lines.[22] Page 7, the social events page of Korean newspapers, published numerous articles and photos of citizens cleaning up the streets, detailing efforts to collect weapons and restore order. University students were always portrayed as innocent. During this period, the newspapers handled the Gwangju uprising in their editorials, and their attitudes were more or less the same. They all stressed a peaceful settlement and advised that readers exercise vigilance over "malevolent rumors." However, in editorials on May 23 and 25, the *Chosun Ilbo* stated that "it was not a time to determine who was right and who was wrong" and called for a rapid settlement, claiming that the Gwangju incident was a serious national security issue. On the other hand, the *Donga Ilbo*, in

19

its May 24 editorial, hinted at some sinister background, using terms such as "bitter grief" and "great indignation" without offering any explanation and then emphasizing the "fact that a makeshift measure, not fair principles and methods, will not do."

The representative discourse that cannot be left out during this period was President Choi Kyu-hah's special press statement aired nationwide on radio and television three times on the evening of May 25. It was a smooth piece of appeasement that emphasized the president's concern for the Gwangju citizens and took pains not to provoke them. He stressed that the situation should be settled through dialogue but expressed his concern over the possibility of the invasion by the North Korean puppet government. The logic of national security and the high time for a crackdown were the keys to the statement. In the morning papers of May 26, prominently printed next to the president's press statement was an article that "hard-liners" had taken over Gwangju's Provincial Hall the previous evening. This mudslinging effort to paint the situation as having reached its savage peak contrasted sharply with the president's statement. From this page, any reader could sense that an armed suppression was imminent. Earlier, published in the evening papers of May 24 and the morning papers of May 25 were articles about the capture of a North Korean spy at the Seoul train station. His mission in the South was to infiltrate Gwangju for the purpose of agitation. What was notable was that he had carried a hallucinogen for strong destructive activities.[23]

The articles about the martial law troops' operation on the morning of May 27 had screaming headlines but were short on details. Afterward, the Gwangju issue was mostly handled on Page 7, in the social affairs section, not on Page 1, the political page. The contents included the efforts of restoration, the government's support, and the nationwide "campaign to help the Gwangju citizens." Needless to say, none of the newspapers was stingy with praise for the efforts of the innocent Gwangju citizens who had maintained order despite difficult conditions.

If there were eye-catching articles, they were printed on Page 7 of the *Joongang Ilbo* on May 29 and 30. The May 29 article hinted at an enormous unresolved issue looming in the city by describing how Gwangju was weighed down by a heavy atmosphere and that the departing governor was at a loss for words when pressed to explain the situation. The next day, an article claimed that virtues had blossomed in anarchic Gwangju with few violent criminal acts, a sharp contrast to previous reportage about the "lawless world" where dark smoke billowed out all over the city.

3) Period of Judgment

With the armed crackdown by martial law troops on the morning of May 27, the Gwangju incident came to an end after 10 days. In the sky, helicopters showed off their armed prowess; orders came down through loudspeakers: "Citizens, stay home," "Civil servants, report to work early," and "Rioters, surrender yourselves." Thus the messages suggested, visually and orally, that everything was over, and made sure that the citizens knew who was in power. Soldiers sprayed disinfectant all over Gwangju, as if it were a city cursed by an epidemic, probably in an attempt to erase the shouts, sweat, and smell of blood permeating many parts of the city. For the time being, military authorities monopolized the privilege of defining the 10-day period beginning May 18. On May 31, the Martial Law Command issued a statement called the "Gwangju Incident." The entire text and its explanation were printed on Page 1 of all the dailies. Next to it, an article about the establishment of the National Defense Emergency Measures Committee attracted readers' attention. The Martial Law Command's announcement was a statement carefully drafted with its own logic.

An emphasis was placed on the fact that only in Gwangju did students cause a problem after the expansion of martial law on May 17. As if conscious of the weight of reality, the statement admits to, and simultaneously dismisses, "excessive suppression." With exquisite deftness, it notes that "the young soldiers and students, both full of vigor, lost their heads and ended up in confrontation with abusive remarks and shouts." The rest expands the previously published scenario. As before, "malevolent rumors" are singled out as the sole source of the Gwangju citizens' power: "Words stimulating and fanning regional sentiment, which are unimaginable with cold reason, instantly spread all over Gwangju, agitating citizens and pushing demonstrations to extremes." The statement goes on to say that spreading "malevolent rumors" and agitating citizens were "premeditated actions of fixed spies and impure elements." For evidence, it cites a clash in front of a correctional facility and the publication of the *Fighters' Bulletin*. In addition, it states that most of the "rioters" were "hooligans and impure elements who had particular political goals," emphasizing that students made up only about 30 percent of the throngs.

This statement fingers two groups as those pulling strings: "impure elements and spies," and "Kim Dae-jung, who manipulated the students' disturbances behind the scenes to achieve his impure political goal." The statement continues: "Kim's manipulation and instigation of his followers at Chonnam National University and Chosun University in Gwangju ignited the disturbance. During the investigation process, the fact that his diehard followers in Gwangju worsened the situation and intensified the course of the riot in a step-by-step, organized way kept coming to light" (JSRI 1998, III-4, 173-175). This statement gave military authorities an alternate conspiracy to blame for Gwangju: "impure elements and spies" or Kim Dae-jung's "die-hard followers."

According to this announcement, 144 civilians died during the ten days of the uprising. The analysis of deaths is quite interesting. In front of the correctional facility, 28 died and they were "impure elements" who tried to release leftist prisoners. Next came "32 who died in traffic accidents including overturned cars and collisions due to drunk driving and speeding" resulting from a "lawless world." There were 15 who died from gunshots, accidentally fired by their own side, and 17 who died in the process of controlling riots—these figures are the same as the announced death toll during the military's re-entry on May 27; if we accept these numbers, no one died before the final suppression. The rest were "murders committed in a clash between the hawks and the doves within the same group." Although the figure of the last category was not revealed, a quick calculation indicates that the number reaches 52.

The *Jeonnam Ilbo*, which resumed publication on June 2 after a long silence, printed a series of articles about the uprising. The title of the series, "Mt. Mudeung Knows It," moved the Gwangju citizens to tears. "Citizens" was the word mentioned continuously by articles that could not speak the truth. "Citizens" and "Gwangju citizens" named a community that affected the people of Gwangju during the uprising, and these terms were also lauded by the national media. These citizens included "armed rioters" and "disgruntled elements." The association of surviving family members of victims adopted the term "righteous rebellion" to link the uprising to the 1960 student uprising. On the same day, June 2, the *Jeonnam Maeil Sinmun* published the poet Kim Jun-tae's poem, "Ah, Ah, Gwangju, the Cross of Our Nation! " though a considerable part of it had been censored. The Gwangju citizens burst into tears after reading this poem. Many of them bought tens or hundreds of copies to send to their friends and families in other parts of the country or overseas. Soon after, the *Jeonnam Maeil Sinmun* was forced to close.

In June, leaflets penned by anonymous writers began to circulate. They rejected the May 31 Martial Law Command's announcement head-on. "The Truth of the Gwangju Situation," printed in June in the name of Roman Catholic priests in the Gwangju Archdiocese, accused the paratroopers of atrocities and claimed that a high civic spirit existed during the struggle (JSRI III-5, 177-179). Representative pieces of writing regarding the uprising were "Torn Flag" and "Truth About Gwangju Citizens' Righteous Rebellion," both of which were printed anonymously and distributed in June of 1980. Although they were written in contrasting tones and from different perspectives, both declare an intention to refute the Martial Law Command's statement.

"Torn Flag" details personal experience, vividly describing the writer's emotional journey. The gist is this: The most primeval sense of humanity drove them to fight, and such ethical judgment coalesced and was confirmed as a warm community of struggle. The tragic end and the promise of a second coming were symbolized in the image of a "blood-stained flag, torn and fluttering, that national flag of Korea with holes" in the hand of a child who had been gunned down and lay in the street. The meaning of the bloody struggle was symbolized as infinite love for the national flag and hometown, which was like a "mother's breasts" (JSRI III-8, 186-191).

On the other hand, "Truth About Gwangju Citizens' Righteous Rebellion" was a serious academic paper. After asserting that the uprising was not an unforeseen accident but "a concrete expression of democratic capabilities cultivated under Park Chung-hee's 18-year dictatorship," this paper systematically reviews the history of the democratization movement from the 1970s. It goes on to expose the airborne unit's atrocities with examples and rebut the government's arguments one by one, in particular the accusations against rioters, "impure elements," and regional sentiment. Going a step further, the writer argues for a change in perception about the United States, the first of its kind coming from a freedom lover, or a liberalist. He insists that Koreans have turned a blind eye to the United States' numerous unjustified actions. He posits that it is impossible to forgive the United States for approving a massacre in Gwangju targeting fellow Koreans and insists, "We must closely watch the United States with a new eye" (JSRI III-9, 193-207). This important work opened a new chapter in the discourse of the

Gwangju uprising. First, it points out that the uprising was far from accidental, but inevitable in the context of the democratization struggle. Second, it enlightens the Koreans, telling them to break away from the one-dimensional viewpoint of considering the United States a blood ally.

In June, another statement, titled "Truth About the Gwangju Situation," was issued in the name of the Army Headquarters. It appears that this release had a strategic relationship with the writings mentioned above and at the same time, it had the goal of revising and fleshing out the May 31 Martial Law Command's statement. It strengthened the mudslinging campaign against "rioters." The new statement dramatized the situation: the "impure elements" seized rifles on May 21 and "fired indiscriminately," caused more than 120 casualties by acquiring and spraying two light machine guns, and "at night, violent rioters staged shootouts in many parts of the city with the guns they had seized." The major change, however, could be found in its explanation about how the incident began and what caused it.

The statement lifted Kim Dae-jung to stardom by changing the primary political forces from "impure elements and spies" to "the followers of Kim Dae-jung": "When it proved impossible to carry out anti-government activities in Seoul in the wake of the May 17 measure, the problem students, including Kim Dae-jung followers, at such universities as the Seoul National University and Korea University—the students originally from Honam who had led the student demonstrations in Seoul—colluded with hooligans and infiltrated Gwangju. Joining forces with the local hooligans, they fanned regional sentiment, already rife with misunderstanding of the government." This time, "the pro-communist elements, including fixed spies" were pushed aside to play second fiddle. Naturally, once again a decisive role was assigned to "malevolent rumors," but another factor was added. The statement elevated the urban lumpen classes to stardom, placing them just below Kim Dae-jung: "Shouting the slogans such as 'all wealthy people must be captured and put to death,' they encouraged the participation of disgruntled forces, such as shoeshine boys, scavengers, junk dealers, factory employees, people with criminal records, and the unemployed." On the list of behind-the-scenes forces, in order of importance, were: Kim Dae-jung followers, hooligans and lumpen classes, and pro-communist spies. As for "excessive suppression," the following sophistry was offered.

> Although an argument has been raised that we should find out who was responsible for starting it all in the beginning, with the opinion that some of the military personnel's excessive deterrence fanned citizens' emotions immediately before the outbreak of the riot, on the whole it is extremely wrong to make it sound as if the cause of the worsened situation lay in the eruption of regional sentiment, and the general public believes that some impure elements acted the way they did with the calculation that the provocation and ill use of regional sentiment would make it easy for them to achieve their goals.

This sentence, quite a mouthful, is a good gauge of the military authorities' intelligence. The intention was to establish connecting links between discourses by binding the paratroopers' atrocities, malevolent rumors, and regional sentiment into one. Toward the end, the statement classifies 730 persons who were arrested. Among them, students accounted for only 18 percent, and then an unreasonable assertion was put forth: the rest were "the jobless, workers such as factory employees and day laborers, and scavengers" (JSRI III-13: 221-226). This passage seemed to have been drafted with a long-term goal in mind. Before, the Gwangju uprising was branded the handiwork of "impure elements" and "fixed spies," but now "the Kim Dae-jung followers" replaced them, putting Kim in the same boat as the uprising. To spoil the view of the incident being seen as a "righteous citizens' uprising," a spotlight was thrown on the urban lumpen classes and groups with a criminal bent as the majority of the "rioters." It was of course designed to push the middle class to turn its back on the Gwangju uprising.

If, by the end of May, the Gwangju citizens' discourse was a process to find the significance and direction of the struggle, the military authorities' discourse was controlled and strategically devised. We cannot say that the Gwangju citizens' discourse successfully linked justification of their actions with the meaning of the uprising. In particular, for five days in liberated Gwangju, citizens had to struggle for a long time, faced with a dilemma of discourse. By contrast, the military authorities adjusted their tone according to the conditions of military power and means of violence at the time, and when the two sides were at a standstill, they imposed self-restraint on the discourse. When the superiority of power was determined and the time came for them to define the case, the military authorities returned to the original version and relentlessly pronounced their verdict. They used the theory of "malevolent rumors" as the justification to round up people who talked about the Gwangju uprising, and they resorted to the rhetoric of "impure political groups" to remove annoying politicians and torture arrested people. At the same time, the theory of "malevolent rumors" branded the victims culpable by noting that the ultimate cause was "regional sentiment" harbored by the Gwangju citizens, a latent inclination that had been impossible to prove objectively until they went through an incident like the Gwangju uprising.

3. Language of Regeneration

Soon after June 1980, talk about the Gwangju uprising was all but stopped. It was of course due to Chun Doo-hwan regime's oppression. The discussion resumed only after the revival of student activist circles in the wake of the self-regulation measure granted to schools toward the end of 1983. A profound change had gestated during the hibernation of three years. Through study of the Gwangju uprising, student activists viewed the world with a different perspective, set the direction of struggle, and justified their existence. In 1984 and 1985, they published articles reinterpreting the uprising (Gang Sin-cheol et al. 1988, 95). By this time, student activist circles monopolized the discourse of the Gwangju uprising. They were the only ones who could dare bring up the forbidden subject.

"Ah, May! Permanent Flame of Democratization," published on May 19, 1984, by the Youth Alliance for the Democratization Movement, found "minjung" in the Gwangju uprising and proposed a new line of struggle. The word "minjung," the political lingo of our era, was invented by this group. Minjung was a third word starting with *min*, a concept embracing the two meanings ahead of it: "'democracy [*minju*]' that toppled dictatorship, the 'nation [*minjok*]' that rejected foreign powers and cried for reunification, and the 'masses [*minjung*]' who intended to realize economic equality in May 1980, are still vivid in our memory of Gwangju that May." (Minjung Culture Movement Council 1985, 428). If the nation was the main force of reunification, the minjung were the "mainstay of the democratization movement." Minjung were inclusive, meaning "all people other than a small number of the privileged class"—in other words, excluding a small number of the ruling classes—encompassing workers, youths, students, farmers, and religious people. It was a class that "intended to realize economic equality." The spectrum of the minjung cut across class, nation, politics, and economics. By 1984, in the discourse of activists, the main force of democracy was not citizens, but the minjung. The theory of minjung soon acquired a sweeping persuasive power.[24]

"Ah, Gwangju! The Cross of Our Nation," published in April 1985 in the name of the General Federation of Korean Christian Students, insisted that the uprising gave several important lessons to the student movement on several issues: First, the Korean people's potential; second, the issue of the United States; third, the attitude of the true struggle; fourth, the need to organize; and last, a thorough scientific perception and more intense practice. This essay is typical of its kind, which puts importance on three principles—attainment of democracy, reunification of the nation, and liberation of the minjung. The purpose of their movement is "to establish true democracy," "to secure the nation's right to survive among many foreign powers," and "to realize liberation of the minjung to eradicate their exclusion and inequality from the economy, politics, and culture" (JSRI 1988, III-20: 262). It goes on to insist that the three concepts of nation, democracy, and minjung are a single unified organism; therefore, it is not acceptable to entertain the idea of accomplishing the three goals step by step, because "there is no other way but to carry them out simultaneously." This article indicates that by 1985 the direction of struggle aspired after the revolutionary line, having already overcome bourgeois democracy.

The pursuit of three concepts beginning with *min* was the paradigm for student activist circles and dissident groups around 1985. What they meant by a "thorough scientific perception" was an effort to flesh out the logical structure of this framework. It should be pointed out that there is no logical explanation as to why the "three concepts" need to be solved simultaneously and why it is unacceptable to conceive a step-by-step solution. It is a dogma in keeping with the belief of wholeness. A similar dogma in this essay is the logic of self-reliance, a further indication that the student movement in this period had departed from the framework of bourgeois democracy. Finally, by 1985, the exaggeration of some realities of the Gwangju uprising began to appear, depending on the needs of the movement.[25]

During the students' struggle in May 1985, new interpretations of the Gwangju uprising appeared. Two writings—"Reexamination of Gwangju People's Resistance From a Perspective of Contemporary History," by the National Democratic Students Alliance and "Inquiry Into the Character of the Minjung Revolution for the May 18 Uprising," by the academic group of

Chonnam National University General Student Association—offered truly radical explanations.

The former analyzes, in a relatively objective light, the background and development of the Gwangju uprising and specific economic and class traits in the Gwangju area. This interpretation characterizes the minjung as an entity that reached a mature stage of consciousness thanks to previous movements, rather than a passive emergence of the masses. Going a step further, it claims that "members of the minjung demonstrated strength and a pattern with which reality could be changed and history could be created." When it comes to the issue of the armed struggle, however, the article assumes a cautious attitude, emphasizing that the armament and violence of the minjung were a means of self-defense (JSRI 1988 III-22, 273-281).

By contrast, the essay by the Chonnam National University General Student Association paints the minjung involved in the uprising in a romantic light and asserts that they were already fired up with revolutionary zeal. According to this argument, the uprising was manifested among the minjung as a "revolutionary explosion in a situation where political and economic contradictions" had piled up in South Korea, a "semi-feudal, new colony," since the 1945 liberation. The Gwangju minjung were clearly aware of their exclusion and waged a creative revolutionary struggle from May 20. Equipped with anti-American sentiment and high revolutionary awareness, they made "a qualitative leap into a civil war, the highest form of the minjung revolution" (JSRI 1988 III-34: 389-402). This essay, published to celebrate the fifth anniversary of the insurrection, attempted to recover the honor of the deceased by endowing them with revolutionary consciousness, paying scant attention to historical facts. According to this writing, the Gwangju uprising was not a tragic history, in which people were massacred, but a revolutionary struggle by the minjung, armed with acute awareness, to overcome the contradictions faced by the Korean nation.

During the nationwide students' protest in May 1985, a shocking "front-line struggle" was prepared, and the student movement, following its dramatic development, proposed radical interpretations of the Gwangju uprising. These interpretations, however, were based on examinations introduced in 1984. May 1985 was merely a period in which the direction, already set, was streamlined and popularized. In addition, "Re-examination of the Gwangju Minjung Struggle from a Perspective of Contemporary History" introduced a new term, the "minjung uprising." The minjung was discovered within the Gwangju uprising, and then it defined the event itself. The term "minjung uprising" was used to stress that the masses had waged a heroic struggle. The expression "Gwangju massacre" was employed when truth-finding and seeking punishment of those responsible were called for and the emphasis was placed on the minjung as victims.

The forcible seizure of the US Information Center and the subsequent sit-in, staged on May 23, 1985, in the name of the Committee for the Punishment of the Chief Instigator of the Gwangju Massacre, under the National League of General Student Associations, sent shockwaves throughout Korean society. Although the event manifested hostility against America, the very sentiment that spread in the Gwangju area after the uprising, it was, at the same time, a strategic choice by nationwide activist circles. The United States had aided and cooperated with the clampdown of the uprising. In addition, the US Information Service was a place of "extraterritoriality," where Korean police could not enter. For activists, this was the only place in which they could widely publicize their views. Only after this incident did the Gwangju uprising come to the fore as a topic of public debate. On May 30, 1985, the oppositional New Democratic Party submitted a parliamentary resolution to conduct an administrative fact-finding probe into the Gwangju incident. On June 7, Defense Minister Yun Seong-min was forced to submit a "Report on the Gwangju Incident" to the National Assembly

Defense Committee. It was the first and last report submitted by the government after its June 1980 announcement, and the contents of the two statements were more or less the same. The only difference was that, this time, the argument of "excessive suppression" was partially accepted, although it had been brushed off in June 1980, and the word "disturbers" replaced "rioters."

From July 1985, Korean monthly magazines began to compete with each other to report on the "Gwangju incident," linking it to the US Information Service case. Earlier that year, in May, the book *Beyond Death, Beyond the Darkness of the Era* had been published. The sale of this book was soon banned, but its publication caused enormous ripples. A limited number of copies were circulated in Seoul, other parts of the country, and overseas, but they still made a great contribution to changing the understanding of the Gwangju uprising. From this point, the national media began to write about the uprising from the Gwangju citizens' viewpoint and most Koreans refused to take the military's statements on the uprising seriously (Jo Gap-je 1988, 176). In the same year, Hong Gi-il burned himself to death in Gwangju, awakening numerous youths to redouble their struggle.

The June 1987 democratization movement was a result of the Gwangju uprising, but it in turn brought about a big change in the discourse of the uprising. The first factor of this change was the presidential election. The ruling party knew that Roh Tae-woo could win if Kim Dae-jung's political rights were restored to compete with Kim Young-sam. To restore Kim's rights, it made sense to rehabilitate the Gwangju uprising. Politicians scrambled to express their views of the Gwangju uprising and democratization; Roh expressed his opinion on July 2. After the December 1987 presidential election, the Committee for Democracy and Reconciliation was formed in February 1988, and started collecting testimonies about Gwangju. At the committee's recommendation, the government announced "Measures to Heal the Gwangju Incident" on April 1. "Excessive suppression" was admitted and apologies were offered to the general public. In addition, the statement officially rehabilitated the uprising to a certain extent by saying that "it was part of democratization efforts," and it announced a plan to compensate the injured and surviving family members of the dead. However, it put forth the position that it was unnecessary to punish those who had been responsible.

During this period the number of student activists, dissident groups, and labor activists swelled along with the spread of the Gwangju uprising discourse, and language became more radical.[26] Yi Jeong-no's "Shift in Revolutionary Viewpoint Regarding the Gwangju Rebellion," published in the May 1989 issue of *Labor Liberation Literature*, vividly exposes a political interpretation of the uprising. Earlier interpretations were simple treatises based on activists' internal testimonies. Yi Jeong-no's article targeted labor activists and intellectuals all over the nation. It attracted attention in that it dared to criticize the theory of minjung from the viewpoint of democratization, two previously inseparable concepts.

Yi stresses that the "working classes were the mainstay of the struggle" in the civilian militia and the minjung. The word "minjung" already held a class-oriented character in 1984, but efforts at the time were made to form a wide-ranging alliance against the military regime by emphasizing their inclusiveness, and for this reason, the importance of petit-bourgeois groups was not overlooked. By contrast, Yi Jeong-no, who seems to be aware of the swell in the activist sphere in the wake of the nationwide June 1987 democratization movement, asserts that the main force of the Gwangju struggle was the working classes. If the minjung had the propensity for struggle, it was because the working classes played the main role. With this, the Gwangju uprising was universalized by the Marxist logic of class struggle and revolution, going beyond its Korean, Honam specifics. Yi goes on to criticize liberals who defined the minjung as victims, as the "innocent" people who resisted, infuriated by the fact that the incident had been premeditated by the military. He asserts that the working classes in the Gwangju uprising had a guiding organization, organized a "struggle," and managed to establish a "temporary revolutionary authority." Although they were not successful due to time constraints, they possessed clear class-oriented hostility, the will to struggle, and revolutionary consciousness. Going a step further, Yi regards the Gwangju armed revolt as an event that incubates the minjung's will for revolutionary struggle. He asserts that the key lesson is the "issue of government power" and that the working classes must say goodbye to the bourgeois groups advocating free democracy and play a leading role (Yi Jeong-no 1989, 24-36). By this time, activist circles' interpretation of the Gwangju uprising rushed headlong toward the theory of class revolution and praise for armed struggle.

In 1989, the domain of social science entered the fold. On the one hand, this change came about because the interpretation of the Gwangju uprising from its citizens' viewpoint had been accepted as an established theory in Korean society. On the other hand, the shift was the result of a concern that the discourse of the uprising might be limited by the extreme revolutionary theory adopted by the activists. The spread of the discourse to social science was important, partly because the underground language of activist circles was lifted to university lecterns. No less important, the Gwangju uprising discourse began to reach an audience of intellectuals.

Nevertheless, it is difficult to agree that social scientists have adopted scientific rigor in debating the uprising. For example, they have yet to delve into the vagueness and duality of the concept of minjung. Also, their free use of words like "fascists" and "fascism" without precise definitions do not appear to have a theoretical ground, other than expressing distaste for bad people and regimes. In addition, most scholars studying the uprising make it abundantly clear that their goal is to carry on the spirit of the Gwangju uprising and the struggle itself. Thus in the sphere of social science, people with agendas have driven the discourse of the uprising. Indeed, the discourse of the Gwangju uprising in social science, which began to appear in 1989, has hardly departed from that of student activists before 1985. It is hard to escape the impression that social scientists took a step back from the crisp revolutionary theories that began to emerge in 1988.

From the start, the social scientists' discourse on the Gwangju uprising found a dogma in the methodology of social science. It may have derived from the student activists' popular slogan about neo-colonialism and state-monopoly capitalism, applying sociological methodology. At the time, social scientists agreed that the interpretation of the uprising should start with the explanation of structuralism.[27] They mean that the Gwangju uprising was a manifestation of the inconsistent structure in South Korea's modern and contemporary history after liberation from Japan in 1945, and that this inconsistency has national and class contradictions, a product of the global as well as monopolistic capitalist system. The two-pillar structure of contradictions triggered the emergence of new military authorities, which cracked down on democratization, in the wake of President Park's assassination in 1979. Then during the uprising, Gwangju became a place of explosion, with the accumulation of these structural inconsistencies.[28]

However, the foundation of the argument—that the Gwangju uprising was an inevitable incident triggered by unpreventable structural causes—is not derived from empirical research of the particular event. Rather, it is based on the linguistic structure of social science, in particular, of Marxist politics and economics. In other words, the discourse of social science dealing with the Gwangju uprising is a direct application of the discourse of positivist social science in the West. A serious problem is that such a discourse did not view the uprising as a specific event; by viewing it as but one link in a series of events or as a manifestation of "structural conditions," it buried the uprising. Social science leaning toward Marxism in South Korea is definitely a product of the Gwangju uprising. South Korean intellectuals accepted Marxist theories of economic determinism and class struggle at a time when revenge for the uprising was envisioned and a colossal struggle and revolution were hoped for. The discipline of social science in Korea, given birth by the theory of struggle for the uprising, rewrote its own history.

In May 1993, President Kim Young-sam issued a statement to express the government's position on the Gwangju uprising. This announcement, in its own way, restored the uprising as a democratization movement. It reiterated the Roh Tae-woo regime's definition, the "Gwangju democratization movement," depicting the event as peaceful in intent, not as the bloody, fierce struggle implied in "righteous rebellion" or "revolt." President Kim went on to place the Gwangju uprising in the tradition of a longtime resistance, centered on intellectuals, against military dictatorship. He offered ambiguous expressions to describe the meaning of the uprising, such as "occupying an imposing peak" and "blood in Gwangju was fertilizer for this country's democracy." As for fact-finding, he proposed leaving it "to history many years from now." Invoking a "new Korea" then eliminating room to re-discuss the spirit of the uprising, President Kim claimed that he himself had made efforts to publicize the event, and had gone through hardship for this reason. The "new Korea" was the legitimate inheritor of the uprising, whose "spirit must be transcended to the open spirit of participation and creativity toward creating a new Korea." Although the Kim Young-sam administration thereby rehabilitated the Gwangju uprising, it pulled out the event's claws and teeth by binding it together with the bourgeois notion called the "democratization movement." The emergence of another government discourse may be evidence that the Gwangju uprising is isolated from the perspective of the whole society, despite its place in Korean social science since 1989.

The Gwangju uprising was revived. It returned with a robust look, toughened up during its long isolation and silence.

The revived face was different, and its new name, the minjung, had two faces. "Minjung" now referred to a large number of people, everyone except monopolistic capitalists and their mercenaries; it included the endless throngs of people gathered on Geumnam Avenue on May 20. These people from different walks of life were a community of absolute love, where "words were not necessary," and the Gwangju citizens experienced the Korean nation at first hand in this community. Secondly, the minjung were the urban poor and lumpen classes at the bottom of the social hierarchy, who fought fiercely against paratroopers and died while resisting. So, the "minjung" were a beautiful incarnation of love but also were comprised of brave fighters. The minjung, with two simultaneous faces, were reborn from the burial places of "citizens." Intellectuals wanted the beautiful minjung and a vast community for democratization, whereas activist circles wanted brave fighters for a new country. As if these two faces were one, they were called by one name. "The structural conditions," to which both the activists and social scientists clung with tenacity when they talked about the Gwangju uprising, might have been a chant in a rite praying for the resurrection of the minjung.

4. Discourse and Reality

1) Theory of "Rioters"

Although examining the validity of this rhetoric may have little meaning today, it is necessary to review this concept. The word "rioters" was used continuously from May 19 in various official government statements, including loudspeaker urgings and press relations material. The word was replaced by "disturbers" in the defense minister's "Report on the Gwangju Incident" in June 1985 and disappeared after the establishment of the Committee for Democracy and Reconciliation. On the surface, "rioters" refer to those who participated in violent rallies and to those who committed violent acts. This is not only a term that refers to people who simply committed violent acts; it also judges certain violent actions morally and condemns those who committed them. This is why Gwangju citizens were infuriated by the word "rioters." The word was openly used to justify the use of arms against them, and this discourse was put forth with government power looming large in the background.

"Rioters" refers further to people who went around using violence routinely, not simply those who exercised unjust violence. As Prime Minister Bak Chung-hun put it in a conversation with journalists, "The armed rioters—they are the problem." They were seen as the lumpen proletariat classes, hooligans, scavengers, the jobless, laborers, shoeshine boys, and beggars—who were referred to as "disgruntled elements" by the military from the outset. The term "rioters" was continuously used to define the character of the entire incident; the groups listed above took the opportunity to express their deep-seated discontent and resentment against society by resorting to violence and setting fire, which propelled the incident to spread out of hand.

This rhetoric is sufficiently refuted by the fact that these classes that participated in the uprising showed a civic spirit during the liberated period of the struggle.[29] The logic of class revolution—that they were on the forefront of the struggle and demonstrated civic spirit because they constituted the lowest rung of society—is not persuasive. That these classes exhibited civic spirit while standing at the vanguard of the struggle can be primarily understood with the logic of circumstances and the social system. The uprising was a struggle in which all citizens participated, not only these groups. The situation was an extreme emergency, where everyday life was suspended; grandfathers and grandmothers were clubbed, not to mention students and youths, and even children were slaughtered. In such a situation, it may be logical for the community to expect people who rely on their physical strength to make a living and are good at fighting to come forward voluntarily, and that the rest of the citizens demand that they play frontline roles.[30] If the struggle was a battle of spoken or written words, professors and university students would have stepped forward as a matter of course. In their own way, the intellectuals did perform such duties. What we must keep in mind is that at the time of the incident, the Gwangju citizens' system of voluntary division of work and impromptu organization worked to a surprising degree. The fact that the urban poor stood in the vanguard of street fights, and criminal gangs declared their cooperation with citizens' self-governing activities, was the manifestation of their civic spirit; their participation did not compromise the spirit of the uprising at all.[31]

It is apparent that the Martial Law Command put forth the theory of rioters with the goal of justifying itself. Given that the uprising was long misunderstood in Korean society, we may regard this goal as having been accomplished to a certain degree. It also appears that this rhetoric brought about several political results. Some Gwangju citizens accepted the "rioters" argument during the liberated period, and for this reason the civilian militia was disarmed rapidly. In Gwangju and the whole South Jeolla Province, this rhetoric was an important mechanism to repress all citizens who had participated in the incident—the "rioters" troubled the participants for a long time, as much as using violence did. Many of the injured and arrested could not help being aware of the sharp eyes on them, as arduous to bear as physical pain.

2) Theory of "Impure Political Groups"

The argument of "impure political groups" was officially raised by the Martial Law Command soon after opening fire on the afternoon of May 21. The military authorities were able to propose it because they monopolized investigation rights, legal authority, and the apparatus to inflict physical violence. The purpose of this discourse was to threaten demonstrators that inordinate violence would be meted out, and, at the same time, to alienate citizens from one another. In a series of the Martial Law Command's statements, the key elements of the "impure political groups" went through a change. At first they were "fixed spies and impure elements," later to be replaced by the "group following Kim Dae-jung." Political considerations seem to have triggered this change.[32]

None of those arrested was indicted as a spy. According to various testimonies, military authorities had initially intended to torture many detainees in a bid to brand them spies, but they shifted the gears midstream and prosecuted "the group following Kim Dae-jung." Among those indicted as ringleaders of Kim's followers, Yun Sang-won, who orchestrated the revolt in the final hours of the uprising, had a continuous relationship with the National Alliance (National Alliance for Democracy and National Reunification) led by Yun Bo-seon, Ham Seokheon, and Kim Dae-jung.[33] However, Yun Sang-won cannot be viewed as a person who acted on someone's instigation or was backed by operational funds, for he had been deeply involved in the movement for workers and the poor, and possessed a considerable level of social and political consciousness.

The explanation that the Gwangju citizens fought under the sway of lies and instigations concocted by Kim Dae-jung, fixed spies, or North Korean spies lacks credibility. We must ask these questions: How much operational money and by whom would make people fight against paratroopers? How much instigation would it take to make them fight?[34] This explanation may lead to an assertion that those who were agents of such groups agitated the demonstrators to worsen the situation. But such exhortation can be effective only when many are already risking their lives at the forefront of the fight. In conclusion, the rhetoric of "impure political groups," no matter how it is revised, has no persuasive power. We may understand that this explanation came from a commonsense belief that an incident like the

Gwangju uprising could not have happened without someone's organized action behind the scenes. As I will explain in detail, however, this particular uprising went beyond common sense.

We may have to leave room for further research on North Korea's activities. Although the actual effect of any such operations is doubtful, the North may have made its own efforts. According to many testimonies, the North Korean radio reported the uprising as if it were broadcasting a live event, and many Gwangju citizens learned the news through the North Korean radio (ICKHD 1990a, 1035; 2008; 2034; 2038; 3006; 3021; 3078; 3123; 6044, etc.). It is certain that a considerable number of North Korean agents were active in the region at the time.

3) Theory of "Malevolent Rumors"

The rhetoric of "malevolent rumors" constitutes the most crucial part in the military authorities' discourse of the uprising. It appears that in the short run this argument was put forth to conceal the paratroopers' atrocities with a preemptive attack on reports of atrocities. In the May 21 press release, the Martial Law Command cited eight examples of "malevolent rumors," and most of them had to do with the airborne unit's cruelty. Most of these rumors have been since proved correct through citizen testimonies. At a higher level, the practical function of this rhetoric was to punish those who told the truth about the event; many, including journalists, were arrested on the allegation of spreading malicious rumors.

The biggest problem of this theory is that it blamed Gwangju citizens' regional sentiment as the fundamental cause of the uprising. The discourse claims that someone intentionally fabricated rumors to influence citizens, such as "Gyeongsang Province soldiers came to annihilate the seed of the Jeolla people." In this case, regional sentiment, unconsciously harbored deep in the hearts of Gwangju people, is offered as a factor that is impossible to rebut objectively. It cannot be denied that regional sentiment—more concretely, the resentment over discrimination against Jeolla Province (Gang Jun-man 1995)—played a role in the uprising. I will return to this point later, but it is impossible to regard resentment over discrimination as the prime cause of the uprising.

It may be impossible to find the person who first made up the rumor about the Gyeongsang Province soldiers. Was it the Martial Law Command? Was it a certain group in Gwangju? Did it come from the Gwangju citizens' misunderstanding? However, many soldiers and officers in the airborne unit went around shouting at the top of their lungs with thick Gyeongsang Province accents: "We will be killin' all Jeolla bastards!" "We're gonna annihilate their seed!" It is also true that commanders and commanding officers with thick Gyeongsang accents ordered operations through bullhorns (ICKHD 1990a, 3053; 650; 3055; 652; 7082: 1358; 7106: 1402; 7131: 1445; 7155: 1506). On May 20, demonstrators witnessed that intelligence agents instigated the crowds by playing up regional sentiment.[35]

Whatever was the case, the theory of malevolent rumors does not work as the direct cause for citizen participation. According to testimonies, many Gwangju citizens heard rumors about Gyeongsang soldiers through their families and friends on May 18 and 19. Few of them were thickheaded enough to swallow them and plunge into a demonstration. Upon hearing them, they doubted their ears and wanted to find out whether they were true. Most went out to the streets to check, and the paratroopers' actions convinced them in the streets that such rumors were practically true.[36]

A number of people, including Kim Yeong-taek, who covered the scene as a reporter and published a testimony later, raised a question whether the military can justify itself for mentioning malevolent rumors as a reason for its action. According to testimony in the National Assembly hearing by Brigadier General Choe Ung, commander of the 11th Brigade, Special Warfare Commander Jeong Ho-yong expressed concern over rampant rumors and ordered him to take caution while telling Choe to go to Gwangju around 3 o'clock on the afternoon of May 18. It was before the 7th Brigade launched an operation in Gwangju; logically, it is impossible that rumors existed then. If General Choe's testimony is true, we must conclude that the military leadership at the time was poised to spread rumors. If it is not true, why did General Choe give false testimony to the National Assembly? (Kim Yeong-taek 1996, 59-60; Gwangju City 1997 IV, 362-363; Jeong Sang-yong et al. 1990, 166)

4) Theory of "Excessive Suppression"

The awkward conjoining of two words—"excessive" and "suppression"—may show that the party that came up with this expression had not given it deep thought. The phrase first appeared in the May 24 document, "Report on Consultation During our Visit to Martial Law Sub-Station," distributed to citizens in the name of "all members of the May 18 Incident Settlement Measures Committee." According to it, the committee members during their May 22 visit to the sub-station complained about "extreme suppression" and the deputy commander of the Combat Training and Doctrine Command immediately said, "After hearing on-site explanations, I admit that it was excessive suppression" (Gwangju City 1997 II, 51). The general's jargon revealed the military's penchant for pedantry. This discourse appears to have been created through a sort of agreement in the process of dialogue.[37]

It was a tactical agreement reached at a deadlock of power. Contained in it are a shred of objectivity and the intention to avoid provoking the other side. Upon regaining strength, the military denied using "excessive suppression," and it was officially brought up again only in a situation where power was in balance during the Roh Tae-woo regime.[38] Intellectuals representing the Gwangju citizens perceived this discourse as blaming both sides. We may admit at least that this explanation contains a thread of truth, not simply unilateral self-justification or mudslinging. To understand the citizens' motives for struggle, we need to follow the direction indicated by this expression. This term ultimately means that the suppression was too harsh. The chief of staff of the Combat Training and Doctrine Command later insisted, however, that the suppression of the uprising was far from harsh.[39] On the other hand, in the eyes of the Gwangju citizens, the paratroopers did not appear to be "guys who came to Gwangju to control a demonstration" (The Association of Surviving Family Members of Victims 1989, 68). They argue that the purpose of the paratroopers' entry into the city was to kill people, not to quell a demonstration. The problem begins with the fact that the paratroopers' repression could not follow standard riot police methods, in particular the ways of the US forces. In Korean society, if the government opens fire on its citizens, it means the end for the regime, as was the case in the 1960 students' uprising. Therefore, at first the military did not intend to open fire during the incident and thoroughly controlled live ammunition.

The paratroopers during the 1979 Busan-Masan incident and the Gwangju uprising relied on special control measures, which might have been suitable for the characteristics of the South Korean army and its paratroopers. The airborne unit's suppression was what could be called "demonstrative violence." Fear was to be instilled in observers by meting out relentless violence on captives. The onlookers would be too frightened to stand around, let alone to participate in a rally. The target of the paratroopers' violence was not its recipients, but the gathered spectators.[40] Gwangju during the uprising was a theater of violence. To kill or not to kill was not an issue. The basic principle of suppression was to create terrifying pictures—beating, stabbing, slashing—that were excruciating to watch. Special riot police sticks had been ordered in April for this purpose, and bayonets were in use from the start of the crackdown. The paratroopers' atrocities had their origins in the government authority's unusual use of violence in South Korean society. They pandered to South Korean society's tolerance of routine violence, though it will not forgive opening fire on citizens. In other words, the military turned the tables regarding the ethical standard, or more precisely, the standard of political legitimacy—a demonstration that "violence is all right as long as there is no shooting."

Such violence was neither a repression of demonstrations nor a garden-variety beating. It was a visual language conveying a crystal-clear message: "To us, you are not human beings." The violence—in particular the terrifying acts that are still remembered as the stuff of legend—showed adroit skills acquired through intensive training and long exercises, mostly honed during the Vietnam War. These acts were not an offensive instinct of human beings, an expression of fury, or the effect of hallucinogens. The paratroopers during the uprising represented barbarism crafted by civilization on the foundation of reason. If the Gwangju citizens' desperate resistance inherited the spirit of the Naktong River battle during the Korean War, the paratroopers' violence harked back to the Vietnam War.[41]

The 1979 Busan-Masan disturbance was easily quelled by paratrooper violence. In Gwangju, it is difficult to say decisively what conditions drove the citizens to resist. Their protest cannot be explained as a reaction against the paratroopers or as a response based on primal instincts. The victims of violence felt wronged, and were furious about the injustice. Many people said they experienced enormous fury when they saw others being beaten and murdered. Fury aside, they were scared, which was the aim of the paratroopers' violence. Some overcame fear and participated in the struggle, but many more ran away instinctively. Many of them testified that they had felt so ashamed of themselves afterward that they got drunk. Cruelties inflicted on the weak triggered particular fury, such as when they saw grandfathers and grandmothers being beaten and women being sexually harassed. A common expression was, "I felt as if blood were surging to my head." Frequent expressions found in testimonies referred to the deliberately dehumanizing effects of the violence: "They beat people as if they were dogs" and "dragged them like dogs and put them in trucks."

The next-stage emotion was guilt. Those who ran away were woefully aware of their helplessness and wretchedness. This emotion went beyond pity. It was anger at acts that violated human dignity, complete with humiliation and fury over their own helplessness to respond and fearful trembling in the aftermath of violence. Paratroopers treated human beings like animals, and at the same time, this violence made those who were forced to confront their own weaknesses feel like subhuman entities. The Gwangju citizens' anger was double-edged.

The fury over humiliation and dehumanization had its origin in the fear of violence. And so, the Gwangju citizens risked their lives to fight paratroopers. They struggled to recover their humanity. The message of the violence was that the human beings who suffered from it, those who watched it, and, by extension, all the people of this era and all over Korea were not human. Furious, the people of Gwangju lost their senses and crossed the death line.[42] By joining the ranks of the struggle, they were liberated from beastly humiliation and became dignified human beings. We can fathom the meaning of Father Kim Seong-yong's sermon on May 25.

> Now, we must crawl with four paws, stick our mouths into bowls when we eat like dogs and pigs, and live like beasts. It is because the heirs of Yusin treated us as animals, beat us, dragged us around as if killing dogs, stabbed us, and shot us. . . . If we want to walk on two feet and live like human beings, we must plunge ourselves into the struggle of democratization. We are now paying for our silence in the past, the price of cowed silence (ICKHD 1990a, 1008:177).

Dignity is a basic human moral need. It is a basic value in any society, well beyond the values of the era and the ideology written by theorists, such as democracy, freedom, equality, and human rights. The Gwangju citizens' resistance to the paratroopers' violence was not instinctive; it was a conscious claim of basic human value.

Fury over inhumane violence does not explain everything about the uprising, however. It was a primary factor; but when this trigger was pulled, many other factors—each of which could not be separately developed into a protest—kicked in. Ideological justifications, such as democratization, were offered atop this primary justification.

5) Theory of Democratization

This was the most general explanation persistently put forth during the uprising, and it occupies the status of orthodoxy in South Korean society, comprehensively defining the uprising. It appears to have become the orthodoxy after the political forces that called for democratization named themselves the descendants of the uprising and glorified the event. In this discourse, the uprising was triggered by the students who participated in demonstrations before May 16, and paratroopers were dispatched with the goal of crushing their demands for democratization. The decisive ground for this explanation is that in many treatises published after the withdrawal of the martial law troops on May 21, democratization was the theme that appeared most frequently. The fact that many participants in later years explained their struggle as a drive for democratization supports this view. It has a dimension that cannot be brushed off.

However, the relationship between the Gwangju uprising and democracy is not simple. Although President Kim Young-sam likened the Gwangju uprising to an "imposing peak" in Korea's democratization movement, Father Jo Bi-o called it "a hardship and a historical turmoil."[43] In reality, there is a gap between the event and the struggle for democracy. The situation after May 18 consisted of a struggle against the paratroopers with the participants' lives on the line. The paratrooper unit was dispatched by "Chun Doo-hwan and his group" to Gwangju after staging a coup d'état and arresting Kim Dae-jung. It was therefore known that the paratroopers were composed of an element representing dictatorship, the opposite of democracy. Fighting dictatorship is a necessary condition for democratization, but there is no guarantee that it is sufficient. Furthermore, many citizens did not know who Chun Doo-hwan was and what the slogans in the rallies were. The demand for democratization triggered the Gwangju uprising, but in the big picture of the event, it was merely a blueprint or a background.

In fact, the demand for democratization was forgotten until May 22 or 23 after the paratroopers' retreat. When the citizens cried out for democracy after May 23, it had a different meaning from the democracy call prior to the uprising. Students and intellectuals shouted for democratization more loudly than anyone else, but many of the people who resisted to the end were not familiar with democracy. It appears that the values—which the leadership of liberated Gwangju and the civilian militia hoped to defend to the death although they failed to describe them precisely—cannot be embraced with just one word: democracy. These values could not be compared to a democracy that can be obtained through political negotiations and compromises.[44]

Democracy seemed to have two meanings to the citizens of liberated Gwangju. First, the paratroopers' atrocities originated from dictatorship, and only when democracy was established could the violence that trampled on human lives and dignity be eliminated. To this end, the paratroopers had to be repelled from their region, even if it meant resorting to violence. In this case, democracy was a systematic goal to be achieved by means of violence. Therefore, democracy had a secondary value and a secondary means between a realistic method and an ultimate goal. Democracy appeared to be everything, but it could not help being vague and double-faced in its relationship with violence. This is equivalent to the theory of democratic revolution.

Second, the demand for democracy appears to be part of an effort to break away from isolation and dilemma in the face of the revolutionary atmosphere, which they had not intended. The rhetoric of democratization links the event to peaceful student demonstrations prior to the Gwangju uprising, and at the same time it is connected with the universal political ideology of Korean society at large. Democracy during the uprising had two discourses. The first, related with the theory of revolution, was that a "democratic country" had to be created and defended, even if by force. The second indicated that democracy was a universal political ideology of South Korea. The first was a realistic notion of democracy during the uprising, and the second was a discourse with a political purpose, suggested by the Gwangju citizens in order to overcome a dilemma they found themselves in.

6) Theory of the Minjung

Although the word "minjung" had been used in the catchphrase, "the police are the walking sticks of the minjung," it was not until around 1984 that the word began to carry socio-political baggage. This unique concept came into being in the course of interpreting the Gwangju uprising. The concept is not derived from foreign social science theories; it appeared as a "*synthese*" of the experience during the uprising, the flag of the uprising's regeneration.[45] The word "minjung" is a unique double-edged concept that embraces almost all Gwangju citizens on the one hand, but on the other connotes exclusivity, referring to the groups at the very bottom of the social hierarchy that participated in the final struggle of the uprising.

Calling the crowds and fighters in the uprising "the minjung" negates the existing concept of citizens; this negation sprouted from the "disgruntled forces," whose weight continued to increase after their first appearance in the Martial Law Command's May statement. The command attempted to alienate the Gwangju uprising from the Korean middle classes with the assertion that most demonstrators belonged to the lowest rungs of society—hooligans, scavengers, the jobless, and factory workers.[46] If the "impure political elements" of the Martial Law Command's statement—whether they were "fixed spies" and "impure elements" or "Kim Dae-jung's followers"—were the producers in the theater of violence, the groups of the lowest social echelon were the main actors on the stage, the antagonists of the paratroopers. Around 1984, student activists revived "disgruntled elements" as the minjung in interpreting the Gwangju uprising. The rhetoric of the minjung can be then understood as a discourse created in the process of dialogue and mutual exchange, rather than one imposed by one side.

When this "minjung" theory was first presented, its inclusive character was emphasized. The minjung comprised people from all walks of life who participated in the uprising, except for undemocratic political elements that were not part of the uprising and some members of uncooperative bourgeois classes. With just a minimum of exclusiveness, therefore, the minjung formed a tripod with the existing concepts of democracy and nation. Although this third leg appeared last, it was the most important. Now, after the emergence of this third leg, democracy and nation could stand on their own, buoyed by a poetic cadence. At the same time, their exclusiveness made it possible for the minjung to become a main force of the struggle, the mainstay of the nation's self-cleansing. In the late 1980s, particularly after the nationwide democratization protest in June 1987, more focus was placed on the lower-echelon social groups who had fought to the end during the Gwangju uprising as an example of the congruence of the theory of the minjung with Marxism, which stresses the working classes. The minjung became paratroopers of a new country, fighting fiercely against military dictatorship.[47] The assertion that the uprising should be called the "minjung uprising" was first raised in 1985, and it caught on by 1987 or 1988.[48] The strength, and simultaneously the weakness, of the concept of the minjung is that it connotes class and at the same time has a politico-economic meaning. Empirically and objectively, the crowds during the uprising exhibited traits of class. But we cannot know that they subjectively fought for class. Even in liberated Gwangju, demands or slogans concerning economic issues, in particular redistribution, were extremely rare. From May 23, student activists and youths led by Yun Sang-won, a representative personality when it came to advanced struggle consciousness, urged "ordinary citizens" to "return to normal life" through "Democratic Citizens' Platform" and "To Democratic Citizens" (Gwangju City 1997 II, 47). The conscious exclusion of social reform led to a dilemma. The intention of returning to a semblance of society prior to the uprising gave rise to the logic of "settlement factions" calling for the "annulment" of the uprising. The minjung did not fight for their interests as a class. The question whether the minjung, as a class, struggled for democratization yields a skeptical answer. The theory of the minjung is logically linked with that of democratization, and therefore the two explanations are not mutually exclusive, but in conflict.

If the minjung participated in the uprising as a congregation of several classes, it must be understood as ethos, or *habitus*, rather than class interest. If there existed a "structural factor," rather than economic factors in the emergence of the minjung as a main force of the struggle, its roots might be found in the class-oriented worldview and lifestyle achieved over a long period of time on the foundation of economic factors (Bourdieu 1985). During the uprising, the issue of participation in the struggle was a decision as to whether to risk life to join the community. The bourgeoisie, in possession of family members and assets, were expected to control their fury with their characteristic individualism and rational thinking; they stayed at home or took refuge. In short, the participants had a more class-oriented understanding or desire for democracy, while the bourgeoisie, who were reluctant to join the demonstrators, lacked courage in the face of physical violence.

The more educated the citizens were, the less they participated. The basic principle of education, prior to acquiring knowledge, lies in discipline, which encourages people to control emotions and obey authority. The lumpen proletariat perhaps jumped into protest without mental conflict, because they did not have family members or assets. They were not used to rationally controlling their emotions, but were accustomed to a lifestyle in which "loyalty is paramount." Thus they put community before individuals.[49] Besides, as members of the rock-bottom class of society, they might have been more infuriated than anyone else about the paratroopers' violence. For them, it also could have been compensation to belong to the same community as other classes while standing on the forefront of the struggle.

The "[revolutionary] dynamics of the minjung" that emerged in the uprising, as often quoted by Han Seung-won (1987), must be approached in a realistic way. The rock-bottom classes were quick to respond to the daily deprivation of human dignity, before they sought democracy, socialism, or economic compensations. The lifestyle and worldview of the downtrodden might have prompted violent fury in them, which was much stronger than that of any other groups. They may have felt that they had nothing to lose when they stepped forward to the front lines of the struggle, and they may have been buoyed by the other citizens' applause and cheers. Both the urban lumpen classes, who found themselves in a situation perfect for their temperament, and the middle classes, who watched them with some distaste over their newly arrogant appearance, must have smelled a strong whiff of revolution and sensed that the world had turned upside down. The primary motive for retrieving firearms from the civilian militia lay in the citizens' anxiety over these lumpen classes and armed youths. The Gwangju citizens struggled against "devilish" paratroopers. But the minjung's dynamics was structural, rather than a circumstantial response to the struggle.

Dull and outdated though it is, "class consciousness" explains that differences in social classes manifest themselves in the degree of human dignity distributed within society; economic goods and production means are merely part of it.

7) Theory of Revolution

The theory of revolution grew from the theory of the minjung. It was put forth in 1989, but already some part of the minjung theory seemed to thrust toward the revolutionary explanation.[50] The gist of the revolutionary theory is that the Gwangju uprising took place as the minjung were in the process of acquiring revolutionary consciousness in 1980. No revolutionary theory claims that the minjung started the Gwangju uprising. It claims that amid the uprising, the minjung and working classes consciously attempted to stage a revolution and carry out an armed insurrection in an organized manner. There is no need to point out that this argument exaggerates and distorts the Gwangju uprising, and the full-fledged form of this theory is not empirically valid.

Yet this theory is important. First, it may be valid for liberalists to criticize the defense of the "minjung"—who were said to have voluntarily waged the struggle without any organization. The Gwangju citizens' community did, in fact, play an important political role. Second, the Gwangju uprising had a definite "whiff of revolution." It was far from a rally or a demonstration calling for democratization. Armed citizens waged battle with martial law troops, and briefly liberated Gwangju. The overturned Gwangju was enveloped by a revolutionary atmosphere. However, the uprising and revolution were neither simply quelled by arms nor frustrated by a failure of social consciousness. The mood of revolution was strongly rejected by the Gwangju citizens, and for this reason the discourse of the Gwangju uprising was bogged down and developed into an indecipherable form.

Those who carried out organized activities from the beginning were few in number, including student activists centered on the Nokdu Bookstore, led by Yun Sang-won, the Wild Fire Night School team, and the theater activist group, Clown. Yun Sang-won and his followers encouraged organized resistance from the afternoon of May 18, printing leaflets and manufacturing Molotov cocktails (JSRI 1991, 226). The Nokdu Bookstore was a sort of situation room in the early hours of the resistance. But it is difficult to accept that the organization, centered on Yun Sang-won, played a leading role in pushing forward the uprising. As soon as the martial law troops withdrew, the members of this group debated whether to step to the forefront. In the end, they centered their activities on the YWCA, keeping a distance from the Provincial Hall. On the evening of May 25 when the mood was leaning toward surrendering weapons, Yun Sang-won armed some 70 university students and entered the Provincial Hall. In effect, he formed the Democratic Citizens' Struggle Committee, a leadership body of the revolt. Little came of it, however.

If an effective political system was in operation throughout the uprising, it was the community of Gwangju citizens. This emerged on the evening of May 20 when the paratroopers were put on the defensive and the space for citizens' activities was secured. Impromptu organizational activities took place; Jeon Ok-ju and others mobilized citizens and exhorted them to struggle. In markets, middle-aged women provided food and beverages to demonstrators. All citizens voluntarily sought suitable activities to do, and the young members of the lower social strata took turns staying up all night on the front lines of the demonstration.

More than anything else, the demonstrators in vehicles that appeared on the evening of May 20 were organized on the foundation of the community, rather than the minjung or working classes. What pushed them into action was that some drivers had been killed, but these drivers joined an all-citizen struggle with the mightiest weapons in their possession. Such an undertaking was impossible without the cooperation and tacit approval of many car owners; it will not do to exaggerate a few car owners' lack of cooperation.

The decisive index of the community's activities was blood donations. Anecdotes involving barmaids' "clean blood" reveal the status of the community at the time. Blood was a part of the body for all citizens to share in order to keep each other alive, and at the same time a symbol of the gruesome struggle.

It was not only a few leaflets that defined the military authorities and paratroopers as enemies. The Gwangju citizens were practically unanimous in saying that "we should protect our region and families with our own hands," and such an imperative was expressed in various phrases—"defending the right to survive," "we must fight in order to live," and "self-defense." These clearly constituted a political discourse created within the community. If individuals wanted to survive, they could run away or hide; many people, in particular the bourgeoisie, behaved this way. The phrase, "we must fight in order to live," means that life and death, having already gone beyond the dimension of individuals, were defined at the community level. The phrase indicates that such a definition of life and death was common sense for many citizens, including children.[51] The description of the paratroopers—"it was impossible to imagine that they were of the same nation"—fell into the political discourse of the same vein. The community carried out the political action of separating the "enemies" from "our side" in the manner of the German political and legal thinker Carl Schmitt, and all citizens felt that life and death were an affair of the community, not that of individuals (Schmitt 1976). The community's definition of enemies was absolute.

The paratroopers were regarded as enemies and of an alien nation because even communists had not behaved the way they did. From the citizens' perspective, the paratroopers' operation targeted Gwangju with the definition that all citizens were their enemies. As a result, the struggle between citizens and paratroopers rushed headlong toward Carl von Clausewitz' concept of absolute war (Clausewitz 1976). There were no rules or norms in this battle and Gwangju turned into a "city of darkness." Although the expression "self-defense" referred to a common norm, the language of revenge—"Let us dispel the resentment of our dead sons and daughters," often uttered among Gwangju citizens—was the formula that confirmed the absence of law. With large-scale shooting by paratroopers on the afternoon of May 21 and Geumnam Avenue soaking in blood, the "war" began against the unforgivable paratroopers.

The community's struggle took place with all the citizens' bodies and everyday language as vehicles, without leaders or theorists. The community of Gwangju citizens defined life and death by the community as a whole, and defined the military authorities and the paratroopers as enemies in a bid to protect the community's life, people's lives, and humanity. "Our side" was painted as "patriotic citizens," "the Korean nation," the South Korean flag, and the South Korean anthem, which were taken from the existing logic of the state and its symbols. Citizens sang war songs and created an odd scene by singing the national anthem as if it were a war song, fast in staccato. This indicates that the community against the South Korean Army manifested its identity as an alternate state and symbolic system. At the same time, they denied that the barbaric paratroopers were "the troops of our country," and the community claimed itself as an orthodox state authority. Before it had its own independent language and symbols, the community was absorbed into a nationalistic discourse system.

Community politics created the discourse of struggle, but it faced a dilemma when Gwangju was liberated. After the community repelled some South Korean military forces by resorting to a language of the state and its symbolic system, the emergence in liberated Gwangju of another sovereignty corresponding to the incumbent Republic of Korea's government authority might have been something to shout for with joy, and at the same time a nightmare. A majority of the citizens and militants were filled with patriotism as the founders of a new country, and the mood of revolution was strong in many parts of the city. The citizens in liberated Gwangju ferreted out suspected spies, pledged loyalty to the Korean nation and the Republic of Korea, recovered reason, and called for a return to normal life in order to get rid of the lurking temptation of revolution. To do so, they asserted that weapons should be retrieved and surrendered, which led to the conclusion that everything that had happened during the uprising was to be annulled. However, the civilian militia and many citizens involved in the struggle were strongly against collecting arms. Splinters coming from the clash of discourses between the revolution and anti-revolution flew in all directions.

Some citizens went back to where they had started and sang about the beauty of and love for their region, while others rediscovered the cry for democratization, which had rung out at the dawn of the uprising. The Gwangju citizens raved about the pain of shackles, cursing the military dictatorship and the paratroopers' atrocities, which had pushed them to the verge of sedition. The issue of democratization kept surfacing in different contexts. Some argued that democracy could be achieved by prolonging the struggle, while most citizens returned to the semblance of a typical peaceful student demonstration from the realm of a new state power and called for their fatherland's democratization. At first, the discourse of democratization was a path that allowed them to escape from isolation; a little later, this discourse constituted the final words of the militants, who sensed death awaiting them.

Ultimately, to turn away from the threshold of revolution and break away from the confines of discourse, the Gwangju citizens changed the definition of themselves from a state to a civic community. The stance of the so-called "uprising faction," which wanted to fight to the end, was that instead of causing more bloodshed, the "price of blood" up to that point had to be paid by the government. Then they would disarm themselves and return to the rule of state power. Simply put, the payment of the "price of blood" was the so-called "recovery of sullied reputation." In concrete, it was to draw out the government's apologies and compensations and officially confirm the Gwangju citizens' ethical superiority. However, the military authorities, at the crossroads of life and death in their own way, could not admit to the paratroopers' atrocities. Perhaps it was destined from the outset that the negotiation between the Gwangju citizens and the Martial Law Command could not be carried out in a peaceful manner. The recovery of sullied reputation and "defending Gwangju to the death" were the last justifications for the civilian militia. To protect these justifications, some of the citizens had to be sacrificed. The fighters of the Gwangju uprising accepted their fates in order to maintain the community's superiority, to get a pledge of the uprising's rebirth, and to protect the nameless embryos of the revolution. As far as the relationship between the uprising and the revolution was concerned, the youths who defended the Provincial Hall to the end vetoed with their own deaths the rejection of revolution. The military authorities branded them "impure elements," the "comrades of the South Jeolla Republic," and traitors.[52] The theory of revolution that appeared in the late 1980s was a sort of foreign name attached to the posthumous idea of the Gwangju uprising. Activist students embraced this theory to interpret the Gwangju uprising, but it soon lost its validity. The socialist revolution theory leads to intellectual schizophrenia; this rhetoric was consciously chosen, having escaped to a different reality after realizing the dilemma in the discourses of the Gwangju uprising. The abstract discourse of "reunified fatherland" found its place in reality only after sacrificial lambs were offered. On the other hand, the "Jeolla Republic" was a sad joke about a fantasy that had been reached during the uprising by keeping in close touch with the idea of the hometown in a visceral manner every day, while stubbornly maintaining the logical consistency in the struggle and in the discourse of a state. Of course, tragedies in Gwangju originated from the political choice of the military authorities, "which demonstrated to fellow Koreans real examples of atrocities in massacring innocent civilians in the Vietnam War."[53]

5. Conclusion

Discourses began at the time of the struggle. The key to modern Western politics is that politics is an issue of state power, whose core is violence. The new military junta's belief in the omnipotence of violence, dramatically expressed during the Gwangju uprising, was also a product of the West's modern political discourse and the actual form shaped by this discourse— a militaristic modern state and capitalism. However, this political viewpoint, prevalent in South Korean social science circles, overlooks the importance of language in politics. The military authorities at the time, in slavish worship of violence, continued to monopolize arms, but for several days could not overwhelm the strength of Gwangju citizens' battle cries, moans, and fury— in a word, the specter of the Gwangju uprising. The military inflicted violence that could never be justified with any language, spouted sophistry to hide its shameful secrets, and going a step further, made a futile effort to obliterate language itself.

The military authorities' discourse of violence from May 18 to June 1980 had the purpose of masking disgrace, justifying itself, and then concealing reality with additional violence. The various arguments put forth by the military—"rioters," "impure political groups," and "malevolent rumors"—were its unilateral discourses manufactured in full awareness of its power, and these theories now remain empty, lacking validity.

However, the discourses did not purport to describe reality as it was. Yet they were not unrelated to reality or just empty words. They were based on violence—a power prior to reality—and were an essential means to re-create reality. For years after the event, many Gwangju citizens were greatly pained by the discourse of "rioters" that the government authority forced upon them, even after it abandoned the "Kim Dae-jung's conspiracy theory" with the amnesty of all persons who had been imprisoned following the uprising. This theory stripped many people even of sorrow (The Association of Young Comrades of May 18 Gwangju Righteous Uprising 1987, 57). A "reality" was created that painted many deaths in an ugly light, denying citizens the right to openly mourn their dead. The continuing struggle for democratization after the uprising was tantamount to a battle on how to depict the event.

Since the late 1980s, everything about the uprising has been written from the Gwangju citizens' viewpoint; the citizens now find themselves holding a monopoly on the truth of the event. They are the witnesses, participants, concerned parties, and victims, but their roles do not necessarily stop here. The Gwangju citizens made the greatest contributions to the struggle against the military regime and for Korea's democratization. Recently, a number of academic institutions and organizations have made decisive contributions to disclosing the truth of the uprising. But although the words of the concerned parties may be the most accurate testimonies of the uprising, there is no reason to accept that they are the most authoritative, valid discourse for the event. Their stance, emotions, and defensive arguments as the concerned parties may complicate their discourse. Many citizens, in reality, did not understand why they fought while they were in the thick of it; the meaning of this battle was often taught by intellectuals and learned people on battle sites, between fights, and in the detention barracks at the Combat Training and Doctrine Command when the uprising was over. Ethical judgments of the fight itself and of its historic significance are two different matters; historical meaning is created through interpretation, which is not limited to those who were there and witnessed what was happening.

In analyzing the discourses of the uprising, what is most difficult is the discourse of the Gwangju citizens that was formed for about 10 days during the uprising. In comparison, the statements of the Martial Law Command and the discourse of interpretations are simple. The words, which had pushed the citizens to fight in the face of unexpected violence, encouraged fellow citizens to join, justified their struggle, and set the direction of struggle, were not easily formulated amid the violence and restraints of the discourse structure in society. As soon as citizens defined their enemies, a nationalistic discourse threw a net over an alternate state that resembled that of the enemies. When "we" took shape of a country, this state power and the anti-communist ideology drove the citizens to the verge of treason. Most Gwangju citizens rejected all discussions of revolution in liberated Gwangju, where the whiff of revolution was strong, in order to escape from the nightmare of revolution. Liberated Gwangju was swept by a torrent of discourses; in the end, citizens returned to where they had started and cried for the love of hometown and the fatherland's democratization, with guns in hand. The love of the hometown continued to take shape in literary and artistic activities after the uprising, and the discourse of the fatherland's democratization remained a legacy to be fulfilled, together with the hatred of the dictatorship that had triggered the massacre of Gwangju citizens. At the time of the uprising, the Gwangju citizens' first discourse was not a logical language. Their first expressions were poems, not prose or academic papers.

Democracy, as the spirit of the Gwangju uprising, was inherited by Korean intellectuals and the minjung. Ultimately, democracy in South Korea is the fulfillment of the Gwangju uprising's legacy. At this juncture, however, the gaps between the reality of the armed struggle and the discourse of love and democracy have pushed the uprising into a new isolation. The discourse of democratization was a struggle to escape from this isolation. The brave fighters of the uprising, finding themselves in a dilemma following the rejection of the revolutionary discourse, attempted to secure their position in time and space by linking their uprising with democratization, the dominant political discourse in society. They did so by linking the demonstrations that had called for democratization prior to the Gwangju uprising with their own armed struggle. The legacy of the fighters in the uprising was a discourse to extricate themselves from the isolated situation at the time; it is difficult to accept that it was a discourse that reproduced the period of struggle. The legacy was merely what they wanted to say, and could say, to their descendants. The revolutionary idea—the posthumous idea of the uprising—was a product of a discourse reflecting the times, rather than the meaning and spirit of the struggle. What the fighters of the uprising demanded as their final wish, after their return to their prior positions, was not a crude Western-style menu of South Korean politics, such as democracy, socialism, and revolution. It was the recovery of their reputation and their ethical superiority over dictatorship. They did not ask for charity. Democracy, agreed within the current South Korean society as the foremost spirit of the uprising, is merely the lowest possible standard of their demands.

The discourse of the uprising is not monopolized by the two sides: the military and Gwangju citizens. The theory of "excessive suppression" was created in the course of dialogue between the military and the representatives of the Gwangju citizens, while the theories of the minjung and the revolution were the products of long-term verbal exchanges. The Martial Law Command's rhetoric of "rioters" was ultimately revived as the theory of the minjung, and the rhetoric of revolution was the reversal of the argument that blamed "impure elements." These three discourses possess fragments of the uprising's truth, having steered clear from the differences in stance between the left and the right. The analysis and criticism of these discourses provide a channel through which we can approach the reality shared by the two sides.

The reasons that compelled the Gwangju citizens to fight during the uprising remain scattered in many pieces of writing and testimony. The Gwangju citizens' struggle cannot be explained with any ideology or justification prepared prior to the event. At the same time, no terms implying human desire for material goods—exploitation, extortion, bribing, and control from behind the scenes—can satisfactorily explain what made citizens risk their own lives to fight the paratroopers. In addition, we cannot view it as violence against the paratroopers' violence, an explosion of instinctive violence. On the individual level, what infuriated the Gwangju citizens was the violence that trampled upon the dignity of human beings who were victims and witnesses. The motive of the citizens' struggle was to recover human dignity, to become human beings again.

The Gwangju citizens' community was based on respect and human love for dignified human beings, who had overcome fear and had been liberated from the humiliation of being subhuman. In such a community, individuals and the community coexisted in perfect harmony. Ultimately, human dignity could not be resolved at the individual level. "My" dignity and the dignity of those fellow citizens battered to death shared the same destiny; the joy of regaining dignity by participating in the struggle was confirmed in the joy of fellow comrades fighting side by side. The Gwangju citizens were infuriated over the word "rioters" because they knew that they themselves were dignified beings who had fought for human dignity. From the community level, the motive of struggle was the protection of lives. The Gwangju citizens' community defined life and death at the level of community; they wanted to protect all lives, protect their young, their families, their women and children, the land of Gwangju and all who live there—and to love them all. Whereas the struggle for human dignity was waged with fear, fury, and a sense of liberation, the struggle to protect lives and defend the hometown stemmed from cool-headed resolve.

The recovery of honor, for which Gwangju citizens clamored from those May days up till now, is far from abstract or materialistic. In liberated Gwangju, when the citizens escaped from the trap of the nationalistic discourse and found their place in the discourse of community, they felt that the "price of blood" was the true motive and the value of their struggle. This was to be human, to carry out what human beings were supposed to do. If they are still "animals" and "rioters" after such bloodshed, or if they go down in history as sharing culpability with paratroopers, Koreans may have to spill more blood. What they wanted on the condition of putting down arms was to get their fighters' picture back—the image of being human. Toward the end of the uprising, dignity became the tableau of the entire community, not just of the individuals.

The motive of the Gwangju citizens' struggle does not boil down to the demand for democracy, this quintessential modern political ideology and system. The Gwangju uprising originated from the demand of democratization. However, Gwangju citizens stumbled upon toxic elements located deep in the dictatorship and exposed them, going beyond democracy as a political ideology, through a desperate struggle for human values and community. Only through the uprising was the dictatorship exposed as a fount of violence that eradicated human life and dignity, not to mention an undemocratic political system; also because of the uprising, democracy, this Western political ideology, began to take root in South Korea. However, the fundamental value of human ethics and community is not absorbed into democracy, and it cannot be resolved by a political system called democracy. During the dark period of the 1980s, the South Korean democratization struggle was not propelled by the force of democratic ideology; rather, it was led by the fury over the images in which human dignity and values of life were destroyed, such as the tragic experience of the Gwangju uprising and a series of torture cases.

The value of human dignity and life, which led the Gwangju citizens to a struggle that brought them immense sacrifice, cannot be replaced with human rights, a legal concept of the modern West. The defense of humanity and community, which appeared during the uprising, is not limited to that particular era. The most basic human values travel beyond history and culture; they began with the birth of mankind and will continue into the unknown future. The Gwangju uprising may prove to be a pole with which to leap over democracy, the tragic value of our time. In the new epoch, the tale of the Gwangju uprising will be read as a giants' adventure story.

The reality and spirit of the Gwangju citizens' struggle in the uprising have yet to find a systematic discourse, and my book cannot complete this task. The term to refer to this primeval instinct has not been found in South Korea's narrow arena for political discourse and ideology. Although the spirit of the Gwangju uprising has not been set in stone, its giant outline has appeared before our eyes. The memorial monument at the new section of Mangwol-dong Cemetery eloquently tells the meaning of the deceased's fight. The two imposing columns will firmly defend silent life, the prototype of life, from high above.

ENDNOTES

[1] The total number of airborne troops dispatched to Gwangju at the time was 2,901, of which 504 were officers, from two battalions of the 7th Brigade, the 11th Brigade, and the 3rd Brigade.

[2] The exact number of the dead is still disputed; the government announced the toll to be 200, but many people still believe it was over 2,000.

[3] Other theories exist about the MBC arson. Many witnesses say that the arsonists were not citizens but martial law troops (Institute of Contemporary Korean Historical Data [ICKHD] 1990a, 1040: 306; 3058: 661; 3065; 675; 4011; 890 etc.). However, the citizens did have the intention to set fire and threw Molotov cocktails. In fact, the citizens caught soldiers trying to set fire to the Mokpo train station on April 22 (ICKHD 1990a, 6011:1046).

[4] Kim Yeong-taek, who covered the scene as a journalist, gives the following testimony: "At 10:08 in the morning, a military helicopter landed on the square in front of the Provincial Hall, followed by the distribution of bullets, at 10:10, to the paratroopers stationed at the back, in the vicinity of Sangmu Gymnasium. I learned later that each soldier received 10 bullets. The soldiers belonged to the 66th battalion of the 11th Brigade. . . . When dialogue became impossible with the demonstrators and it was no longer possible to appeal to them via bullhorns, Governor Jang stood in the hallway next to his office on the third floor of the main building. I was there with him. Below us, we could clearly see that the bullets in boxes were being distributed" (Kim Yeong-taek, 1996, 101).

[5] General Yun Hong-jeong, the then Combat Training and Doctrine Command chief and the division head of the Martial Law Command, gave the following testimony during a National Assembly hearing: "On the evening of May 18, I received many phone calls from my acquaintances in Gwangju. They asked how martial law troops could act as they had and how they could beat up people

as if they were dogs. I had been briefed that the crackdown operation on May 18 was winding down well . . . so I was astonished; it was not just one or two people who called me; many did. . . . On the morning of May 19, I immediately summoned the commanders of important posts, including the 31st Division commander and the airborne brigade head, telling them to call a meeting involving the military, government office, and civilian defense councils, such as the governor, mayor, superintendent of educational affairs, top prosecutors, and religious leaders. About the issue . . . at the time, from the officials I heard stories that shamed me for wearing a military uniform. . . . I heard many stories and during the meeting I sincerely requested that the military not carry out such actions and also ordered so" (Gwangju City 1997 IV, 124). In addition, around 8 o'clock on the evening of May 19, reserve generals from Gwangju and influential citizens complained about the airborne unit's method of suppression (ICKHD 1990a, 38). Such protests might explain why the 3rd Airborne Brigade, sent on the morning of May 20, attempted to show a different attitude.

[6] According to the testimonies of the arrested people, investigations into the *Fighters' Bulletin* (tusa hoebo), the notable underground paper penned by citizens during the uprising, took place only toward the end. Those involved in the bulletin generally received light sentences. By contrast, heavier sentences, including capital punishment, were meted out to people who had been directly engaged in the armed struggle (ICKHD 1990a, 4004: 859). In a May 31 statement outlining the incident, the Martial Law Command emphasized the role of political conspiracy groups. It threw the spotlight on the role of *Fighter's Bulletin* as an example of organized conspiracy, together with the role of "malevolent rumors," by saying, "[the groups] printed carefully drafted fliers and even an underground newspaper (issued nine editions from May 18 to 26)" (Jeonnam Social Research Institute [JSRI] 1988, III-4:173).

[7] The poet Go Eun, analyzing one of the fliers, "Time for Decisive Battle has Arrived," (Gwangju City 1997 II, 23), stated as follows: "Rejecting all modifiers, this flier shouts facts succinctly and breathlessly. If there is a possibility for qualifiers, it is the

addition of a desperate combat cry of, "Brothers! Let's die while fighting!" Although not all of the information in the leaflet is accurate, the sense of urgency—brimming with a burning, unconditional militant will to fight as the Gwangju minjung uprising is spreading into an armed struggle—resembles the absolute austerity of poetic language" (Go Eun, *Literature After the May Gwangju Minjung Uprising*, ICKHD 1990b, 226).

[8] The "plea" dated on May 19 (JSRI 1991, 236-237), created by Yun Sang-won's Field Fire Night School Team, cries out as follows: "What makes them different from communists? . . . Now the only way for us to survive is to make all citizens unite in one, protect youths and students and smash the bastards of the Airborne Special Warfare Command, who are composed of the remnants of the Yusin faction and the cruelest devilish murderer Chun Doo-hwan and his gang, every one of them, without sparing a single one. . . . We have seen everything. We have learned everything . . . why the students shouted at the top of their lungs. Our enemies are neither the police nor the army. Our enemies are none other than the remaining Yusin faction and the Chun Doo-hwan gang, who are driving the entire general public to the scene of extreme fear" (Gwangju City 1997 II, 22).

[9] "Democratic Citizens, Rise Up," issued on May 19 in the name of the Chosun University Democratic Struggle Committee, says: "Those dog-like bastards of the remaining Yusin faction—Choi Kyu-hah, Sin Hyeon-hwak—and the bastard Chun Doo-hwan, the son of the Yusin dictator" (Gwangju City 1997 II, 23). An article entitled "You, Democratic Citizens," penned by a so-called citizen's representative, said, "What are we doing now? . . . We are gathered here to overthrow that heinous son-of-a-bitch Chun Doo-hwan, who murders people as easily, as cruelly, as if killing flies" (Gwangju City 1997 II, 47).

[10] On May 25, Yun Sang-won changed the *Fighters' Bulletin* back to *Democratic Citizens' Bulletin* while continuing with its issue number. In other words, from No. 9, it was published again as *Democratic Citizens' Bulletin* and printed up to No. 11. The final edition was not distributed due to the martial law troops' reentry into Gwangju.

[11] During the Korean War, soon after North Korean troops invaded the south on June 25, 1950, they took the peninsula by storm and reached the Naktong River on July 25. The South Korean Army and US forces put up desperate resistance until September when they broke the deadlock and pushed northward.

[12] Yun Seok-nu, head of the civilian militia's mobile strike unit, said the following during a National Assembly hearing: "If one sees human blood—if it is from a traffic accident—one avoids it, thinking it is unclean and disgusting, but in my eyes, the blood shed by the citizens was not dirty. It was the kind of blood one could scoop up and drink and feel refreshed" (Gwangju City 1997 V. 335). Apart from the poetic value of this remark, the illogical and passionate character of the uprising is vividly revealed.

[13] Kim Seong-seop, a member of the *Fighters' Bulletin* team, testified as follows: "What we had was the *Fighters' Bulletin*, and at first it wasn't the *Fighters' Bulletin* but a leaflet in the title of *Democratic Citizens' Bulletin*. . . . On the morning of May 19, the first issue was printed, followed by No. 2 in the afternoon, and No. 3 in the evening. . . . On May 20, we judged that guidelines were necessary to encourage citizens to exhibit unified behavior, rather than let them be engaged in random fights. I am not sure, but I think it was from No. 4 that the name was changed to the *Fighters' Bulletin*" (ICKHD 1990a, 4004:856).

[14] Hwang Seog-yeong (1985) was the first to use the expression "liberated Gwangju," referring to the days from May 21, when paratroopers withdrew from Gwangju, to May 27, when they reentered the city.

[15] The result of this negotiation caused controversy when it was announced at a 5 o'clock rally on the same afternoon. The part mentioned here is the literal quotation from the "Report on Consultation During our Visit to the Martial Law Sub-Station," published in the name of all members of the May 18 Incident Settlement Measures Committee (Gwangju City 1997 II, 51). It stands to reason that the quoted words have been reproduced after a long, hard deliberation. However, it is more likely that the writing may not truly reflect the May 22 negotiation. According to Father

Jo Bi-o, who was on the negotiation team at the time, the visitors obtained nothing; they were threatened and sent home. He also asserts that he suggested that the conversation at the negotiation site be recorded on a tape recorder or by shorthand, but everyone balked at the idea (Jo Bi-o 1994, 35-36). Due to this document, the citizens' settlement committee became the target of fierce criticism and was put on the defensive by the citizens, in particular the crowds at rallies. It is likely that the May 24 document could have been revised to a certain degree by the committee with the purpose of eliciting citizens' trust. Nevertheless, the expression "excessive suppression" could have been used by General Kim Gi-seok, deputy head of the Combat Training and Doctrine Command at the time.

[16] The martial law troops sent spies, Jang Gye-beom and Jong Hyang-gyu, to the Provincial Hall and when they were suspected by the members of the civilian militia, they collapsed, pretending that they were hit by a poisoned needle, and escaped the Hall. The martial law troops claimed that North Korean agents amid the citizens used poison and circulated this rumor throughout the city. Given various circumstances and testimonies, it is certain that this incident was an operation staged by the South Korean intelligence authorities to weaken the resistance.

[17] According to the testimony of Kim Jong-bae, vice chairman of the student settlement committee, who opposed surrendering weapons, Kim Chang-gil, the committee chairman and the leader of those in favor of returning weapons, said during a meeting: "Kim Jong-bae, that guy, is suspicious. Nothing good will come of it if we listen to him." This shows that the faction arguing for the weapons surrender branded the opposing members as "impure elements." Kim Jong-bae felt danger to his person, and Bak Nam-seon, head of the civilian militia Situation Room, found a security guard for him (ICKHD 1990a, 1014:207).

[18] It appears that the committee had a special reason to take such a stance on May 25. The demand for retrieving weapons, which was promoted by the May 18 Measures Committee, faced resistance. The measures committee that visited the Martial Law Sub-

Station on May 22 was disbanded on the afternoon of May 25 and this particular settlement committee was a new organization in which a large number of "dissidents" participated.

[19] A May 23 flier entitled "You, Democratic Citizens" insisted that citizens must protect the youth, repair damage, and devote themselves to their daily activities (Gwangju City 1997 II, 47).

[20] The demand for democracy began to appear in all leaflets and statements from May 23. However, according to a written arraignment, it was included as an official condition for the surrender of weapons following Yun Sang-won's suggestion upon the establishment of the revolt leadership on the evening of May 25 (ICKHD 1990a, 109).

[21] The Army Headquarters' "True Face of Gwangju Incident" printed in June 1980 discusses "malevolent rumors" as follows: "Needless to say, malevolent rumors originated from the tricks of the North Korean puppet government's agents and fabrications based on vague guesswork by impure inciters of demonstrations and disgruntled forces. Such contents were reported in a number of foreign press outlets as if the Republic of Korea were gripped by fear and anxiety. This tarnished the image of the country and was used by the North Korean puppet government for its smear campaigns and slanderous propaganda toward the South, leading to the grave result of falling in line with the North's tactic to communize the South" (JSRI 1998, III-13:223). This statement seems to confess the military's internal thoughts.

[22] For example, the chronology of daily events printed on May 22 hinted at something lurking below the surface with the use of phrases such as, "The demonstration participated in by all citizens starting May 19," "in the form of a protest involving all citizens," "shouting that they should die together," and "the use of extreme methods infuriated the citizens and fueled them to join." For some reason, this chronology was composed in reverse order, from the most recent to the earliest.

[23] Each newspaper gave this news a different weight. The *Maeil Sinmun* of Daegu printed it in prominent letters right next to an article about Gwangju. Underneath, it reported an article about

three spies in Gwangju, including a woman named Jeon Ok-ju under the header, "Three Captured by a Throng Verified as Fixed Spies." This paper did not fail to mention each time that the two news agencies—Hapdong and Dongyang—verified all articles on the Gwangju incident to make sure that readers would not get the impression that the newspaper was responsible for possible errors.

[24] On the occasion of the fourth anniversary of the Gwangju uprising, Jeon Gye-ryang, head of the Association of Surviving Family Members of Victims of the May 18 Gwangju Righteous Rebellion, put forth the "victory of minjung" as the historical goal. In his commemorative speech, he said, "But if those who departed intended to sacrifice their lives and follow righteousness only for democracy and reunification of our divided country, we realize that only the real victory of minjung is the true compensation, comfort, and great praise" (Minjung Culture Movement Council 1985, 432).

[25] For example, "The Gwangju minjung uprising broke out in order to protest against the political military force, which mercilessly trampled on Korean people's fervent desire for democratization through the May 17 military coup d'état. Despite the May 17 military coup d'état [many people believed that Chun and his group encouraged student demonstrations and expanded martial law on the pretext of a demonstration in front of the Seoul train station], 300,000 Gwangju people carried out a peaceful demonstration, calling for the 'repeal of martial law,' 'the immediate resignation of Choi Kyu-hah's transition government,' 'Chun Doo-hwan's resignation,' 'immediate release of Kim Dae-jung, democratic figures, and students,' 'establishment of a transitional democratic government to save the country,' and 'immediate withdrawal of martial law troops stationed in downtown Gwangju.' However, Chun Doo-hwan's military forces dispatched an airborne special warfare unit and instituted a bloody crackdown, which triggered the drama of the Gwangju massacre and left scars that will never be completely healed in the history of the Korean nation" (JSRI III-20, 260).

[26] The representative organization that commanded the radical, emotional language regarding the Gwangju uprising was the Alliance for Democratic Reunification and Minjung Movement [Mintongnyeon]. The group did not advocate radical ideology; its members simply seemed to use the language of instigation within the framework of the democratization movement. Of course, "democracy" and the inflammatory language that encourages people to "rise up" do not go together. The so-called "dissidents" and "activist circles" seemed to call for something more than "democratization" (National Democratic Research Institute [Minminyeon], 1989).

[27] For example, Kim Jin-gyun and Jeong Geun-sik said as follows: "The effort to approach the Gwangju minjung uprising in a scientific manner, from the perspective of the entire national movement history, focuses on the structural causes that triggered the incident, rather than the direct causes, and it is carried out in the direction of explaining why the minjung uprising was inevitable amid the shift in class domination and the picture of struggle in contemporary Korean society" (ICKHD 1990b, 65-66).

[28] Considerable differences are found in the interpretations of the Gwangju uprising. For example, in a 1989 discussion, Seo Jung-seok viewed the Gwangju uprising as a "watershed event in the nation's history," meaning that it was an occasion that "exploded" in Gwangju and moved toward other events in history. In the same discussion, Jo Hui-yeon asserted that the Gwangju uprising was an occasion in which "the ruling power's violent character" had been exposed. In other words, they mean that the uprising was not an isolated event but just a moment in which the truth was revealed. Going a step further, they claim that "the Gwangju resistance was a general expression of South Korean society's overall inconsistencies and a manifestation of general political advancement in the process of the minjung's self-liberation (Choe Jang-jip et al. 1989, 26-75).

[29] A typical example that opposed describing Gwangju during the days when the paratroopers withdrew as being orderly and calm, in other words a utopia, is Kim Yang-o (1988).

[30] Bak Seog-yeon, who was managing a shop specializing in electrical appliances, recalls his feelings at the time: "I thought, 'I don't know what the hooligans in Gwangju are doing now. What do they save their strong fists for? If I had a gun with a silencer, I would gun those paratroopers down'" (ICKHD 1990a, 397:744).

[31] On May 22, the first day of liberation, the honchos of the Obi and Hwasin factions, the two major gangs in Gwangju, ascended the podium of a citizens' rally and promised that they would cooperate with the citizens' struggle (ICKHD 1990a, 86).

[32] Kim Sang-yun, who managed the Nokdu Bookstore and led Gwangju activists, was locked up during a preliminary roundup on May 17. He gave the following testimony. "Later, I heard it from professor Song Gi-suk that a certain lieutenant colonel of the military security unit had opposed dyeing [the involved people] in red, arguing that if the Gwangju incident were defined as a Reds' riot as had been the case for Yeosun, its aftermath would be immense and it would not do any good for maintaining the regime. That was why they linked me to Kim Dae-jung's conspiracy of sedition. I became an important person engaged in this sedition...." (ICKHD 1990a, 3014:559). According to Kim Dae-jung's National Assembly testimony, he was arrested on the evening of May 17 and was interrogated in the basement of the Korean Central Intelligence Agency. For the first 20 days or so (until early June), no question was asked about his relationship with Jeong Dong-nyeon, a purported handyman of Kim. On several occasions, Kim Dae-jung emphasized that he had never met Jeong until 1985 (Hangminsa 1989, 63). This testimony supports the hypothesis that the Martial Law Command made a decision in early June to put forth Kim Dae-jung as the mastermind of the uprising in place of "impure elements and fixed spies."

[33] In May, Yun Sang-won reluctantly accepted the role of working-level official at the South Jeolla Province chapter of the National Alliance, where Kim Dae-jung was the general affairs manager, on

the condition that he would resign if a new political party was founded. He made this agreement because he could not refuse the requests of Kim Sang-yun of the Nokdu Bookstore, and Yun Han-bong of the Current Affairs Research Institute. The National Alliance leadership was slated to launch on May 22. During the Gwangju incident, a young man from the National Alliance went to Gwangju to see Yun Sang-won on the morning of May 19 to plan nationwide demonstrations for May 20 This young man had no idea that Gwangju was in turmoil on May 19, and that the rally on May 20 would be meaningless. Needless to say, Kim Dae-jung had been already arrested at this point (JSRI 1991, 197; 230; ICKHD 1990a, 4011:889).

[34] What is of interest is the example of the North Korean spy dispatched to the South, who was said to have been arrested at the Seoul train station. According to a press release, he had in his possession a hallucinogen. Of course, it is impossible to confirm the story's verity, but it was common to believe at the time that people in their right mind would not be able to fight against paratroopers.

[35] Yim Chun-sik, who ran a gallery at the time, gave the following statement: "On May 20, it rained in the morning and only cleared up in the afternoon. That day, unlike the previous day's inhumane violent suppression, paratroopers quelled the crowds in a relatively mild way, saying, 'We are not from Gyeongsang Province. The paratroopers who controlled the crowds yesterday and the day before have been pulled out.' Right then, I spotted some intelligence agents I knew among the crowds. Standing amid the demonstrators in front of the Catholic Center, they blurted out remarks that agitated the demonstrators. 'Those bastards are from Gyeongsang Province,' 'They came to kill all the Gwangju people,' and 'Let us kill them off.' I think these shouts were intended to leave room for excuses later that the paratroopers had no choice but to resort to excessive suppression in response to provocation of the demonstrators and the incitement of radical actions" (ICKHD 1990a, 3082:713).

[36] Bak Si-hun, who witnessed the scene as a conscripted police aide, said, "Starting on the afternoon of May 19, many stories smacking of farfetched rumors reached us. Savage tales, such as 'the seed of the Jeolla people will be annihilated' and 'pregnant women's bellies were cut open' came through our walkie-talkies. I had no doubt that they were true. It was a belief formed after two days of observation" (ICKHD 1990a, 8002: 1536).

[37] As mentioned before, it is questionable whether the deputy commander of the Combat Training and Doctrine Command admitted at the time that "excess suppression" had been used. Although the settlement committee claimed he had admitted it, some of the people who were part of the negotiation team, i.e. Father Jo Bi-o and Professor Myeong No-geun, testified that no concession was made.

[38] During a 1988 National Assembly hearing, Yi Hui-seong, the martial law commander during the uprising, formally confirmed that excessive suppression was one of the causes of the Gwangju uprising (Gwangju City 1997 III, 212; 220).

[39] In an interview with Jo Gap-je, he said, "An American film was shown during training on how to suppress demonstrations. It had to do with control methods under martial law. According to this film, you make the demonstrators kneel. If they resist, you control them by bashing their collarbones with riot control sticks. If they run away, you open fire on them. The suppression of the Gwangju incident was much milder than the actions shown in this movie" (Jo Gap-je 1988, 192).

[40] Wi Gye-ryong, then the medical officer of the 7th Airborne Unit, testified as follows: "The suppression method was this. At first you instill fear and awe in the demonstrators to make them disperse. If it does not work, you catch a few as examples and treat them mercilessly to make the demonstrators run away. . . . When a rally is suppressed, troops are supposed to congregate in one place and let the demonstrators continue with what they were doing, to give each side the latitude of placating the other. When they cracked down on them without giving such an opportunity, the incident escalated" (ICKHD, 8001: 1532). Another testimony observed:

"The slaughter by the paratroopers seemed definitely to be intentional. They committed such acts in front of as many people as possible, and when the citizens stamped their feet with fury and helplessness, they were emboldened and committed their acts with more gusto" (The Association of Surviving Family Members of Victims (1989, 67).

[41] Gang Gil-jo testified about what had happened in a classroom of Chonnam National University on May 20, "A considerable number of the airborne unit would talk about what they did during the Vietnam War. One of them pulled out a bayonet and boasted, 'This bayonet is a souvenir sword. It cut off more than 40 breasts of Vietnamese women.' He then swooshed it over the head of a man in front of him. His long hair was cut off and he now sported a cropped haircut" (ICKHD 1990a, 7134:1451).

[42] Regarding the citizens' armament, Kim Jong-bae, who was the chairman of the revolt leadership, said the following in a 1988 National Assembly hearing: "At the time, because the paratroopers were massacring indiscriminately, I wanted to throw an atomic bomb, not just a grenade or a bomb, at the bastards of the airborne unit" (Gwangju City 1977 III, 579).

[43] "How Will We Resolve Gwangju: Gwangju of 1980 Told by Participants and Measures of Settlement," *Wolgan Chosun*, August 1987, 291.

[44] In July 1984, Kim Young-sam, the co-chairman of Congress for National Unity, said in an interview with the *Far Eastern Economic Review*, "I am willing to set aside the Gwangju incident on the condition that the recovery of democracy is pledged." The organizations related to the Gwangju uprising bristled and released a letter demanding apologies, in which they said, "How can one individual, in what capacity, argue for or against the pain of history, in which numerous human lives were lost and injured, and blood, tears, sorrow and oppressions were strewn everywhere? How can a person who did not personally experience the pain in such an immense tragedy act and talk as if he were a central figure in the event? . . . Mr. Kim Young-sam! . . . What intention do you have in spouting a gaffe that dares place the Gwangju righteous rebellion on the altar of sacrifice for

political negotiations? If there is no measure whatsoever to heal the wounds of deaths, injuries, imprisonments and slave-like oppressions, we make it clear on behalf of the dead that we cannot forgive political words and actions to gloss over the solemn fact—the Gwangju righteous rebellion" (Minjung Culture Movement Council 1985; 436-437).

[45] During a witness interrogation of the 1985 seizure of the US Information Service, regarding the concept of people being beneficial to the enemy North Korea, Hong Seong-mun, an expert on communism and seditious documents, answered that it was a new word whose concept had not existed before ("Witness interrogation protocol for the USIS incident trial (data)," *Wolgan Chosun*, October 1985, 187-188).

[46] Kim Sang-jip (younger brother of the Nokdu Bookstore's Kim Sang-yun), a key figure in activist circles and one of Yun Sang-won's confidants at the time, claimed that the Martial Law Command intentionally played up the roles of the urban poor and the lumpen proletariat as crafty tactics. "In actuality, many students participated at the time, but [the Martial Law Command] sent them home with a warning, except student leaders. This is evident by the fact that the students I had divided up into squads in front of the YWCA in 1980 were not arrested." In addition, he argues for the reconsideration of the theories of the minjung and the minjung revolution currently circulated in a one-sided manner (ICKHD 1990a, 4011:897).

[47] In 1988, the Catholic Justice and Peace Committee of the Archdiocese of Gwangju officially declared the minjung as the main players of the uprising, named the incident the "minjung uprising," and defined it as a "democratization movement with the minjung as a main force." Going a step further, the Archdiocese established the relationship of the minjung with the citizens: "It will not do to confuse the fact that all citizens participated in the struggle and that the people at the bottom ladders of society stood at the forefront to fight actively." Until May 1984, the Catholic priests of the Archdiocese of Gwangju used the term "Gwangju righteous rebellion" (Minjung Culture Movement Council 1985, 435).

78

[48] In 1988, the "Association of Surviving Family Members of Victims of the May 18 Gwangju Righteous Rebellion" changed its name to the "Association of Surviving Family Members of Victims of the May 18 Minjung Uprising" (ICKHD 1990a, 3072). On the other hand, the Association of Youth in Gwangju Righteous Rebellion was created in 1986. In 1987, the Association of Young Comrades of the May 18 Gwangju Minjung Uprising was formed. In the same year, the Association of Wounded Comrades of the May 18 Gwangju Righteous Rebellion separated itself from the Association of Comrades, over the issue of supporting President Chun Doo-hwan's pledge to protect the constitution. All these organizations were unified in the Association of Young Comrades of the May 18 Gwangju Minjung Uprising in 1995 (Na Gan-chae, Jeong Tae-sin 1996). It appears that the "minjung uprising" became generalized in 1987. That year, the Association of the Young Comrades of the May 18 Gwangju Uprising published *Testimonies of the Gwangju Minjung Uprising*. In an opinion poll conducted in early 1988, while 28.7 percent expressed their opinion that the event should be called "the righteous rebellion," 56.3 percent opted for the "minjung uprising" (Catholic Church 1988, 33).

[49] A well-known theory regarding this issue is suggested in Jeong Do-sang's short story, "Tale of Fifteen People." "Do you know why the guys who make a living scrubbing people's backs in bathhouses fought as if their life depended on it?" a character says. "Students have their knowledge, so they can fill their stomachs even if they didn't do it. So they ran away. The body-scrubbers are resentful because they have no education. Body-scrubbers are body-scrubbers and factory hands are factory hands whether they demonstrate or not, so they fight. More than anything else, to them loyalty is everything" (Jeong Do-sang, "Tale of Fifteen People," Han Seung-won, et al. 1987, 316-317).

[50] "Flag I," a pamphlet that had an important impact on student activists in the early months of 1984, specifically put forth the line of struggle as a "violent revolution based on the minjung uprising." This booklet, of course, is not a commentary on the Gwangju uprising (Gang Sin-cheol et. al 1988, 66).

[51] Regarding the situation on May 20, Bak Si-hun, a conscripted police aide at the time, testified: "It appears that instinctively a sense of unity was formed among citizens. They took to the streets, shouting such slogans as, 'We must protect Gwangju. With our own hands,' and the demonstrators running toward us from all directions were united in one, from grandfathers to children" (ICKHD 1990a, 8002: 1536). The quoted words were not a suitable slogan for the demonstrators. It seems that he did not hear the exact words at the time. It is presumed that Bak, a native of Gwangju, described the scene in recollection. In this case, we may judge that everyone used this particular expression as a matter of course, and he testified with the conviction that it was natural for all demonstrators to have the same thought.

[52] According to Kim Jun-bong's testimony, when he was taken to Combat Training and Doctrine Command, investigators greeted him, "Welcome, Comrade of the South Jeolla Republic!" and beat the daylights out of him (ICKHD 1990a, 1020:234).

[53] Quoted from "Chun Doo-hwan's Slaughter Operation in Gwangju" of May 20, 1980 in the name of the Chosun University Democratic Struggle Committee (JSRI 1988, II-4: 109).

Chapter Two

Dialectic of Violence and Love: Emergence of Absolute Community

1. Words and Bodies

Around noon on May 18, 1980, university students demonstrated on Geumnam Avenue, in the heart of Gwangju, South Jeolla Province, calling for democratization and the lifting of martial law. A mobile police squad came to quell the rally. In South Korean history, it may be of little importance how many students were involved, how many riot police were mobilized, exactly where they stood, and how the two sides moved. This was the kind of event that had been common in South Korean cities for the previous several months, even years. The meaning of such an occurrence was, and still is, easily conveyed as the expression (*signe*), "university student demonstration," a common term in South Korean society. Although martial law was in effect, this particular demonstration was not out of the ordinary. The citizens' responses were varied as well; some encouraged the students, others were indifferent, and still others were critical. Some said, "They are doing this because they don't feel like studying."[1] We may assume that citizens had formed their opinions after watching, listening to, thinking of, and discussing similar rallies for several days, or perhaps over a long period of time, and they must have expressed their feelings frequently.

What happened only a few hours later, however, was far from typical. This occurred at four o'clock in the afternoon, soon after an airborne unit, more precisely the 33rd and 35th battalions of the 7th Airborne Special Warfare Command, was mobilized to Geumnam Avenue and its environs. The people who witnessed the unfolding scene could not express what they saw in any language they knew, and they would have been unable to convey what happened to those who were not there. The observers could not help but doubt their eyes. When they described the details of what happened, most listeners—whether from Gwangju or from other regions—did not accept the reports as factual accounts. At the time, *The New York Times* was perplexed after getting reports from local journalists that it was "a situation that is beyond description" (The Journalists Association of Korea et. al 1997, 64). The *Donga Ilbo* journalist Kim Chung-geun remembers as follows:

> While covering the Gwangju struggle, I lamented my lack of descriptive power as a reporter. I experienced viscerally the fact that there were situations that could never be conveyed in writing or words. . . . As a reporter, I couldn't find words to adequately describe the scene. "Atrocity," "reckless violence," "indiscriminate attack"—I wasn't satisfied with any of them because they were too bland. . . . The word I came up with as the last resort was "human hunting." (Although this term was not printed in papers at the time due to the Martial Law Command's censorship, this has been continuously quoted as one of the expressions conveying the tragic scope of the Gwangju incident.)

> Violence targeting young women was worse; the better dressed and the prettier they were, the worse treatment they received. How can one describe it when certain parts of the female body were the targets of violence and the clothes covering them were torn to pieces? The expressions—"rape in broad daylight," "violent debauchery," and "armed suppression fraught with sexual perversion"—flitted through in my head, but they were also inadequate to convey what happened in Gwangju.[2]

Those who witnessed what happened in Gwangju at the time must have busily rifled through the dictionary in their heads.[3] Even yet, there is no name, no definition, nor understanding of what happened between the afternoon of May 18 and the early hours of May 27 when the Republic of Korea's forces attacked Gwangju from all directions and occupied it.

The overall character of this event, referred to as the May 18 Minjung Uprising, or simply May 18 by many people, was the clash and destruction of bodies, with language occupying only a secondary status. Then, all words were auxiliary, used either to conceal reality or encourage the clash of bodies. The analysis of the uprising's discourses confirms the gap between language and reality. To the Gwangju citizens, the uprising is still an incident that sends chills down their spines. Since the event, there have been attempts to understand and convey it with language, but so far words have failed to approach real experience and memories. Although academic research was attempted on several occasions, theoretical tools and conceptual terms completely betrayed the reality and experience.

The exclusivity of those who went through the uprising may not be the only reason that they have continued to dwell on the event. Attempts to understand the uprising with the vehicle of language, at least until now, have failed to approximate the vividness of the experience of those concerned; what they went through was enough to induce the so-called "May 18 syndrome," comprising extreme fear—the likes of which, seemingly, will never be felt again in their lifetime—rage, hostility, a sense of unity, joy, and inspiration. Those who participated in the revolt have lived with a pride often incomprehensible to others, and this feeling may have led to a deep-seated sense of isolation, alongside a sense of victimhood.

The Gwangju citizens could never understand the paratroopers' cruelty. It was incomprehensible how the soldiers of the ROK Army beat up anyone in sight—regardless of age and sex—in broad daylight with intimidating riot sticks, drove bayonets into them, ordered them to strip before subjecting them to inhumane disciplinary measures, and loaded them onto truck beds as if they were parcels. In such a situation, the "malevolent rumors" that are said to have played an important role in escalating the incident—"Gyeongsang Province soldiers came to annihilate the seed of the Jeolla people," "The unit is exclusively made up of soldiers from the Gyeongsang Province,"—may have sounded plausible.[4]

It was not only the citizens who were struck by such an incomprehensible situation. Despite the paratroopers' atrocities—the kind that had completely emptied downtown Busan in about 10 minutes in 1979—in Gwangju, demonstrators surfaced again a little later, the number of them increased the next day, and finally a majority of citizens were united as one in resistance. For the soldiers at the scene and the scholars who would later study the uprising, this was hard to believe. The soldiers, ordered to defend the Provincial Hall to the death, must have trembled in fear in the face of a mysterious power approaching them, while the scholars reading the accounts may have been gripped by unforgettable emotions. Conspiracy theories about the uprising may have arisen because the situation defied words. A conspiracy theory may be effective in ethically criticizing the opposite side. Nevertheless, it may eventually erase the shouts and screams from history and memory by explaining them away as a puppet show staged by a handful of people.

This chapter is an attempt to understand how the Gwangju minjung struggle unfolded. My intention, as a person from another region, is to recompose the development of the event as an experience that can be understood by every Korean. The focus will be on how the resistance developed from May 18 to May 21. This is an attempt to find answers to the question of what made all the citizens rise up and fight off 3,000 soldiers in three brigades of the most elite paratroopers of the Republic of Korea. This chapter intends to describe how the Gwangju citizens triumphed, because from the current historical viewpoint, they won the struggle of the Gwangju uprising.

First, I will critically review still-circulating conspiracy theories. Then, I will discuss the reasons and motives that drove citizens to participate in the revolt, which was followed by the emergence of an absolute community, the apex of the Gwangju minjung struggle. The experience of this community may provide an important meaning of the Gwangju uprising in modern Korean history and also in human history. In this community, there was no private ownership, other people's lives were as important as one's own, and time stood still. In this community, discriminations disappeared, individuals were merged into one, and fear and joy were intermingled. Distress at the end of one world coexisted with confusion at the beginning of a new world, in which emotion and reason were reborn.

2. Conspiracy Theories

At present, two decades after the uprising, it might seem meaningless to bring up this rhetoric again. Although the military officially raised the argument that North Korea was involved, it was not fully exploited for political reasons and was soon abandoned.[5] On the other hand, although the military authorities were cautious when they first raised the argument that Kim Dae-jung was involved in the conspiracy, they established it as an official theory on May 31 to explain the uprising, alongside the argument that North Korea was involved.[6] In June 1980, the theory of North Korea's involvement was thrown out and that of Kim Dae-jung's conspiracy emerged as the centerpiece. Political consideration engendered this change.[7] This pushed Kim Dae-jung into a sudden spotlight as a national leader, and Kim Dae-jung's conspiracy of sedition was adopted as an official offense to punish a number of people, including Kim himself. All these sentences were suspended later, however. According to a number of testimonies, many of the charges against a majority of those arrested, alleged to have been participants in Kim Dae-jung's sedition conspiracy, were fabricated. New grounds must be supplied to bring up this argument again.

At this point, no conspiracy theory involving the Gwangju citizens is persuasive. It is unnecessary to reiterate that, at the time, the citizens had no organization that could consistently lead a protest. We may question, however, the conspiracy theory involving Kim Dae-jung. Who, unarmed, could fight against the Republic of Korea's airborne unit? Who could have paid them to take action? How much operational money would have been enough to embolden them? How much instigation would it take to make them act the way they did? Operational funds and exhortations cannot make human beings give up their lives. It is possible, of course, to argue for their supplementary roles, saying that those who were incited or received operational funds exhorted demonstrators and exacerbated the situation. In this case, too, instigations could be effective only in a situation where many people were already fighting with their lives on the line. If such organizations really existed, they would have taken refuge on May 18 and 19. On the contrary, we may consider that the resistance grew strong because citizens' participation was voluntary, with no organization present. The theory of Kim Dae-jung's conspiracy has no ground or logical backing.

The conspiracy theory that does have a strong persuasive power is that of the military authorities' involvement. This alleges that the new military leadership created a scenario to foster a sense of crisis and fear—fanning a large-scale riot and cracking down on it intensively—and put it into practice in Gwangju to find justification for the official seizure of power. The best, and simultaneously the thorniest, part of this theory is that the paratroopers were supposed to have two goals: to create an atmosphere of fear and, at the same time, to provoke citizens to accelerate the demonstration. This theory was suggested by Kim Dae-jung, a presidential hopeful, in a press conference during the 1987 presidential campaign, and was subsequently taken up by the researchers of the uprising (Kim Dae-jung, 1987 etc.).

Few social scientists have officially adopted this theory, however. By nature, it can never be proven until the military's top-secret documents are declassified, and it is possible that relevant documents have been destroyed. The main reason for the emergence of this particular conspiracy theory is that it is impossible to explain the paratroopers' actions in rational terms. At the same time, citizens' resistance went beyond the range of rational comprehension. The demonstrators seemed to be subdued toward the evening of May 18, but they resumed their protest on the morning of May 19. Around noon that day, it appeared to be over, only to be restaged more fiercely in the afternoon. Rain seemed to end everything that evening, but a full-fledged resistance recurred on May 20. The student activist leaders, intellectuals, and professors—who had watched the situation rationally—decided to hide themselves during this period. The paratroopers clamping down on the demonstrators were also convinced that the incident would soon come to an end.[8] Conspiracy theories seem to have surfaced when the situation was spinning out of control despite the two sides' rational assessment of the situation.

The argument that paratroopers used brutal tactics of suppression from the start to provoke Gwangju citizens rests on the fact that the violence used in Gwangju was different from that employed in Busan and Masan in the previous year. Both in Busan and Gwangju, paratroopers randomly beat up people in the streets. But similarities end there. In Gwangju, lethal riot sticks, 70 centimeters in length, were used, and unlike in Busan, soldiers cursed and assaulted the elderly and committed perverse sexual acts on women. There is no evidence, however, that such actions were planned by the military or that orders came down from the superior ranks, and it is difficult to presume so.

Rather, what should be pointed out first is that the Martial Law Command's operations and actions had no consistency throughout the revolt period. As some military generals have mentioned, the dispatch of different troops into the city each day must be viewed as an operational mistake.[9] Many people bring up the possibility of conspiracy, saying that the May 19 dispatch of the 11th Airborne Brigade was decided in the early afternoon of May 18 before the 7th Airborne Brigade launched a suppressive operation. It must be pointed out, however, that it was when Molotov cocktails appeared in downtown Gwangju for the first time in contemporary South Korean history, and it may be understood as the new military junta's extremely sensitive response, obsessed with the belief that disturbances had to be quashed strongly and rapidly. What must also be pointed out is that the 3rd Airborne Brigade, which entered Gwangju at dawn on May 20, treated citizens politely, contrary to what the 7th Brigade and the 11th Brigade had done until the previous day. The Martial Law Command, which prohibited any news coverage in the beginning, changed its policy and issued an official statement on May 21 in the name of the martial law commander. From this point on, the command carried out propaganda warfare by mobilizing all the mass media, claiming that the country faced a national catastrophe with the outbreak of a colossal "riot" in Gwangju, instigated by the North Korean puppet government. In the initial stage, the military authorities maintained a strict control over live shells, but they ordered mass firing on the afternoon of May 21, and officially adopted self-defense rights that evening. These facts are enough to raise speculation that the military authorities ran pell-mell, rather than acting on a consistent scenario.

Military operations are always based on plans, however. The lack of consistency mentioned above must be understood as a revision of the initial plan in response to the unexpected development of the situation after the launch of the paratroopers' operation. According to the testimony of Jeong Dong-nyeon, who was arrested prior to the expansion of martial law, the members of the military security unit where he was detained were visibly flustered on the afternoon of May 19, and the detainees were urgently moved to the military jail at the Combat Training and Doctrine Command (ICKHD 1990a, 3002: 517). This indicates that the core of the new military was thrown into confusion on the afternoon of May 19 after sensing that the situation was rapidly developing in an unexpected direction. Around 1 o'clock on the afternoon of May 20, the entire central government cabinet under Prime Minister Sin Hyeon-hwak resigned without stating a reason. On that afternoon, General Jeong Ung, the commander of the 31st Division, was stripped of his nominal commanding rights; three senior officers—the head of the Second ROK Army, the assistant deputy chief of staff for operation of the Army Headquarters, and the head of Special Warfare Command—personally appeared in Gwangju and began to command the operation from the situation room of the Combat Training and Doctrine Command (Jeong Sang-yong et. al 1990, 217).

According to testimonies of Gwangju citizens, Korean Central Intelligence Agency operatives mingled among demonstrators on the evening of May 20 and encouraged radical behavior (ICKHD 1990a, 3082:713). Although these agents' activities are not judged to have had a great impact on the development of the situation, we may detect the drift of the military's policy. At 8 o'clock in the evening of May 20, an order was issued for the 20th Division to depart for Gwangju. Three brigades of the division headed for the city immediately, and joined the other troops in the Gwangju area on the evening of May 21. At the time, almost 20,000 troops were gathered in the area. On the afternoon of May 21, the head of No. 505 Security Unit, who was in charge of the Gwangju region, was replaced; this may be interpreted as a reprimand for the unexpected development of the situation (Gwangju City 1997 IV, 259).

The next day, on the morning of May 21, several important changes took place. The martial law commander issued an untrue statement that the military and police had been dealt serious losses, thus actively beginning to paint the uprising as a "riot." Around 10 o'clock in the morning, military troops began withdrawing from the Provincial Hall in four helicopters belonging to the 31st Division. Around this time, journalists covering the incident at the government building witnessed live ammunition being distributed to paratroopers. We cannot help but raise the question why firing was being prepared while troop withdrawal was under way. Furthermore, live cartridges were doled out secretly, away from the eyes of the demonstrators. No demonstrator was aware that shooting was in the offing. Nothing concrete has come to light about the order of shooting, either in hearings or research, but when all known facts are put together, the suspicion that someone had thoroughly planned and ordered an infliction of considerable losses with the sudden opening of fire is inescapable.

In addition, many witnesses have questioned whether the military turned a blind eye on the citizens' armament. The armories and powder dumps of many police stations were almost unguarded, and certain testimonies have it that the soldiers in ambush at the city border looked on while cars loaded with guns and live cartridges entered Gwangju.[10] Many have also asked why the paratroopers were pulled out of the city (for example, Kim Yeong-taek 1996, 119-120). They insist that there was no good reason for them to withdraw, given the comparative firepower between the civilian militia and the martial law forces.

To sum up, it appears that the military dispatched paratroopers on May 18 and 19 to crack down harshly on the demonstrations. With the situation unfolding in an unexpected direction, the military came up with a new plan midstream. There must have been a scenario or conspiracy over the timing of sending the airborne units into the city. It appears that the military authorities had a plan to seize state power by installing the Emergency Measures Committee for State Security: they may have wanted to created a sense of crisis throughout the country with the relentless suppression of demonstrations in Gwangju and the thorough control of the media, and then foster an atmosphere of fear throughout the country with the spread of "malevolent rumors" about the paratroopers' atrocities as they had done during the Busan-Masan incident. Until the martial law was expanded on May 17, the military appeared weak as it handled student demonstrations in Seoul; it may have wanted to take the opportunity in Gwangju to impart the impression of strength. In this sense, we may say that Gwangju was selected. However, I do not have concrete evidence to judge whether Kim Dae-jung was arrested on a political scenario to provoke a protest in Gwangju.[11]

It appears that on the afternoon of May 19, when demonstrations spread gradually despite the paratroopers' ultra-hardline suppression, derailing the initial plan, the military authorities switched to another scenario. When the situation heated up and passed the point of no return for the Gwangju citizens, the military could have thought that another measure was necessary to overwhelm the citizens and turn the tables. We may conjecture that the scenario—allow the citizens to accelerate the demonstration and arm themselves while the martial law troops would withdraw briefly, cool the situation by alienating citizens from each other, and then overwhelm them in a flash with the mobilization of heavy weapons—was drafted in a cloak of total secrecy between the afternoon of May 19 and the evening of May 20.[12] The citizens' armament could have been a precondition to mobilize heavy weapons and accumulate justifications for harsh repression.

It is difficult to judge that the paratroopers' brutality displayed from May 18 was a premeditated action to provoke the citizens with the goal of escalating the demonstration; and on the same extension, it is hard to believe that the large-scale propaganda campaign from May 21 using the mass media and the May 27 armed suppression were mapped out from the start. The State Security Emergency Measures Committee was created simultaneously with the fall of the Provincial Hall on May

27. However, we cannot say with certainty that the new military leadership could not have installed this committee if the Gwangju situation had developed differently. Going a step further, we also cannot say that the new military authorities hoped that Gwangju citizens would repel the paratroopers, that they would be quelled with arms, and that armed citizens would put up a final resistance. The young people's final resistance bore witness to the truth of the Gwangju citizens, and their sacrifices cast dark shadows over the destiny of the Chun Doo-hwan regime from the outset. In this regard, the armed suppression staged in the early morning hours of May 27 must be evaluated as a political failure.

It is impossible that events like the May 18 minjung resistance are made of a series of accidental occurrences. It is unreasonable, however, to think that one of the two sides took the initiative from the very beginning and turned everyone involved into puppets. The military always engages itself in an operation with a plan. Just as Carl von Clausewitz said that war was a gamble, a war or a war-like action can lead to an unexpected outcome due to accidental situations, even if it is waged with all uncertainties kept at minimum (Clausewitz 1976, 148-150). We may have to consider that the Gwangju uprising was escalated into an unexpected incident by citizens who acted without calculation, triggered by rage, emotions, and immediate judgment, while the citizens and students who had been judging the situation in a rational, strategic manner went underground. As many people have pointed out, "the capabilities of the minjung" exploded into a scale beyond imagination, and the military authorities must have abandoned their initial scenario and coped with the situation with another plan, another conspiracy.

Conspiracy theories are by nature a discourse of power. The military authorities introduced the conspiracy theory with a plan to make their opponent—their enemy—an entity of conspiring power similar to themselves, and to create evidence in support of their argument by suppressing citizens with their authority and torturing those arrested. In addition, soon after the uprising was over in early June, the military authorities switched from the conspiracy theory involving the North Korean puppet government to the one asserting Kim Dae-jung's involvement. This was a political choice. It is possible that the conspiracy theory involving the military authorities was brought up by a presidential candidate in the arena of power struggle to draw the voters' attention to the true face of the incoming regime, and this may have been based on vague fear and awe of mighty military power, in addition to fragmentary information.

Cases that plainly show the irrational character of the Gwangju uprising include stories about hallucinogens. A rampant rumor had it that the paratroopers sent to Gwangju in the initial period were high on alcohol and hallucinogens, and it was obvious that some of them were drunk. On the other hand, national dailies reported that when a spy named Yi Chang-yong was arrested at the Seoul train station, he was in possession of a hallucinogen, and he intended to infiltrate Gwangju to provoke the citizens.[13] At the time, it was difficult to believe that both sides of the uprising were in their right mind. That the issue of hallucinogens was put forth by both citizens and the military indicates that both sides perceived the Gwangju uprising as being irrational.

3. Explanations of the Citizens' Participation from the Social Science Perspective

It is rare that everyone in an incident that involves a large number of people participates in it with an identical motive. Individuals join with different motives and they create its meaning through common interpretations during a struggle or afterward. In the case of the Gwangju uprising, it is unrealistic to presume that everyone participated in the demonstrations with a single motive, and for this reason, it may be impossible to look for a single cause. It is natural to assume that a number of causes and motives prompted a majority of Gwangju citizens to rise up. At a certain point during the incident, a variety of individual motives were melded into one, and when it happened, all citizens were united as one. Up to now, many researchers suggested social, structural factors from the viewpoint of social science. The factors that are often raised may be summed up as follows: first, yearning for democratization and the students' movement that represented it; second, discontent and resentment over discrimination against the Honam people; third, the history and tradition of the minjung-oriented resistance movement; fourth, the economic structure; and fifth, the traditional community-based culture.[14] Nevertheless, if such objective factors are not linked to each individual's motive of participation, they may end up a mere play on words using abstract theories of social science.

1) Democratization Movement and the Gwangju Uprising

The yearning for democratization was an idealistic justification; we may view it as the most abstract of the uprising's suggested causes. Democratization was the outspoken demand of the student demonstration, which sparked the Gwangju uprising, and it emerged as an important topic of discourse in liberated Gwangju. As I have mentioned before, it is difficult to put it forth as a primary cause or motive of the overall event. Although the theory of the minjung, which began to emerge in 1985, has the tendency to stress the roles of the working classes or the downtrodden while playing down those of the students, it is judged that democratization and the students' organization played a significant role in the uprising. What must be kept in mind regarding this issue is that the military authorities at the time intentionally downplayed the students' roles with the purpose of undermining the middle-class citizens' support by emphasizing "hooligans," "vagabonds," and "disgruntled elements."[15] In fact, starting on May 19, most of the participants in demonstrations were ordinary citizens and working people. Social scientists tend to interpret their participation as being linked with their interests—in other words, class-oriented interests. According to many testimonies, they joined the rallies without realizing who Chun Doo-hwan was, but they learned of his identity during the demonstration, and their hatred of him grew as they became more involved. A rally site can be an arena of political education; the participants' awareness may differ considerably before and after joining a demonstration. In other words, the fact that general citizens or those at the bottom of the social hierarchy outnumbered students is not proof that the demand for democratization was not a cause of the Gwangju uprising.

More than anything else, we must reconsider the argument that the arrival of the airborne unit on May 18 was premeditated. The clash in front of Chonnam National University on that particular morning was a result of the university student association head Bak Gwan-hyeon's promise during the May 16 demonstration that the demonstrating students would meet there if there was trouble. Although the students' demonstration began on a small scale, it soon flared into a serious situation in the afternoon and Molotov cocktails appeared for the first time in contemporary South Korean history.[16] The demonstrators soon torched a pepper-spray vehicle, assaulted a police substation,[17] and held riot policemen hostage. Around noon, a considerable number of citizens joined the demonstrators, who multiplied by leaps and bounds. Around 3 o'clock in the afternoon, the riot police were overcome with fear (ICKHD 1990a, 3020:571; 8002: 1534-1535). It is judged that the citizens' participation on May 18 was an extension of the May 16th torch demonstration, in which citizens actively and favorably responded to the students. Therefore, the student demonstrations until May 16, in particular the torch rally that day, must be regarded as an important background factor of the Gwangju uprising (ICKHD 19901, 1007: 154-155). Although it is not easy to find accounts of the May 16th torch rally, we may get a clue from the demonstrations that took place in many parts of South Jeolla Province outside Gwangju after May 21. These demonstrations generally copied the Gwangju rallies. In the case of Mokpo, where demonstrations were best organized, citizens repeated as many as three torch demonstrations during the protest period (ICKHD 1990a, 6011).

The Chonnam National University students' organization failed to participate in the uprising because most of its members either were arrested on May 17 in a preliminary roundup or took flight around May 19. Independent activist circles still operating at the time contributed a great deal to mobilizing citizens by making and distributing Molotov cocktails and leaflets.[18] The Nokdu Bookstore, located at the Jang-dong Rotary, was managed by Kim Sang-yun, who was arrested before the start of the uprising as one of the leaders of the Gwangju activist circles. The bookstore, a gathering place for remaining activists, played the role of a situation room, where information was exchanged, Molotov cocktails were sent to designated areas, and leaflets were printed. Yun Sang-won, the leader of the Field Fire Night School, Kim Sang-jip, Kim Sang-yun's younger brother, and Kim Sang-yun's younger school friends contributed considerably to the development of the situation throughout the uprising.

In addition, students were an important symbolic factor in the citizens' participation and support. Middle-aged and older generations of Gwangju citizens actively supported the demonstrations because they felt a serious sense of crisis over the community's future, having heard that "the paratroopers are rounding up and killing all the students" and "the airborne unit's soldiers are killing all our children." It appears that the Gwangju citizens regarded the necessity to nurture youth as an ideological direction for the region's development.[19] Also, with regard to the women who prepared food for the demonstrators, which was a decisive factor in forming an absolute community after May 20, the symbolic meaning of young students proved to be a crucial motive. Relevant testimonies often contain the expres-

96

sion, "I said to myself I shouldn't tolerate it as a person who was raising children."[20] Many citizens, especially those who did not take to the streets, must have thought that the people who fought and got killed downtown were mostly students, the talented youth who would carry the future of Gwangju on their shoulders, and believed that the least they could do was to support them in hopes of reducing losses. In this respect, students and the yearning for democratization were important factors in the uprising, and Kim Dae-jung's arrest should be discussed in this context.[21]

It is likely that the citizens in Mokpo, Kim's political stronghold, were more infuriated over Kim Dae-jung's arrest than the Gwangju citizens were. In Mokpo, however, despite an uneasy atmosphere, no agitation occurred until demonstrators arrived from Gwangju. Having heard that demonstrators were coming to Mokpo, some citizens went out to meet them. The dissidents and activists of Mokpo judged that they could take action after the arrival of the Gwangju warriors. On the afternoon of May 21, when some of the Gwangju demonstrators arrived in Mokpo soon after paratroopers opened fire on their fellow demonstrators in Gwangju, citizens of Mokpo immediately began to demonstrate, arm, and stage a torch rally (ICKHD 1990a, 6002: 1024; 6007: 1038-1039; 6012: 1049). The important difference between the two cities is that, in Mokpo, citizens did not fight in solidarity.[22] As soon as news came that the Gwangju Provincial Hall had fallen on May 27, the demonstrators in Mokpo began to disperse. Ultimately, large-scale demonstrations in Mokpo, Kim Dae-jung's political turf, depended on the struggle in Gwangju in many respects.[23]

2) Resentment over Discrimination Against the Honam Region

Discrimination against Honam, southwestern Korea, is also an abstract element; the testimonies do not reveal to what extent citizens were aware of this issue during their participation in the demonstrations. It is clear, however, that the remarks about how the soldiers from Gyeongsang Province were targeting the Jeolla people had a strong effect. The fact that such rumors sounded realistic and spread throughout Gwangju in a short period of time demonstrates that awareness of discrimination against Honam was an important factor in one way or another.[24] There were few observed cases of resentment and fury over discrimination against Honam; this issue was rarely mentioned in real-name testimonies. There is no evidence that the rancor coming from regional discrimination was expressed in the early hours of the rebellion. Some part of this issue came to the surface on May 21. That morning, a big-character poster entitled "South Jeolla People, Rise Up" was pasted on a downtown wall (Kim Yeong-taek, 1996, 108). Around 1:30 that afternoon, a bare-chested young man, riding on an armored vehicle racing toward the Provincial Hall, waved the national flag and shouted, "Long Live Gwangju!" Soon a shot was fired and he slumped forward, lifeless. This shocking scene would be seared into the minds of the Gwangju citizens. The next day, May 22, the first day of liberated Gwangju, a big-character wall poster was found on the side wall of the Catholic Center. Its title was "You and I are Brothers, What is This Slaughter, What Is This Regional Color?" (Kim Yeong-taek 1996, 130). In other words, resentment over discrimination against Honam was first expressed by citizens around May 21, not during the first days of the uprising. Some people nevertheless believed that the cause of the Gwangju uprising derived from regional discrimination (ICKHD 1990a, 3032: 606; 3061: 666-667; 7106: 1401).

The issue of regional discrimination was more vividly demonstrated on the outskirts of Gwangju. The demonstrators in Hwasun and Mokpo expressed rancor over regional discrimination as a justification of their protests.[25] We may have to understand that demonstrations and armed protests occurred in South Jeolla Province outside Gwangju because the entire region identified itself with Gwangju. The forms of protest in many parts of South Jeolla Province copied the Gwangju citizens' struggle. For example, the Mokpo citizens held torch rallies on three occasions and staged "vehicle demonstrations" as well.[26] What could not be copied was the unity of citizens formed in Gwangju; in other words, the absolute community to be discussed later. Nevertheless, all state authority withdrew, afraid that the residents might rise up by forming an absolute community in the style of Gwangju, and there was a vacuum in public security. Also all police forces were dispatched to Gwangju to crack down on the demonstrators. Another reason for the expanded demonstration throughout South Jeolla Province is that martial law troops shut off the roads leading to Gwangju from the evening of May 21, which prompted those who intended to join the Gwangju civilian militia to move around in the vicinity.

The military, however, was an institution in which regional discrimination was practiced openly. If we want to examine regional discrimination as a cause for the Gwangju uprising, it is the military that needs to be scrutinized, not the acts of the Gwangju citizens. For a long time, overt regional discrimination took place in all aspects of military life, from the promotion of officers to everyday life in the barracks. Most Gwangju citizens who had been conscripted into the military had the experience of openly being discriminated against, abused, and beaten for the sole reason that they were from Gwangju. In the military, the expression "double back" symbolizes blatant discrimination against Honam.[27] The Gwangju citizens with such experience may have thought plausible the stories of the Gyeongsang soldiers' atrocities or that only those from Gyeongsang had been sent into Gwangju. In particular, the reservists and reserve commanders, who made decisive contributions in the stage of arming citizens, may have remembered similar incidents during their days of active duty. In the military at the time, the leadership of the Gyeongsang soldiers was entrenched, from generals, to non-commissioned officers, to enlisted men.

People frequently ask: If paratroopers had committed such atrocities in cities other than Gwangju, would they have elicited a similar reaction? This question needs to be changed: "Could the paratroopers have acted in other cities as they did in Gwangju?" The comparison between the Busan-Masan incident and the Gwangju uprising reveals many differences. Most officers and enlisted men in the airborne unit may have generally believed that they could do anything they pleased in Gwangju, the heart of Honam, while the soldiers from Honam had no choice but to obey the orders and adapt themselves to the atmosphere, swallowing tears.[28] The code name of the paratroopers' operation—the "glorious vacation"—allows a glimpse into the odd sense of liberation felt by the paratroopers in Gwangju.[29] If the airborne troops had been mobilized to other regions at the time, the atrocities that went beyond the operation of quelling Gwangju citizens—beating grandmothers and grandfathers and unimaginable brutality targeting women—might not have occurred. In this sense, Gwangju was selected in a tacit manner. The regional difference and the resentment over it were important factors that worked in all stages of the unfolding situation.

3) History of Resistance

In explaining the uprising, the role of history and the tradition of the minjung's resistance may be more difficult to prove. It is likely that few participants in the demonstration at the time were aware of history and tradition. However, many university students involved in student activism were aware of the history of resistance, which must be considered along with democratization and the student movement. Considering the roles and responses of middle-aged and older people at the time, it is clear that history and tradition cannot be regarded as a vague factor. To begin with, the older people's laments, frequently found in testimonies—"We saw many intimidating policemen during the Japanese occupation and we experienced the communist People's

Republic, but even they did not act like this."—played an important role for the youngsters' participation in the demonstrations. These remarks, through historical comparison and analysis, assured young people that they could consider their resistance a just act beyond doubt; as a result, many youths remembered these words and mentioned them in their testimonies.

At the time, middle-aged and older people actively encouraged youngsters to fight in places where people from all walks of life gathered, such as the Daein Market and the Yangdong Market. According to many testimonies, older people advised the youths to take up guns soon after the paratroopers opened fire. Although the actual battle involved young people, they were able to risk their lives in a brave fight because they were convinced that their struggle was the right thing, thanks to the active support of the older people, who prepared food and other necessities and cheered for them in the streets.

Going a step further, the motto of the demonstrators— "We must defend our region with our own hands"—though it is not clear who said it first, may have been wisdom obtained from the experience of immense losses when the 14th Regiment revolted in Yeosun in 1948.[30] Finally, distrust of public authority rooted in the history of resistance could have been an important factor in the genesis and development of the Gwangju incident. Following the expansion of martial law, it was only in Gwangju and Jeonju that demonstrations took place on May 18; the students in Seoul, so vocal until then, fell silent. The conviction that fighting against state authority was doubtlessly a just act might have been impossible without the tradition of resistance.

4) Community and Class Structure

The economic structure has often been offered as an explanation for the uprising from a sociological viewpoint. This issue has been presented as a decisive factor in the "theory of the minjung," which is concretely linked with social class. This issue, however, must be understood at a community level. The Gwangju region lagged in developed commerce and industry; few outsiders moved in, while many of its citizens migrated to other parts of Korea. For this reason, the residents' homogeneity was intact. In a nutshell, "everybody knew everyone else through acquaintances"—and they were aware of the Gwangju region's strong community characteristics.[31] In other words, because industry was undeveloped, a traditional agrarian community existed in Gwangju. The Gwangju citizens did not regard the paratroopers' violence against the youth as something that was unrelated to them; in fact, they witnessed their own acquaintances being assaulted. Thus, the possibility of citizen participation in the demonstrations, despite the fear of the paratroopers' brutality, may have been higher than in other regions.

In addition, the perception that "everyone knew everyone else through acquaintances" must have provided a great reward for those who put up a brave fight. The Gwangju citizens encouraged young ones risking their lives with enthusiastic applause. Whether or not young people joined the demonstration and what roles they played may have been directly related to their status in the community. When the struggle spread to involve all the Gwangju citizens, the sense of obligation to contribute in any way possible was universal, and they may have been unable to resist the obligation to the community if they wanted to live in Gwangju. When some refused to donate their possessions to demonstrators, several young participants said, "Let's see whether you can live in Gwangju with that kind of attitude," and such a remark might have been perceived as a real threat.

The large number of the poor within the city was a decisive factor for many citizens to join. The structure of a marketplace city—in which small-scale shops were concentrated in the downtown area with few of the large-scale factories or industrial complexes that are commonly situated outside a city—made it easy for workers to join rallies held at the heart of town. The sense of community encouraged them to volunteer for the frontline of the struggle, and they were given the status of honorable citizens.[32]

4. Theory of Fear and Fury

The various factors discussed above cannot cause a minjung rebellion on their own. The Gwangju citizens have lived for a long time with such factors, and they may continue to live with them. These elements may provide easy explanations for those who supported the protest by assisting the demonstrators. However, the structural factors—the elements that link individuals' economic interests, ideological leaning, and resentment—are not sufficient to explain why some people fought on the forefront of a protest, risking their lives.

In case of the Gwangju uprising, there is no disagreement that people with such interests, resentments, and ideological leanings fought on the frontlines (Son Ho-cheol 1995 et al). Such structural elements kicked in at a certain opportunity or through a certain catalyst. The catalyst was the paratroopers' enormous atrocities, the so-called "excessive suppression" suggested by the Gwangju citizens during the uprising and afterward, which was the primary reason for their fight.[33] The decisive issue in understanding the citizens' participation is how this occasion and structural factors combined to compel them to take action. This issue can be illuminated only when we microscopically analyze the psychology of the Gwangju citizens in such a situation.

The so-called Chungjeong riot-quelling training, which the paratroopers had received for a long time, was described by an army surgeon of the 7th Airborne Brigade: "Instill fear and awe in the demonstrators to make them disperse. If that does not work, you catch a few people as examples and treat them mercilessly to make the demonstrators run away" (ICKHD 1990a, 8001: 1532). This method seems to have been independently developed in a socio-political situation where it was impossible to follow the methods of the U.S. forces' drill book on suppressing demonstrations under martial law.[34] Given that those who ordered the police to open fire on a crowd during the 1960 Student Uprising received capital punishment, firing at citizens is not generally accepted in South Korea, as it may be in American society. The suppression method in question must have been adopted in consideration of the Korean military's long tradition of beating. It was systematically developed after its effect was shown in the Busan-Masan incident, and the military had faith in it.[35] In April 1980, the paratroopers received 70-centimeter sticks made of birch or ash, manufactured by a private company on commission. These sticks were mightier than the 50-centimeter bats used by the riot police, and they proved lethal. The paratroopers' method of crackdown can be understood as demonstrative violence. The method instilled fear not only in those who were the targets of violence, but also in observers. The military must have believed that the more brutal the quelling was, the better it was. The paratroopers' suppressive actions had the goal of creating a theater of violence.[36] It was a cruel transformation of socio-political ethics, holding that "it is all right as long as there is no shooting." On the extension of this principle, the soldiers of the airborne unit used bayonets from the beginning, and going a step further, they started using flamethrowers on the afternoon of May 20.

However, such brutal use of authority is unjust as long as crime and punishment do not correspond; when brutality is used to pursue a goal, it is inhumane. Although such inhumanity resulted in depriving the violent party of legitimacy, the military authorities eager to grab power paid no attention to political or ethical considerations.[37] The airborne unit became an evil being and fed the judgment that the expansion of martial law on May 17 was yet another illegitimate coup d'état. In the eyes of the citizens, it was impossible that the paratroopers were "the same ethnic people." They were "beasts" and "devils," incarnations of evil beyond description.

104

The paratroopers' suppressive method had the goal of sending citizens home in a hurry, evoking their instinct of self-protection when they witnessed the scene in the streets. As we have seen, strong elements of community remained in Gwangju at the time. Initially gripped with fear, the citizens scattered, but in the end they returned. The Gwangju citizens, closely linked to each other, could not betray the conscience and obligation of the community. The paratroopers' crackdown method focused on individual selfishness and instinct for self-protection. Probably it could only have the opposite effect in a group with a strong sense of community. The demonstrations did not continue consistently; they were sporadic from May 18 to 20. This pattern demonstrates the conflict between citizens' individual protective instincts and the obligations they felt as members of the community.

However, the paratroopers sent to Gwangju did not stick to their instructions. They used bayonets from the very first day, threw abusive remarks and relentlessly beat grandfathers and grandmothers who protested against excessive violence. They inflicted violence on women, tore off their clothes, and drove bayonets into their breasts. Such acts turned the scene into a vicious theater of violence.[38] There is no reason to suppose that the paratroopers' frenzied use of violence was based on their superiors' directions or orders. Rather, it may have stemmed from many conditions existing within the airborne unit. Soldiers had not been allowed to take a day off or sleep away from their barracks for more than half a year since the Busan-Masan incident, due to a series of events, including President Park Chung-hee's assassination in October 1979 and the military coup d'état in December 1979. Being subject to continuous riot training, they were filled with discontent and fury. In conjunction with the regional discrimination rife in the military organizations, the operation in Gwangju must naturally have struck them as an opportunity to vent their anger. In other words, their individual and collective attack instincts erupted in the name of cracking

105

down on a demonstration, and this instinct had been systematically cultivated with the paratroop's special training.

A considerable number of non-commissioned officers, the
mainstay of the troop, had experience fighting in Vietnam. They
were well-versed in atrocious techniques, and brutality may have
become their second nature. What enraged citizens was that the
paratroopers seemed to enjoy the exercise of brutality; smiles
flitted across their faces and they burst out with gleeful laughs.
The crackdown by the airborne unit went beyond a daring strike,
conveying the message that "we are not human beings but beasts
and devils" and "you are not human beings to us." These bar-
barians and devils were shaped by a civilized society that had
poured enormous financial resources into their training.

Those who witnessed the atrocities between May 18 and 19
describe the scenes in similar language. Expressions such as "beat
the citizens as if they were dogs," "dragged them as if they were
dogs and loaded them in trucks," and "lifted them onto trucks
as if they were parcels" can be found in many testimonies, and
the scene evoked intolerable fury, making the witnesses' "blood
surge to their heads." They avowed that "even animals couldn't
be as cruel." In particular, many citizens were outraged by the
violence and perverted actions aimed at older people, children,
and women. The Gwangju citizens' rage was not only the resentment of those who had been treated with unjust violence but
also rational fury over the destruction of human dignity. Some
citizens participated in the demonstration at this point.[39] However, a majority of citizens had no choice but to run away, despite their fury. They felt they were "infinitely helpless" for running away in fear (ICKHD 1990a, 1042: 313).

An unidentified witness confessed his feelings after fleeing
from a scene in which troopers slashed open a pregnant woman's
stomach.[40]

Are they really the soldiers of the Republic of Korea, who
carry out the sacred tasks of defending our country, our land?

I began to feel ashamed of myself for having been in hiding, stealing a look at the horrible scene. Realizing my own servility, which makes it impossible for me to protest against such an act, and seeing myself as a shameful being, I felt indescribable contempt for myself. It was not because I saw a woman dying with an open belly, but because I experienced self-hatred for the first time—that I was cowardly and inferior (Gwangju City 1997 II, 123).

This feeling is not merely fury over injustice or pity for neighbors' misfortune; it went beyond rational rage over the obliteration of human dignity. This is a mixture of rational rage, humiliation, and anger at one's own failure to react other than by fleeing in fear. The paratroopers treated demonstrators as less than animals. The spectators of the theater of violence, no less than the targets of such violence, were demeaned into servile, subhuman beings. Some cried out, "It is a curse living in a period like this!"

Fury over their abasement and anger that their fear of violence had ruled them pushed the Gwangju citizens to cross the line of self-preservation and fight the paratroopers. That Gwangju citizens risked their lives and boldly participated in the struggle came from a rational decision to express their fury, despite their fear, in order to recover their human dignity. Human dignity was not an individual matter; it existed between the neighbors being beaten and the witnesses, as well as within individual members of the community. The Gwangju citizens' enraged resistance can be viewed neither as an "explosion of barbaric hatred" and the "instinct of destruction," nor as the escalation of radical demonstrations in response to excessive suppression.[41]

The social structural factors discussed above might have come into play in individual consciousness as humiliation and fury piled up. When they became aware of the shame they felt after fleeing in fear and the helpless picture they cut, memories of how they had lived so far must have flashed by and their shabby, wretched lives must have aggravated their sense of humiliation. Resentment over their poverty and the discrimination they faced as Honam residents may have added insult to injury. It was not that these structural factors independently pushed poor citizens to participate in demonstrations, making them aware of their poverty and resentment, but these conditions dormant in their consciousness were awakened as soon as they realized that they had fled like cowards; coupled with the humiliation they felt at the time, these factors drove them to an uncontrollable rage.

The classes that had relatively few miserable memories might have found it easier to digest humiliation and fury. By contrast, the rage of those who had lived with heavy resentment must have grown out of hand. It stands to reason that the downtrodden would have felt more urgency to recover "humanness," and that those who had been subject to regional discrimination harbored an excruciating sense of pain. Humiliation and fury, mixed with resentment, were triggered by fear of violence, and overcoming this fear promised that they could overcome their sad memories.

To sum up, economic interests and individual resentments cannot make citizens fight against paratroopers. Therefore, they cannot be direct causes for the unfolding of the Gwangju uprising. However, observations revealed that key roles were played by the poor and working classes, and those at the bottom rung of social ladder—in other words, people who had the most economic grievances and personal resentment. Despite it all, the motive of their participation in the demonstrations and struggle was, as I have explained at length, fury over the destruction of human dignity. In actuality, people's participation in a demonstration depends largely on individual characteristics, such as whether they have a strong sense of public spirit or tend to keep to themselves. Nevertheless, in general, the social makeup of those who participate in rallies is decided by the social distribution of resentment—which is likely to mirror social classes—and other relevant conditions.

Such an analysis explains a phenomenon in which objective observation clashes with subjective awareness when it came to citizens' participation in demonstrations. The fact that certain classes of people come forward in such a situation is often described as "expressing their own resentment." However, personal rancor following objective causes must be viewed as a marginal factor.[42] Although most participants were of the classes harboring deep-seated anger, they participated primarily as human beings. The internal process before making a decision to join a rally may take a considerable time; the on-and-off pattern of the Gwangju protest may be understood as the result of such internal processes. While some citizens may have taken to the streets after reaching a calm resolve through an internal process, others may have experienced it during their participation in demonstrations. This on-and-off pattern clearly indicates that the development of the Gwangju uprising cannot be explained as an escalation of violence between paratroopers and citizens.

On the afternoon of May 18, after the paratroopers swept through the city, almost all the students and citizens dispersed out of fear and the streets were empty.[43] The confrontation seemed to be over, but another demonstration began near Gwangju High School at Gyerim-dong around 7 o'clock in the evening, and paratroopers emerged and slaughtered the participants. Soon after, the troops searched the residential areas in the vicinity—Sansu-dong and Punghyang-dong—and indiscriminately rounded up youths. Having witnessed the scene, the citizens, perplexed, phoned their families and friends to find out what was going on. The citizens trembled at the rumor that paratroopers were searching for activist students throughout residential areas all over the city with the students' school records in hand. On the other hand, some citizens fought late into the night (ICKHD 1990a, 3042: 628).

On the morning of May 19, the entire city was filled with a sense of fear as paratroopers roughly inspected passers-by. Parents discouraged their children from venturing out. That morning, paratroopers carried out an offensive crackdown operation. If paratroopers took notice of someone peeking out a window, they searched every hotel and cram school in the vicinity. They caught every youth in sight, gathered them on Geumnam Avenue, stripped them, and imposed disciplinary measures and violence. That day, the paratroopers mobilized armored vehicles, and their cruelty was at its height. Around lunch time, the streets were deserted, and the paratroopers relaxed and withdrew to their base to have lunch. In the afternoon, however, countless citizens spilled out to the streets, forming new ranks. From that point on, the students did not play a central role in demonstrations. At first, a majority was made of downtown citizens— suited salaried men, working people, middle-aged men and women—and soon high school students began to join in.

Fierce battles erupted in many parts of the city, including in front of the Catholic Center. Seizing this opportunity, some of the demonstrators—citizens who joined with determination, having overcome fear—began to arm themselves with all sorts of household fixtures and material from construction sites. They destroyed facilities on the streets and built barricades to put up a staunch resistance. Hwang Seog-yeong described the scenes of violent battles that day in many parts of the city as follows:

> The demonstrators dispersed temporarily and gathered again. It looked as if a giant balloon were losing air, going flat, and then expanded to grow taut with air again (Hwang Seog-yeong 1985, 63).

Such a picture shows that paratroopers were unable to run too far after the demonstrators, and the balance of power between the airborne unit and demonstrators was slowly being struck (ICKHD 8002: 1536). The paratroopers began to see casualties in their midst, and a patrol helicopter started intensive propaganda broadcasting, using terms such as "mobs" and "impure elements." This was tantamount to the paratroopers' confession of their faulty reasoning, which pushed the citizens to become more furious.[44] From that afternoon, the citizens' everyday lives were completely suspended; almost all workplaces and most schools in the city closed their doors.

From this point on, responsibilities were divided among the Gwangju citizens. Young people fought on the frontlines while women broke sidewalk bricks at the back and delivered them to the demonstrators. Construction workers with carts delivered material that could be used as weapons. In the streets, young women gave first-aid treatment to the injured.[45] When the paratroopers felt that they were gradually being overwhelmed by demonstrators, they grew vicious and an immense number of citizens were sacrificed. Around five o'clock in the afternoon, the first gunshot rang out from an armored vehicle under siege. Although many youths fought tenaciously, rain began to fall in the evening and many citizens went home. Some fought throughout the night, despite the rain. Mun Jang-u, who was an active participant in the demonstrations, described how he felt that night.

> That night I couldn't bring myself to go home. If demonstrators went away one by one, everyone would be gone. If I went home, I felt my resolve would be weakened in the presence of my wife and children. There was no good place to sleep. I entered a large concrete drain pipe at a construction site near Jeonnam Technical High School. I was wearing a suit. Afraid that it might get dirty, I took off the jacket before I went to sleep. I woke up because it was so cold. I went to a friend's house near Chonnam University Hospital and left his home on the morning of May 20 and headed downtown (ICKHD 1990a, 2025: 434).

The citizens' anger had already exploded, and they felt re-sponsible as members of a community. On May 19, Gwangju citizens' faces were "filled with seething fury" (ICKHD 1990a, 1045:327). Though they put up a staunch front, they were en-gaged in a lonely battle. Most citizens overcame fury when they joined the demonstrators, but they fled as quickly as possible when paratroopers charged toward them shouting at the top of their lungs, and they had to firm up their resolve before they could come forward again. They did not give up, however. Now, they were not engaged in university students' demonstrations, in which they tried to achieve something with numbers. Rather, they were engaged in a protest of citizens waged by those who had overcome fright with resolve and reason. The demonstra-tors were on the defensive, and they had to run away desper-ately to save their skins. They threw Molotov cocktails, set fire to many cars, and rolled petroleum drums toward the paratroop-ers to ignite explosions. They burned vehicles with Gyeongsang Province license plates wherever they were spotted, and set fire to police substations in Numun-dong and Im-dong. Fire was the citizens' major weapon. It was also a scream in the midst of loneliness, a torch to prompt more citizens to join them, and a firework of the community staged by lonely warriors.[46] When night fell, citizens burned a large arch at Yu-dong and someone set a big fire on a hill on the way to Mt. Mudeung (Kim Yeong-taek 1996: Yim Cheol-u 1997 III, 218-220). Clearly, the fire en-hanced the atmosphere and invited citizens to come out to watch it, thus taking on the significance of a beacon that heralded full-fledged resistance.

Such acts translated into a mammoth destruction of assets; it was an indication that workers and the urban poor, who do not care about bourgeois property and who harbored secret hostility toward the propertied, participated in the demonstra-tions in earnest. Some of the demonstrations took on the form of a "riot" as citizens torched many places in the city, resisting their loneliness, and expressing resentful hostility toward those who did not join.[47] However, demonstrators maintained a modicum of reason; only a few drivers with Gyeongsang Province license plates or Gyeongsang Province people were targets of violence (ICKHD 1990a, 3032: 606). Some argued that such people should be beaten or "killed," but there were always others who discouraged them (ICKHD 1990a, 1045: 328 etc.).

5. The Emergence of Absolute Community

The situation changed dramatically on the morning of May 20. The 3rd Airborne Brigade, which had been sent to the city in the small hours, stood guard in the streets and treated citizens politely; no bayonets were attached to their guns. In the morning, however, a dismembered body was discovered in front of the Jeonnam Brewery. Citizens lost their heads and soon gathered in front of the Daein Market, where a demonstration broke out. The demonstration and its suppression in the morning were not on a big scale, but female merchants in the market began to make rice balls for the demonstrators (Yim Cheol-u 1997 III, 37-38), and thousands of leaflets were distributed. Citizens were solidifying their resolve to fight.[48]

In the afternoon, a considerable number of citizens—young and old, men and women—walked from the outskirts of the city toward downtown. Yim Cheol-u describes the scene of this slow gathering as follows:

> The sound of singing. Whoever started it, the national anthem spread from mouth to mouth. . . . In Mu-seok's eyes, the scene looked like a mammoth funeral procession. The song drifting out of their mouths sounded like a dirge. A funeral that is endlessly solemn and extremely sad. The number of mourners increased with the passage of time, and it looked like the procession would continue forever. Men and women, the old and the young, who ballooned to thousands in an instant, moved slowly toward downtown, creating heavy, dull waves. . . .

Now Mu-seok revised his thought about their appearance resembling a funeral procession. Rather, they looked like a festival procession buoyed by passion. Clearly, something strong and mysterious ruled over them. Amazingly, few traces of fear were visible in their faces. They shouted slogans following a leader, clapped their hands, sang songs, and then burst out laughing—some lightheartedness could be glimpsed from these citizens. . . . What had happened? Once again, Mu-seok was perplexed. . . . Something was definitely different from the expressions he had seen on the citizens for the past two days—terribly distorted with fear, despair, consternation, and rage. The citizens' faces were now brimming with strength. The strength, hot and strong like a ball of fire, concealed an immense explosive power. . . . 'What could it be? Where did that power come from? What makes so many citizens look completely different overnight?' . . . To Mu-seok, it was like a riddle"[49] (Yim Cheol-u 1997 III, 134: 137-138).

At last, a large-scale demonstration took place in the afternoon, and the paratroopers launched flamethrowers at the Seobang three-way intersection at around 2:30, burning several citizens to death on site. Blind hostility flared up among citizens. Around 3:00, the 7th and the 11th Brigades were redeployed in the downtown area, and the citizens and paratroopers plunged into an all-out war. When huge masses of demonstrators emerged, the paratroopers began to defend the city's important positions by the battalion, instead of occupying the city block by block, as they had done the day before. As a result, many liberated areas began to emerge.

A new phenomenon appeared. In the space created downtown in the wake of the paratroopers' defensive entry, for example near the Funny Department Store, hundreds of citizens began a sit-in demonstration amid the smoke of tear-gas bombs. To encourage the participants, a student gave a speech, led the citizens in shouting slogans, and read aloud from a leaflet. The crowd snowballed almost instantly. When it was difficult to hear the student's voice, someone began to collect money to buy a microphone. In no time, 400,000 won was collected. Students began to teach the citizens the songs of activists. Repeated were "Our Wish Is Reunification," "Song of Justice," "Song of Fighters," and the "Hula Song." The citizens had trouble carrying the tune at first, but soon sang with ease. Someone suggested that they sing the national anthem and the folksong *Arirang*, which everyone knew. All burst into tears while singing *Arirang*.

Someone shouted. "Let us all die, following those who passed away!" The slogans now changed from hostile ones, such as "Let us tear Chun Doo-hwan to pieces!" to expressions of tragic resolve, such as "Kill all of us!" and "Let all of us die!" With the start of the demonstration, young men stood at the forefront, holding weapons, such as construction lumber. Women distributed wet towels and toothpaste to help the men better withstand tear gas, and brought water. Some carried wooden poles and steel pipes from construction sites, while others brought small stones in carts. No one stood around watching. The citizens were no longer isolated. They embraced each other, shed tears, and fought desperately. Although the paratroopers soon stormed violently into them, the demonstrators were more ready to die than at any other time. The citizens stood their ground, shouting slogans, singing, and forming scrimmage lines with people they had never met before.

Dusk fell and citizens were tiring. Suddenly, the headlights of numerous cars approached from the Yu-dong three-way intersection. The citizens were seized by fear, their instinct telling them that reinforced paratroopers were coming, but someone shouted. "At last, democratic drivers have risen up!" It was a vehicle demonstration mounted by drivers. Large trucks and buses were slowly approaching the Provincial Hall, followed by hundreds of taxis, with their headlights on and horns honking. The sound of "hurrah!" shook the city. The citizens appeared to be strong enough to drive away the paratroopers in no time.

115

The soldiers were overcome with fear; they destroyed phone booths and large flower pots along the streets to build barricades. Although it was citizens who had erected barricades until the day before, it was now the paratroopers who were compelled to do so.

While the vehicle demonstrators paused before the barricades, numerous tear-gas bombs exploded and paratroopers charged forward, threading between cars and fighting with the citizens one-on-one. Many drivers and citizens were hurt and captured. However, confirming that they were united, demonstrators gained strength throughout the city. Some residents brought seaweed-rolled rice, rice balls, soft drinks, towels, and cigarettes to distribute to the demonstrators. Many people flocked downtown from the outskirts of the city. It may be impossible to explain how the citizens became united in such a short period of time. No explicit words were necessary to help the citizens overcome their fear and join the demonstration.[50]

From May 19 to the morning of May 20, the Gwangju community existed within individual citizens fighting in the streets. Had there not been a traditional community, this battle could not have begun. Nevertheless, the decision to participate in the protest was reached through each person's internal process. At first, the warriors were on their own. They hoped that all citizens would rise up at the same time. Such unity of all citizens seemed to be a wistful wish. Demonstrators ran from place to place to avoid arrests; sometimes they threw stones or set fires to express their rage and encourage other citizens to join them. On the afternoon of May 20, however, their wish came true. On Geumnam Avenue and in other parts of the city, a concrete community of citizens was formed. It was an absolute community, different from a traditional community.

This absolute community was not created by a leader with a microphone in hand, urging the demonstrators to unite. Many citizens anticipated the emergence of someone like Jeon Ok-ju.[51] She was not a leader. Individual citizens were leaders, and she was only a cheerleader. Unlike the military, the absolute community was not an organization created by someone by oppressing individuals to achieve a goal. This was a community whose members overcame fear of violence and personal shame through reason and courage. Citizens braving death gathered to join forces after recognizing and congratulating each other for being real human beings. The human dignity pursued by citizens was objectified by mutual recognition in encounters with other dignified human beings. In this absolute community, citizens found their identity as human beings, and they were reborn.

The first encounter was between students and citizens, which led to the encounter with participants as individuals. Students led demonstrators in singing activist songs that they had sung during their own battles. Then the citizens, the minjung, suggested that they sing their song, *Arirang*, the song everyone knew. Kim Chung-geun, a *Donga Ilbo* reporter who was covering the scene at the Provincial Hall, later described *Arirang* as follows:

> I realized for the first time that *Arirang*, the representative folksong of Korea, conveyed such blood-curdling emotion.... All alone on the Provincial Hall rooftop, as I listened to *Arirang*, sung by the crowds as they came toward the square in front of the Provincial Hall in complete darkness, because power and water had been cut off throughout the city after broadcasting stations and police substations were torched, and as I looked down on the people with national flags in their hands, a violent chill went down my spine and I don't know for how long tears kept flowing down my cheeks (Journalists Association of Korea 1997, 215-216).

The surging emotion in the wake of *Arirang*, the plaintive folksong about the loss of a beloved, was a feeling that everyone was becoming one. The melody, which contains long-held emotions of the traditional Korean community, mysteriously bound the citizens and prompted them to act as one, as they walked together slowly.[52] The weeping contained heart-rending confes-

sions of guilt and shame that the citizens had witnessed gruesome scenes involving their fellow citizens but had failed to come
to their rescue, and at the same time they meant a generous ab-
solution. The melody of *Arirang* was Gwangju citizens' salvation.

Citizens were overjoyed to see that people from all walks
of life joined the community, in particular unexpected classes,
such as barmaids from Hwanggeum-dong and prostitutes of
Daein-dong.[53] After dusk fell, about 50 farmers, clad in white
traditional outfits and holding rakes, hoes, and bamboo spears,
emerged on Geumnam Avenue, as if brave fighters of the 1894
Donghak Uprising had just stepped out of a time machine. The
citizens welcomed them with passionate applause. They put their
arms around strangers' shoulders, formed a scrimmage line, and
fought with a determination to die.[54] The citizens became one in
body and spirit. They chipped in whatever they possessed. They
collected money to buy goods for common use, and, every time,
an amazing amount of money was collected in a short period of
time. Everything—food, cigarettes, wet towels, toothpaste, tools
that could be used as weapons, and even cars—was voluntarily
offered. Citizens sought out ways to help out. Many came out
alone, and fought throughout the night without meeting any acquaintance, but no one felt lonely. All helped one another as if
they were old friends.

The absolute community defined life and death at the level
of community, going beyond individuals. Expressions such as
"We fight in order to survive" and "We defend our region with
our own hands" clearly indicate that individual lives were equivalent to the community's life.[55] The sharing of life grew concrete
with the sharing of blood through blood donations. There was
no private property, and there was no distinction between my
life and your life. They found themselves sharing frequent laughs.[56]

When night fell, small national flags materialized in the hands
of adults and children alike, who waved them enthusiastically.[57]
The citizens, having formed the absolute community, began to

claim state authority, singing the national anthem and waving the national flag. To the citizens, the new military junta that had dispatched the devilish paratroopers was a target for overthrow, and the Gwangju citizens were the ones who represented the real Republic of Korea. Along with this notion came the feeling that their fight was sacred. Now, the fight with paratroopers was patriotism. Citizens began to commandeer goods needed for the battle.[58] Getting an idea from the vehicle demonstrators, the citizens requisitioned buses, trucks, and even fire trucks and commandeered gas. A flame was put to some of them before they were pushed toward the paratroopers. Some young men formed suicide squads and braved death. They carried out reckless attacks; they drove burning cars toward the airborne unit and jumped out at the last possible moment. Others drove around the outskirts of the city and transported people downtown. It was from this time that cars were used to transport citizens. The absolute community, as state authority, commandeered numerous citizens and their lives.[59] Even late at night, citizens could not bring themselves to go home, leaving others behind. Without realizing how time passed, they fought throughout the night.

The citizens began to arm themselves in earnest. If only a handful of citizens held up wooden poles and steel pipes to protect themselves until May 19, many armed themselves to wage a war from the afternoon of May 20. Citizens brought out any objects dull and heavy enough to be used as weapons, such as wooden poles, kitchen knives, steel pipes, charcoal briquette holders, shovels, and hoes. Lumber merchants cut a large number of beams and distributed them.[60] Some shouted that they needed guns, and in the evening of May 20, several rifles were seized but there were no live shells. On the morning of May 21, the citizens began to attack the paratroopers defending the Provincial Hall with armored vehicles commandeered from Asia Motors.

Throughout the night of May 20, citizens, as state authority, condemned public organizations. Munhwa Broadcasting Company, which had routinely reported falsehood, was burned. Citizens torched the tax office and the Korean Broadcasting System building.[61] All such actions were not caused by a simple explosion of emotion. As far as arson was concerned, citizens debated the pros and cons and took action according to discussion results (ICKHD 1990a, 4005 etc). Other decisions were made by the community as well. On the night of May 20, someone decided with sufficient authority that all citizens would "wage a do-or-die battle" with the paratroopers, and this was relayed from person to person and the military intelligence network reported it to the commanders as a serious threat.[62] After the paratroopers were defined as enemies, the citizens intended to have negotiations with the police and form friendly relations with the military troops other than the airborne units. They also attempted to negotiate with paratroopers.[63] When the citizens' absolute community emerged and state authority was assumed, the definition of paratroopers changed from "devils" and "evil spirits," with whom dialogue was impossible, to "political enemies," the citizens' negotiation partner. This change of meaning—from the absolute community to a state—made it possible for citizens to conduct the political action of negotiating with devils to minimize their losses.[64] In addition to singing the national anthem and waving the national flag, the citizens carried out ceremonies of a state. A large national flag was draped over the two corpses discovered at the Gwangju train station on the morning of May 21, and at 8 o'clock that morning, citizens offered a silent prayer for their felled colleagues in front of the Provincial Hall. The slaughter of citizens, beaten to death like animals, now became sacred sacrifices, and in this way their resurrection was promised.

From the evening of May 20, paratroopers, cowed by demonstrators numbering tens of thousands, had to fight for their survival, and that night paratroopers fired sporadically in front of the train station and the tax office.[65] After midnight, paratroopers and police began to use a respectful form of speech through speakers, instead of the high-handed, commanding tone they had employed before. They said, "Please return to your homes where your parents and siblings are waiting. At your homes, your families are worried about you because you have not come home yet (Kim Yeong-taek, 1996: 91; The Association of Family Members of Victims 1988, 83). Only at this point did the paratroopers and public authority begin to recognize the Gwangju citizens as beings who should not be trifled with. In particular, the battalion commanders who supervised the soldiers in action on the morning of May 21, especially the 35th and 61st Battalion heads, extremely concerned about violent clashes, were enthusiastic about the idea of negotiation (Kim Yeong-taek, 1996, 100).

The demonstrators' overall actions after the evening of May 20 cannot be viewed as a riot or as displaying a violent nature. As members of the absolute community, all citizens fought a war, conscious of their authority as a state and without the slightest doubts about their rationality. Just as in most cases there was little difference between citizens' voluntary contributions and requisitions,[66] the difference between acts of riot and waging war was subtle. There were a few violent acts. Citizens threw stones at government offices—such as the city hall, district offices, and police headquarters—and broke windows, but they did not set fires to these big government buildings. On the other hand, the demonstrators set fires to almost all police substations in the city; this must be viewed as some demonstrators' petty individual resentments against the police. When the tax office was in flames, citizens pillaged furniture and appliances.[67] However, no policeman was the target of violence. A small number of paratroopers caught by the demonstrators were killed in a gruesome manner, but in some cases, the captured paratroopers were released without any harm inflicted on them.[68] In addition, many inexperienced drivers caused accidents while driving too fast, but this was not a display of destructive instinct; rather, it may be because they were filled with an inflated sense of obligation or intoxicated with the joy of born-again human beings. In general, the targets of violence, destruction, and arson were not indiscriminately chosen. In most cases, citizens used their power selectively through debates. Citizens made sincere efforts not to lose morality or become "mobs," contrary to the propaganda coming from loudspeakers.

The demonstrators, ballooned to tens of thousands on May 20, fought throughout the night, forgetting what time it was and how tired they were. Some took turns taking a short nap on straw mats spread out in alleys, while others rested in nearby inns and residential buildings. At 4:00 in the morning, citizens drove paratroopers out of the train station; victory seemed to dawn. But two bodies that had suffered violent deaths were found in the station, and citizens began to get worked up. All morning, a continuous stream of people flocked to Geumnam Avenue from the outskirts of town, and demonstrators transported ordinary citizens on trucks and buses, pounding the chassis with wooden sticks and singing songs. Wherever they went, women raised seaweed-rolled rice, rice balls, and soft drinks to their cars, offering encouragement. Food was piled up in the cars and the demonstrators firmed up their resolve, convinced of the citizens' enthusiastic support.[69] The provision of food, which appeared for the first time on the evening of May 20, spread all over Gwangju on the morning of May 21. The neighborhood associations collected money or rice (ICKHD 1990a, 3117; 3118). Around 10 o'clock in the morning, demonstrators on Geumnam Avenue confronted paratroopers in a tense atmosphere, while a negotiation was going on for their withdrawal. At the time, the outskirts of town were filled with a festive mood. The demonstrators filling Geumnam Avenue and encircling the Provincial Hall were almost 300,000 in number. It was an impressive scene in which almost all citizens participated.

Yi Se-yeong, who had been active in demonstrations but stayed at home on May 20 before rejoining the protestors on May 21, describes the moment as follows:

Our hearts burst whenever citizens clapped their hands and
cheered us. It gave us great strength. Wherever we went, women
lifted seaweed-rolled rice and rice balls to our car, telling us to
fight with courage. Sometimes they wiped our faces, smeared
with tear-gas smoke, with wet towels. Women, in neighborhood units, prepared food and distributed it to us. From stores,
people tossed us soft drinks and pastries. . . . The citizens' encouragement and care, overwhelming wherever we went,
brought tears to my eyes. No matter how I tried to hold them
back, my heart warmed, my eyes grew wet, and tears began to
flow down my cheeks. There was no need in trying to find
meaning. Naturally, I was getting ready to die.

In such a situation, what is politics and what is the need of
activist consciousness? It was enough to see the picture of true
human beings. This was none other than the recovery of humanity, and this was the rage derived from the love for human
beings. This was the citizens' fury after witnessing students being stabbed to death with paratroopers' bayonets and citizens
being clubbed with sticks. This was a firm resolve and protective instinct that we could no longer allow them to be killed.
Maybe it was a community of common destiny. Rather than
stopping at being furious at the paratroopers, citizens were
developing consciousness that they should recover the blood
shed by young people through the realization of democracy,
overcoming the region's isolation from society, politics, and
culture (Young Comrades Society 1987, 182).

On the morning of May 21, citizens elected four representatives, including Jeon Ok-ju, and an attempt was made to negotiate with the Martial Law Command. However, live ammunition
had already been distributed to paratroopers, and they were ready
to open fire on the crowds. It is not surprising that the negotiations broke down. Around 1 o'clock in the afternoon, the paratroopers fired on the citizens, using the national anthem as the
signal. In a flash, Geumnam Avenue turned into a sea of blood

and loud weeping. The paratroopers hid themselves in the Provincial Hall and the surrounding buildings to snipe at anyone who came into view. At around 1:30, a bare-chested young man atop an armored vehicle, flying the nation flag, raced toward the Provincial Hall, calling out, "Long Live Gwangju!" As all citizens anxiously fixed their eyes on him, a shot rang out and the man's neck snapped, blood squirting all around him. The witnesses were shaken. Now it was really "war" from which there was no turning back.

Citizens soon headed for armories inside and outside the city to get their hands on guns. They first ran to the nearby Naju Police Station and wrested away guns and live shells at 2:30, followed by seizures at armories in other areas. Around 3 o'clock, citizens returned to Gwangju and distributed guns and bullets to citizens at Gwangju Park. They formed a special attack corps near the park. With the emergence of the "civilian militia," street battles began. At around 4:40, two light machine guns were placed on the rooftop of the 12-floor Chonnam National University Medical School, which commanded an unobstructed view of the Provincial Hall.[70] To the citizens, taking up guns was a natural development; it did not take a lot of mental torment to do so. With the formation of the absolute community and the assumption of state authority from the afternoon of May 20, armament was a natural conclusion. On the evening of May 21, the civilian militia entered the Provincial Hall, from which the paratroopers had already withdrawn. It was an emotional victory. Shouts of triumph, along with the sounds of wailing, shook the city.

In a nutshell, the Gwangju citizens could repel the paratroopers of three brigades after a four-day struggle because they were able to form an absolute community, quite different from the existing community with its traditional rural background. It was a process of change; individual citizens who came forward to become human beings, having overcome fear with reason, met a large number of colleagues, merged into one, and found themselves to be new human beings, without any doubts of their human dignity. This also meant liberation.

In this community, the concept of private property completely disappeared. The community was created because all shared their possessions, rather than taking away someone's assets, as was the case in communist revolutions. The citizens, however, respected commercial activities and protected each other's property.[71] The sharing of possessions was taken for granted when individuals were dignified beings who fought enemies, braving death; this sharing was a natural thing to do when individual lives coincide with the community's life. As long as human dignity was confirmed objectively in the absolute community, individual possessions that marked social status had no meaning. Naturally, there was no class since every individual's supreme dignity was recognized.[72] Furthermore, it was a permanent space in which finitude was overcome and time had no meaning, for individuals were free from the fear of death.[73] The experience of overcoming the fear of death with the absolute community was liberation from all secular sensations and troubles. Here existed only the whole of life itself, in which desires and everyday ideals had no meaning.

The absolute community was achieved by the tight cohesion of all the Gwangju citizens, but when it took shape and changed into state power, it began to show small fractures. When the paratroopers opened intensive fire on the citizens on the afternoon of May 21, citizens took up guns as a sovereign right. The citizens glimpsed something they had not seen before as they stood around the Gwangju Park square and watched guns being distributed and the handling of guns being taught. Hwang Seog-yeong describes this as follows:

> Although their occupations were impossible to confirm, most seemed engaged in physical labor: they looked like laborers, carpenters, and construction workers, or shoeshine boys, scavengers, bar waiters, vagrants, and day laborers. There were also

125

many high school students wearing military exercise uniforms, and sometimes middle-aged men in reservist uniforms (Hwang Seog-yeong 1985, 121-122).[74]

With guns in some civilian hands, the Gwangju citizens suddenly noticed class. Earlier they had been heartened by the realization that those who had been regarded as different were all dignified human beings, but as soon as they grabbed weapons of murder, it occurred to them that they belonged to different classes and consequently their enthusiasm waned. The gun was different from the weapons they had used earlier. It was a homicidal mechanism devised to make it possible for anyone to kill. Children could kill adults, and women could kill men. As soon as the citizens held these instruments in their hands, and as soon as the citizens were born as the "civilian militia," empowered with the feeling of being a state, many expected to win the battle. At the same time, however, they glimpsed the universal equality of one's killing capability in the manner of Thomas Hobbes, a nightmare in reality.[75] They soon felt that they belonged to different groups, to different classes. When the absolute community was transformed into a state and completed with armament, cracks began to appear in the community. Now they found themselves in a situation where there was no knowing who would fire and kill them. The class theory and the minjung theory of the Gwangju uprising were born at this point, which would later prompt the rewriting of the history of the uprising.

The topic of class emerged as early as May 19 with the description of the demonstrators. Some commented that "all students have disappeared" (ICKHD 1990a, 1046: 335), a sentiment similar to resentment of the bourgeoisie. Unlike the working classes, the bourgeoisie could not be expected to fight on the forefront, given their age, and, accordingly, their children, university students, were supposed to represent them. It was mostly after May 21 that questions were raised about the fact that there were no students among demonstrators. The mention of seeing no students from May 19 could be a reconstruction of memories, however, having sensed class in the civilian militia after May 21. The non-existence of university students did not have equal significance to the existence of the working classes who took up guns on the afternoon of May 21. University students, offspring of the bourgeoisie, were those who had already been invited into the absolute community, the most essential members, both physically and symbolically. For this reason, their presence was duly expected. The working classes were not invited, but they were still welcome to join the community.

As soon as the citizens were armed, the working classes occupied honored seats, not some insignificant corner. The resentment over the university students and anxiety over the working classes and those at the bottom of the social hierarchy reveal subtle class relations in both the absolute community and the previous Gwangju community. The fact that most armed people were of the working classes indicates that those who were intoxicated by a dramatic sense of unity and liberation were those who had been looked down upon as people on the fringes of the traditional community. Although all citizens were dignified human beings in the absolute community, the working classes soon became "more dignified" human beings. When the absolute community advanced to a state and began to arm itself, the classes who had felt that they were masters of the previous community were seized with fear and stepped back. In later years, the intellectuals, who had been gripped by fear and shock during the uprising, justified the citizens' armament, lauding it as the supreme form of struggle and giving it a meaning.[76] The turning of the tables was an inevitable result of internal psychological processes experienced by the citizens from the beginning of the uprising. With the absolute community revealing its shape, some of the bourgeoisie felt threatened and were busy trying to protect their properties.[77]

The transformation from the traditional community to the absolute community was a revolutionary situation. The world

127

was turned upside down, and the future community would not be the same. This situation, however, was not created by some revolutionary with ideology or words. It was an internal process achieved in an extreme situation transcending death, while all citizens fought to become human beings risking their lives, met their fellow citizens, and verified their dignity. The absolute community was a holy, supernatural experience.[78]

6. Conclusion

In the beginning, most Gwangju citizens, like most South Koreans generally, believed that university students monopolized the demonstrations. They believed that cheering on the sidelines was the most that was reasonably expected of them. When they witnessed the paratroopers' brutal crackdown on May 18, they simply stamped their feet and protested that the troops were going too far. For a long time, the political confrontation between dictatorship and democratization had been an issue between the military and the university students. Citizens busy with making a living assumed the attitude of onlookers, and the riot police never clamped down on spectators. In this sense, the South Korean public had been depoliticized.

It was the military that removed such latitude. During the 1979 Busan-Masan incident, when some workers joined the demonstration, the Park Chung-hee government dispatched paratroopers (3rd airborne brigade) who wielded riot sticks at anyone in sight. In that incident and in Gwangju in May 1980, it may have been the military that understood the political danger and dormant power of the minjung. Labor circles were displaying menacing actions in the aftermath of a miners' uprising in Sabuk in April 1980. Probably for this reason, the paratroopers dispatched to Gwangju in May beat up citizens in the streets and took them away on trucks.

In addition, the rumor about the Gyeongsang Province soldiers and the paratroopers' abusive remarks uttered in

Gyeongsang accents suggested that Gyeongsang soldiers were pitted against all the Jeolla Province people. The Gwangju citizens understood that they fell within the range of the troopers' targets. None could be safe from the soldiers' violence. Throughout the entire uprising, the paratroopers searched for students and youths from house to house, a practice that shook up the citizens. In addition to residential areas, the paratroopers forcibly entered any place where young people gathered—hotels, inns, cram schools, restaurants, and pool halls—and meted out violence as they saw fit. There may have been many reasons for citizens to join forces, but a common experience pushed them. Various factors came into play: rage over the inhumane brutality; fury at themselves for being cowed by fear and unable to fight; individual deep-seated resentments; a sense of crisis that the young people, the future of Gwangju, were being killed; and the judgment that no one was safe. The main motivation was anger over the violence that destroyed human dignity, and this rage stemmed from a rational decision that was reached after overcoming fear.

Immediately before the Gwangju uprising, Bak Gwan-hyeon, president of the Chonnam National University Student Association, suggested that citizens engage in a nonviolent struggle in case the military authorities used arms. Regardless of how general citizens reacted to his idea, they did not have the option of nonviolence. Nonviolent struggle, as used by Mahatma Gandhi, is a tactic to reveal injustice and evil by intentionally refraining from resistance. Rather than fighting violence with violence, it is intended to shed light on the users of violence and reveal their true face. The precondition for this nonviolent tactic is an audience that watches the use of violence and judges the scene morally.

In the case of the Gwangju uprising, the military thoroughly controlled the media at first, and no one outside Gwangju knew what was going on. The military turned the city into a theater of violence after shutting off the spectator's stand. As long as there was no audience, nonviolence had no tactical meaning. The lack of audience was a pain that was difficult to bear for the Gwangju citizens, who wanted to draw attention to the paratroopers' unjust violence. Military control of the media made it impossible for Gwangju citizens to obtain help from other regions, and it also eliminated the possibility of nonviolence. Citizens attacked the MBC station on three occasions and went so far as to demonstrate an intention to set fire to it, and torched the KBS station as an expression of frustration over numerous sacrifices made in the absence of an available audience. Torching the broadcasting stations was not simply an act to achieve the abstract ideal of punishing the henchmen of the military dictatorship.

Fury drove the citizens to participate in the struggle against the paratroopers, and this fury was not simply a judgment of injustice by a third-party observer, but rage over the destruction of human dignity.[79] In other words, at the outset the citizens' anger was not an action derived from rational judgment that the atrocities ran counter to the principles of justice. Rather, the citizens, as social beings, responded instinctively. The paratroopers' violence trampled on the dignity of the observers, not only on that of the victims. In the process of fury, all sorts of regret and resentment experienced throughout their lives must have been awakened in their consciousness, fanning their anger further. At this juncture, various types of social, economic, and structural factors in the Gwangju area came into play as marginal factors.

By this stage, the citizens' rage was rational, but the individual expression of resentment, glimpsed from time to time, was demonstrated in riot-like acts. The Gwangju citizens, however, strongly refused to appear the same as the troops, and their actions were far from a mechanical, visceral response to violence. However, during the period when only some of the citizens represented the entire citizenry's anger, the recovery of human dignity was only sporadic.

The struggle entered the next stage on the afternoon of May 20. The citizens, for whom it took a long time to overcome fear and recover dignity, finally showed up downtown. With the paratroopers' gentler attitude that day, the threshold of fear was lowered. As the number of demonstrators increased, liberated areas appeared downtown, and in this space, citizens confirmed their solidarity through celebratory rites. Human dignity, pursued by citizens, was realized objectively through the recognition by fellow human beings and in their new community—the absolute community—and also through the brave struggle of individuals. The key to this absolute community was "love"—in other words, a human response to noble beings.[80] With the emergence of this community, the citizens who had been hesitant eagerly joined to receive its blessing. At the same time, they were liberated from fear. There, they were baptized as dignified human beings and they fought more passionately to deserve their status. They were reborn in the absolute community, and the struggle at the moment was an exciting self-creation. The citizens gave everything they had for the youths who were fighting for the community's life, while the young people demanded everything needed in the battle in the name of the holy absolute community. As soon as life was defined as the community, young people called for state power. This naturally led to armament.

Citizens risked their lives to achieve human dignity. Although this goal could not have been more important than individual lives, it could be achieved only through a do-or-die showdown. In this sense, the intuitive nature of human dignity does not lie in the act and the result of pursuing individual interests and social status, but can be found in the act of recognizing a value larger than individual life and dedicating oneself to obtaining it. This value can be the fatherland or God; in case of the Gwangju citizens, it was the life and dignity of the community.

During the Gwangju uprising, human dignity pursued by the citizens was different from human rights, the legal concept of Western-style modern states; by state law, human rights guarantee the pursuit by individuals of their own interests and status while banning acts that destroy a minimum level of values. Human dignity is the recognition that people are more than human through the action of risking their lives for a bigger value than themselves. Therefore, human dignity is the recognition of something that transcends humanity. In this sense, it has the opposite meaning of equality. The joy that intoxicated the Gwangju citizens was the feeling that they were great human beings. Dialectical materialism can never approach the spirit of the absolute community created by the Gwangju uprising.

Human dignity is not a limited, scarce good that is distributed to society in accordance with economic principles. The absolute community provided a process in which human dignity was abundantly endowed, a salvation for all the Gwangju citizens who had trembled in fear. In this community, there were human rights, democracy, and all ideals. The problem is that as soon as each of these terms representing ideals in Western thought is separately employed to discuss the Gwangju uprising, the spirit of the uprising is betrayed—in particular the spirit of the absolute community. In the absolute community, these ideals were interlocked with an unnamable whole. At this point, we may have to re-appreciate the meaning of Friedrich Nietzsche's philosophy of the Übermensch, in which human beings are liberated from the bonds of language, knowledge, and philosophy, and overcome themselves, starting from the natural essence found at the very bottom of themselves.[81]

Those who contributed the most to the formation of the absolute community, who received the largest benefits and blessing from it, and who were intoxicated in it were people whose dignity had been denied in the preceding traditional community. They were the ones who granted state authority to the absolute community. When this community obtained guns—the universal homicide instrument—for armament as a state, these classes had no qualms about killing people. On the other hand, although those who loved the existing regional community and did not intend to leave it were looking forward to the formation of an absolute community and received a blessing from it, they began to feel anxious after the community took a concrete shape and compulsory state authority was given. As soon as demonstrators had guns in their hands, they again felt fear and noticed that those who were holding guns were from a different class. Their anxiety must have come from their "wisdom"—a prediction that such an absolute community could not last long, and that when the extreme situation was over, they would have to become sober and return to reality—on the basis of rational thinking. Nevertheless, the experience of the absolute community, despite small variations, was universal. All citizens experienced the logic of the absolute community's physical being, the logic of life, and primal human values. This experience was being purely human, breaking away from all types of bonds and oppressions of social roles and classifications, and in this sense it was an absolute liberation from all oppressions, a "revolutionary" moment.

This could have been the sovereign entity depicted by Jean-Jacques Rousseau, in which each citizen is not excluded from sovereignty (Rousseau 1964). Just as Rousseau considered citizens' society and sovereignty identical, the state authority was meshed with an absolute community. However, this absolute community was far from the one suggested by Rousseau, in which individuals are isolated from society to make them perfect rational beings like Émile before putting them together in a community (Rousseau 1969). Although the absolute community had the appearance of a combination of individuals equipped with courage and reason who overcame fear, it did not begin with isolated human beings. On the contrary, this community had its origin in a traditional community and was made possible by individuals who were unable to get away from the meshes and obligations of the community. It was created through the mental torment and courage of individual citizens, who could not bring themselves to betray the community's obligations as its

133

members, and through encounters, blessings, and consciousness of such individuals.

In this process, the song *Arirang*, containing the emotions of the traditional community, displayed magical power. The absolute community was not an organization like the military, which was created by repressing human beings for the sake of war, and it was not "mobs" of cowardly people hoping to rely on the power of numbers. The absolute community provided encounters among dignified warriors. This absolute community was formed only from love, with hatred focused on the absolute enemy. The occasional child-like laughs shared by the demonstrators from the afternoon of May 20 kept their spirit uncorrupt. In Western philosophy, reason is derived from solitary individuals (Choi Jung-woon 1996). However, the Gwangju uprising demonstrates that reason was achieved by human beings who were conscious of being members of a community. Reason was the capability of the community, not that of individuals.

The Gwangju uprising's absolute community and the "state" derived from it inherited the Republic of Korea's symbols. But with few common points with the existing Republic of Korea, it was a state that could exist only for a short period of time. The formation of the absolute community was a sacred revolution that was reached with immense and irresistible power. This revolution was a liberation of bodies and lives from the bonds of language and from social, economic, and ethical principles, achieved in a situation of absolute war.[82] The journey to the absolute community was not intended at all. It was what they reached after offering numerous sacrifices amid the flames of hell; literally it was a utopia, a place that does not exist, a place to which it is impossible to return. Attempts have been made to return to this absolute community. The case in point is that many warriors of the Gwangju uprising created new enemies who were as frightening as the paratroopers, for example the United States. It is possible that creating new enemies was an attempt to return to the absolute community. In addition, the absolute belief in violence, infected from the military through the experience of the Gwangju uprising, had the intention of going back to such a utopia. There have been attempts to find a way to the absolute community with language and ideology without going through the uprising's flames of hell. Most of them merely ended up making new enemies. It is not shameful that no clear ideology and theory existed during the Gwangju uprising. We have come to understand the possibility of a new reality, unfound in the ideologies of the West, through the experience of the Gwangju uprising, in which ideologies did not exist at all. The primeval purity of experience may be the most valuable aspect of the Gwangju uprising. We tasted a pure revolution without revolutionaries, though briefly, and this memory will prove to be the raw material in creating a new ideology.

As soon as the paratroopers withdrew on May 21, a thorny problem presented itself: those who had not experienced the struggle, who had hidden at home, and who had come to the Provincial Hall only after the paratroopers withdrew, could not fully understand the struggle or those who went through it in the absolute community. They could not understand why some people intended to fight again at that point, risking their lives for a battle that had no possibility of being won and that would only lead to numerous sacrifices. The warriors could not convey their experience to others with words and failed to persuade the others to defend Gwangju with their lives. The young people who defended the Provincial Hall, fully aware of their impending deaths, might have harbored a wish for a new world—the absolute community that should be remembered for a long time—deeply experienced only by those who transcended death.

ENDNOTES

[1] Kim Han-jung, who watched the scene in front of Chonnam National University's main gates on the morning of May 18 before he joined the demonstrators, testified: "With some 10 students who had run away from the police, I reorganized the ranks at the edge of the park, and went around Chungjang Avenue, Geumnam Avenue, and the intra-city bus terminal to appeal to the citizens for their participation. During our four-hour trip, citizens' responses were largely divided into two: some scornfully said, "They are running around like that because they don't feel like studying," while others expressed sympathy by clapping their hands. . . . Until then I had never dreamed that a mind-boggling event would occur in Gwangju; I predicted that the demonstration would be wrapped up soon in one way or another" (ICKHD 1990a, 1041:309).

[2] Kim Chung-geun, "*Arirang* of Geumnam Avenue" (Journalists Association of Korea et. al 1997, 212-214).

[3] *The New York Times'* Seoul correspondent Henry Scott-Stokes recalled that the scene reminded him, a Briton, of the Agincourt battle in 1415 between Henry V's troops and the mighty French Army. He went on to say that although there were few similarities between the two incidents from historical or political perspectives, he had to go back 500 years in English history to comprehend a situation in which armed soldiers, carrying bayonets, slaughtered human beings at close range (The Journalists Association of Korea et al.1997, 35).

[4] Jeong Yeong-dong, who witnessed many scenes in different parts of town as a taxi driver, remembered: "Of course, now I don't believe that paratroopers were reckless in using violence because only Gyeongsang Province soldiers had been chosen to be dispatched to Gwangju, but anyone who witnessed the inhumane, brutal scenes of violence inflicted by the paratroopers on demonstrators was compelled to believe it" (ICKHD 1990a, 1022:241).

[5] The military alleged that Jeon Ok-ju (alias Jeon Chun-sim), who exhorted demonstrators, was a spy, and it harshly tortured her to indict her as a spy, but this scheme failed in the end. At present, no one doubts that she was an innocent citizen who had joined the demonstrators in the face of injustice, although many people question the details of her background, such as that she had returned to her hometown after years of working at a private dance school in Masan.

[6] "The mid-term investigation report on Kim Dae-jung," released and covered by the media on the afternoon of May 22 did not directly link Kim to the Gwangju uprising. It merely hints at the possibility of his involvement by mentioning the allegation that he pulled some strings behind the scenes for the disturbance involving university students.

[7] Refer to the aforementioned testimony of Kim Sang-yun (ICKHD 1990a, 3014:559). According to Kim Dae-jung's National Assembly testimony, during the interrogation in the basement of the Korean Central Intelligence Agency after his arrest on the evening of May 17, no question was asked about his relationship with Jeong Dong-nyeon, a purported henchman of Kim, for the first 20 days until early June. On several occasions, Kim stressed that he had not met Jeong until 1985 (Hangminsa 1989, 63).

[8] There are few data detailing the thoughts of the soldiers in the airborne unit. A novel written after more than 10 years' research of the uprising (Yim Cheol-u 1997) raises this point repeatedly. The expression of worry about the worsening situation at the time was in the "City Hall Situation Journal" on the afternoon of May 18 (ICKHD 1990a, 28). Unlike other observations, the City Hall sources may have grasped the drift of the citizens' feelings.

[9] This was later revealed by the chief of staff of the Combat Training and Doctrine Command in an interview (Jo Gap-je 1988, 194).

[10] A case in point is the testimony of Kim Tae-hyeon and others who went to Hwasun to get hold of arms (Young Comrades Society of May 18 Gwangju Righteous Uprising 1987; 233-234; ICKHD 1990a, 2013: 382-6026: 1114).

[11] As to whether the military authorities fanned the uprising with Gwangju specifically in mind, the head of the No. 505 Security Unit made a statement during the investigation into the uprising: "It is possible to make such an argument if only the result—the Gwangju incident—is taken into account, but it seems to me that there are no data to support that it was premeditated from the outset" (*Chosun Ilbo* 1999, 416).

[12] On May 19, the Security Command dispatched to Gwangju its planning and coordination deputy director Brigadier General Choe Ye-seop, and he stayed in the auxiliary wing of the commander's office of the Combat Training and Doctrine Command until the clampdown operation was over. He personally reported to Chun Doo-hwan, the commander of the Security Command, but it has not been revealed what he actually did (*Chosun Ilbo* 1999, 416). Around four o'clock on the afternoon of June 21, General Hwang Yeong-si, one of the influential members of the new military junta, phoned General Yi Gu-ho, head of the Armor Academy, and told him "in an ordering tone" to mobilize armored vehicles. Having heard General Yun Hong-jeong's complaints about the new military authorities' unjust crackdown operation, General Yi refused (*Chosun Ilbo* 1999, 408-410). It is apparent that the military junta's new plan was being carried out in total secrecy, with the Army deputy chief of staff kept in the dark.

[13] There has been no further report about the spy Yi Chang-yong. With no information available about whether he died or was indicted, it is difficult to dispel the suspicion that the case was fabricated.

[14] The representative achievement in analyzing the Gwangju uprising from a sociological viewpoint can be found in Jeong Hae-gu et. al (1990). Please refer to Hwang Seog-yeong (1985, 19-20) as well.

[15] Kim Sang-jip testified as follows: "So far, the Gwangju uprising has been defined as a 'minjung revolution' by showing a distribution chart made of different classes of participants. I believe there is definitely room for reconsideration. In an effort to gain the regime's legitimacy, the Chun Doo-hwan dictatorship military au-

thorities at the time had a tactic of describing the Gwangju uprising as the suppression of a rebellion participated in by the urban poor, the lumpen nobodies, and ex-convicts. In actuality, many students participated at the time, but the military released most of them except leaders. Many students, with whom I personally helped to form ranks in front of the YWCA, were not arrested" (ICKHD 1990a, 4100:897).

[16] According to Kim Sang-jip's testimony, it was decided to make Molotov cocktails upon hearing that the Chonnam National University students were to venture downtown. He said, "Thinking it was a good turn of events, considering that we were about to buy gasoline, I gave 50,000 won to Daedong High School students to buy some gasoline" (ICKHD 1990a, 4011:887). At the time, 50,000 won was a large sum of money, so we can surmise that quite a number of Molotov cocktails were crafted. They were made at the Nokdu Bookstore, where Yun Sang-won was present. Refer to Bak Jung-yeol's testimony as well (ICKHD 19901, 3058:660).

[17] The students made a point of attacking police substations at Chungjang Avenue, Jisan-dong, and Dongmyeong-dong, but they did not set fire to them that day. They built bonfires in the streets into which they threw office fixtures and torched motorcycles. The demonstrators started to set fire to police stations mostly on the afternoon of May 19.

[18] *Fighters' Bulletin*, created by the Field Fire Night School team, became a symbolic leaflet of the uprising, but the Clown team seemed to be the first to print a flier. The members of this group made a leaflet soon after witnessing a clash in front of the Chonnam National University front gates (ICKHD 1990a, 4012:899). During the period of struggle, these two groups acted independently. It was on May 23 that they were merged.

[19] Jeong Sang-yong et al. (1990, 150) pointed out an important factor. "In 1980, the Gwangju population was about 730,000. In this medium-sized city, there were 44 elementary schools, 26 middle schools, 38 high schools, nine junior colleges, one teachers' college, two four-year colleges, and two universities. In particular, while the number of middle school students was 28,863 in

26 schools, that of high school students stood at 73,414 in 38 schools. This oddity indicates that a large number of young talents who graduated from middle schools in the nearby Honam area attended high schools in Gwangju. In 1980, the fact that the number of students who attended high school or a higher level of learning had reached 110,000, over one-seventh of the entire Gwangju population, indicates that the influence of students reached far throughout South Jeolla Province. As such, Gwangju was not simply the seat of the Provincial Hall, but the center of education in Honam. The Gwangju students were a bridge with blood ties that linked the city with small and medium-sized cities and rural areas in the vicinity."

[20] Kim Gyeong-ae, a housewife who mobilized neighborhood women and supplied meals to demonstrators, said as follows: "Following the suggestion of an older woman, I told my neighbors to bring as much rice as they could, and they brought two to four scoops each. Eight women gathered at one of our houses and made rice balls. At first, we were scared and the kids on the demonstrating vehicles looked rough, though they were not soldiers. After watching carefully, I realized that they spoke like students and we had heard that students had joined. We arranged about 50 rice balls in two or three plastic-lined steel basins and instant noodle boxes. Standing at the entrance of an alley on the left-side wall of Chonnam National University Dental School, we lifted rice balls to passing demonstrating trucks whenever they passed. We said, 'You're working hard. What will you do if the result is bad? Be careful' and then we shouted, 'We're from Seoseok-1-dong.' The youngsters replied, 'You're working hard. Thank you. Don't worry too much,' as they went on" (ICKHD 1990a, 3117:809).

[21] Kim Mun argues that the news of Kim Dae-jung's arrest was an immense shock to Gwangju citizens, and therefore it triggered the Gwangju uprising (Kim Mun 1989, 23-24). I believe that this is a quite subjective judgment.

[22] Yi Hong-sik, who went to Mokpo in arms on the afternoon of May 21, testified as follows: "Many citizens were gathered in the Mokpo train station plaza. When we arrived, they clapped their

hands. I thought that they were not necessarily clapping to cheer us up. They could have clapped as an outward show of support, afraid of us, who were carrying guns. After getting out of our cars, we distributed extra guns we had brought in our vehicles to young men in Mokpo. They broke the windows of the cars parked nearby with gun barrels and boarded them. Somehow I felt desolate, thinking, 'This is not a protest against the forces of military dictatorship, but a mere act of violence to express our own deep-seated resentment'" (ICKHD 1990a, 6052: 1195).

[23] An Cheol, the head of the Mokpo Citizens' Democratization Struggle Committee at the time, was well aware that the demonstrations in Mokpo depended on the development of the Gwangju incident (ICKHD 1990a, 6011: 1048).

[24] Most Gwangju citizens heard this remark between the afternoon of May 18 and the afternoon of May 19 through various channels. Not many remember who told them in what circumstances. The fact that it spread to all citizens within 24 hours can be viewed as an amazing phenomenon related to the structure of this particular community, regardless of the judgment whether it played an important role in the development of the situation.

[25] Kim Gi-hun, a resident of Mokpo, drove a newly married couple to Hwasun. The young men in the region surrounded his car and tried to pick a fight. They asked, "Do you know how many people were killed and injured? Are you really Jeolla people?" (ICKHD 1990a, 6002: 1024. Also refer to 6005: 1032; 6026: 1112; 6034; 1137; 6054: 1200).

[26] Many testimonies about the Mokpo situation mention vehicle demonstrations (ICKHD 1990a, 6007: 1039). The term "vehicle demonstration" had a totally different meaning in the two cities, however. The vehicle demonstration in Gwangju refers to a procession on the evening of May 20, in which buses, trucks, and taxis proceeded, honking, with their headlights on along Geumnam Avenue toward the Provincial Hall, where the airborne unit was stationed. In Mokpo, there were no riot police. The vehicle demonstration in Mokpo refers to the scene in which demonstrators mobilized or seized vehicles in various places, and encouraged

141

citizens to join as they sang and moved around the city in cars. The two acts are similar in that vehicles were used, but they do not constitute the same action.

[27] In his novel, Yim Cheol-u explains this expression at length: "Suddenly, an unpleasant memory floated up. . . . A military instructor said, 'Do you know why Jeolla bastards have been called "double backs" for a long time in the military? There are different theories. They are light-fingered, and no one is better than they when it comes to stashing what they've stolen in their duffel bags, which has been changed to double bags. This is what people generally think, but the truth lies somewhere else, though this particular meaning is not far off.' When was this sermon given? It must have been during my days in the Training Corps before the assignment to a unit. It was one of the instructors who said this while teaching about mines and booby traps. It was when everyone in Myeong-chi's company was gathered in the training hall after going through a harsh group disciplinary measure all day long for some reason or other. For some strange reason, those from Jeolla Province happened to be a majority among the trainees. The instructor, who said he had graduated from the Korea Military Academy, was on the tall side with a compact body. He was unusually handsome, but perpetual discontent was reflected in his eyes. 'The real meaning of double back is something else. I will teach you what it is. Did any of you graduate from universities? Or did any of you take a leave of absence from your university studies before joining the army? Okay, good. Hey, you, what does the "back" mean in English? You moron, not a bag, but the back, b-a-c-k. Yes, it means behind or behind your back. Double means two or two-faced. So when you put the two together, you get two backs. In other words, double-faced personality. It means that these are the tribes who pretend they are different on the surface, but as soon as they turn around, they are bound to betray. Do you now understand what it means? How's that? If you're not happy with my explanation or have different opinions, step forward and speak up, any of you. Don't worry. Though we're in the military and I'm your instructor and you guys are my trainees, if any of you came forward to argue with me, I'd accept it as an equal, one-on-one.

So, tell me. . . . You bastards, what prevents you from speaking up? See? The guys like you are called "double backs," get it? To be frank, I hate double backs. If you really got what I mean, I will stop talking about it (Yim Cheol-u 1997 II, 19-20).'" I quoted this part in length to give the context in which the expression "double back" is used. In the military, the expression is used to insult Honam people to their faces, as quoted above.

[28] An extreme example has it that one of the officers of the airborne unit, who played a leading role in committing cruelty while speaking in a thick Gyeongsang accent, was later discovered to be a person from Honam. At the time, the Gyeongsang accent was standard speech in the military and it was not difficult for Honam people to copy it. Probably this officer opted for wearing a Gyeongsang mask in order to actively adapt to the atmosphere, going beyond obeying the orders in a situation that was personally difficult to bear.

[29] A sergeant of the 11th Airborne Brigade testified as follows: "After some time (2-4 minutes), we received a command to get off the vehicle. To our ears, this order sounded like an instruction to beat up young men relentlessly. . . . When we got off, demonstrators had already dispersed. We had to vent our hatred on someone, but there were no demonstrators in sight . . ." (Jeong Sang-yong et al. 1990, 179-180). This testimony shows that the soldiers were generally feeling a sense of freedom, even if there had not been any special order.

[30] The 14th Regiment of the South Korean army led by communist sympathizers revolted in October 1948 in Yeosun, which resulted in thousands of civilian casualties.

[31] Bak Ok-jae, who later became the president of the Association of Wounded People, said the following: "Gwangju is a small town. I am careful with everything I do or say. If I had done something bad, Molotov cocktails might have been thrown at my house and I would have been grabbed by the throat" (ICKHD 1990a, 7073: 1343).

[32] In a similar vein, Kim Dong-uk asserted as follows: "In conclusion, in the South Jeolla region centered on Gwangju, despite ba-

143

sically different interests between a majority of residents on the one hand and a handful of large capitalists and high-level bureaucratic petit-bourgeois on the other, they were able to secure firm ties in the aspect of various demands of bourgeois democracy at a political, economic level, and this was the driving force of the Gwangju rebellion. They formed an allied minjung bloc; they were working classes, farmers, lower middle-class urban petit-bourgeois, and small- and middle-sized capitalists" (Kim Dong-uk, "The Contradictory Structure of Korean Capitalism and the Main Force of Rebellion," Jeong Hae-gu et al. 1990, 111).

[33] Numerous articles on the truth of the Gwangju uprising were read during citizens' rallies in liberated Gwangju. Soon after, in June, Roman Catholic priests of the Gwangju Archdiocese put out the "Truth about the Gwangju Incident." There were also the anonymous "Torn Flag" and the "Truth about Gwangju Righteous Citizens' Uprising." These documents are systematically compiled in the JSRI 1988 and Gwangju City 1997 II.

[34] The chief of staff of the Combat Training and Doctrine Command commented several years later regarding a film showing the US military's method of cracking down on demonstrators: "According to this film, you make the demonstrators kneel. If they resist, you control them by bashing their collarbones with riot sticks. If they run away, you open fire on them. The suppression of the Gwangju incident was much milder than the actions shown in this movie" (Jo Gap-je 1988, 192).

[35] When the paratroopers failed to quell the demonstrators quickly, the military continued to issue orders emphasizing "bold attacks" (Jeong Sang-yong et al. 1990, 198-199, Yim Cheol-u 1997). General Jeong Ung, who had a nominal command authority as the head of the 31st Division Command, testified in a National Assembly hearing that he had issued an order for a bloodless crackdown.

[36] "The slaughter by the paratroopers appeared definitely intentional. Acts of killing were committed in front of as many people as possible. When the citizens stamped their feet in helplessness,

it only encouraged the massacre" (The Association of the Family Members of the Victims 1989, 67).

[37] In the beginning, a widespread rumor in Gwangju had it that the paratroopers were not of the ROK military but armed guerrillas dispatched by North Korea.

[38] On the morning of May 19, at the height of the 11th Airborne Brigade's atrocities, the officers, through speakers mounted on the jeeps, shouted to citizens who were looking out from buildings, "Close the windows and draw the curtains." This may indicate that they themselves were aware that the "theater of violence," intended to incite fear in spectators, had become a human slaughterhouse. In a later National Assembly hearing, Yun Hong-jeong, then the head of the Combat Training and Doctrine Command, commented on a meeting of military commanders and city officials on the morning of May 19: "I heard stories that shamed me for wearing a military uniform. . . . I heard many stories and during the meeting I sincerely requested that the military not carry out such actions and also ordered so" (Gwangju City 1997 IV, 112). Regarding the atrocities committed by paratroopers, many tales circulated, called "malevolent rumors" by the Martial Law Command. It is not easy to confirm the truth of those stories. We will satisfy ourselves with the testimony of a riot policeman who watched the clampdown of the demonstration: "Starting on the afternoon of May 19, many stories smacking of far-fetched rumors reached us. Savage tales, such as 'The seed of Jeolla people will be annihilated' and 'Pregnant women's bellies were cut open' came through our walkie-talkies. I had no doubt that they were true. It was a belief formed after two days of observation" (ICKHD 1990a, 8002: 1536).

[39] Kim Si-do, who began to participate in the May 18 demonstration, testified as follows: "Then two paratroopers followed a fleeing student into a tailor shop. They grabbed him by the throat, and snatching an iron away from an employee working with it, they mercilessly struck him with it. They struck him with a hot iron everywhere on his head and face. The witnesses were agape with fury. While the young people stood around, unable to speak out,

older people expressed their outrage. They said, "You deserve to die!" or "Hey, you bastards!" . . . The troopers rounded up citizens and students, not to mention the student in question, and put them in the middle of the road. One of the troopers shouted through a bullhorn, "Citizens, go home as soon as you can." . . . Swallowing fury, I returned to my brother's electronic store. . . . "Forget about work. Let's go out and fight." . . . So, with the shop employees, I walked to Geumnam Avenue. After watching the intolerable act, as a fellow citizen, as a fellow human being, I could no longer sit around and do nothing" (ICKHD 1990a, 3042: 627-628).

[40] This is not confirmed by a real-name testimony.

[41] The Combat Training and Doctrine Command's "Analysis of the Gwangju Disturbance—Collection of Lessons" analyzes the causes of the citizens' resistance as follows: "Pincer attacks with the focus on arrests, rather than dispersion; outbreak of violent clashes with rioting masses in the full view of regional residents during the clampdown period; explosion of barbaric hatred over the destruction of household appliances and threats to family members in the process of pursuing and arresting the fleeing crowds . . .; provocation of residents' emotions by delayed handling of the casualties and the arrested people (left in the streets for a long time) during the period of suppressing the disturbance" (Jeong Sang-yong et al. 1990, 200-201). This shallow analysis indicates a failure to fathom the Gwangju citizens' motives. "Escalation" has been put forth as an explanation inside and outside the military; before and after National Assembly hearings, many military personalities resorted to this explanation. This is a similar explanation to the theory of "excessive suppression," which blames both sides. In an interview with journalist Jo Gap-je, the 11th Brigade chief expressed strong discontent over the theory of excessive suppression put forth by Martial Law Command Chief Yi Hui-seong in 1988 at the National Reconciliation Committee. He said, "I hear that Mr. Yi Hui-seong used such an expression, but did he ever come to the actual sites? Those above battalion leader have a hard time grasping the situation accurately. I believe that the true nature of the Gwangju incident is that a spark was caused when the two excited parties clashed" (Jo Gap-je 1988, 194). During a

1988 National Assembly hearing, General Seo Jun-yeol, the chief of the Martial Law Sub-Station during the uprising, explained the incident as an "escalation" (Gwangju City 1997 IV, 266). Even a book published by the Association of Family Members of Victims assumes a similar attitude: "The citizens, who witnessed a series of paratroopers' brutal massacres, could no longer afford to sit back, swallowing resentment and fury. Fundamental violence, derived from destroyed human dignity, began to explode. They began to resolve that they would die while fighting because they were going to die anyway" (The Association of Family Members of Victims 1988, 69).

[42] An attempt to explain the cause of the Gwangju uprising by integrating structurally contradicting factors with paratroopers' violence was made by Kim Jun (Kim Jun, "Situational Development and Confrontational Structure in 1980," Jeong Hae-gu et al. 1990, 156).

[43] Lieutenant General Gwon Seung-man, then the head of the 33rd Battalion of the 7th Airborne Brigade, testified during a National Assembly hearing that the operation had been concluded at 4:40 (Gwangju City 1997 IV, 442).

[44] The airborne unit's soldiers are said to have felt fear during the afternoon of May 19 (Jeong Sang-yong et al. 1990, 184). Although this is based on a paratrooper's testimony, it may be difficult to generalize that this feeling was widespread.

[45] Citizens carried the injured on their backs to nearby clinics, but some were treated in the streets. A citizen testified that although he received first-aid from some women at the Jang-dong Rotary, he could not see their faces in the dark (ICKHD 1990a, 2015: 389).

[46] Organized student activists, centered on the Nokdu Bookstore, manufactured Molotov cocktails en masse and used them to set fire to many places throughout the city. Kim Sang-jip remembers that he acquired the nickname "Bomb Master" at the time (ICKHD 1990a; 4011, 887-889). Setting fire was not a result of the "instinct to destroy" but an act intended to excite onlookers.

[47] Printed material entitled "Rise up, Democratic Citizens" in the name of the Chosun University Democratic Struggle Committee, with the date specified as May 19, had the following expressions: "Those dog-like bastards of the remaining Yusin faction—Choi Kyu-hah, Sin Hyeon-hwak—and the bastard Chun Doo-hwan, the son of the Yusin dictator . . ." (Gwangju City 1997 II, 23). It was the first time that such foul language was used, and no similar leaflets followed. The expression of hostility seemed to be at its peak at this point. The May 20 manifesto titled "The Moment of Decisive Battle has Arrived" in the name of the Student Revolution Committee of Pan-Citizens' Democratic Struggle Committee, likely to have been written on May 19, put forth following action guidelines. "Manufacture weapons! (prepare dynamite, Molotov cocktails, privately made bombs, fire arrows, fire drums, and all types of oil) . . . All citizens must burn up government offices! . . . Seize vehicles! . . . Organize a special commando unit to capture military weapons! . . . Ah, Brothers! Let us die fighting!" (Gwangju City 1997 II, 23). According to testimony by Bak Nam-seon, the head of the Situation Room of the civilian militia, he read this wall poster on the afternoon of May 20, before a full-fledged demonstration began, in the company of many citizens near the intra-city bus terminal (Bak Nam-seon 1998, 136-137). The radical content of this writing seemed to reflect the atmosphere of May 19. The two leaflets mentioned above are the most radical of all that were printed during the uprising. Hwang Seog-yeong explained the May 19 situation as follows: "The paratroopers' cruelty worked as a provocative initial explosive that pushed the struggle capability latent in people to respond and erupt against violent techniques. With the disappearance of fear, only a fierce sense of alliance and hatred remained. . . . The fight entered a more offensive stage as the minjung began to display their own fundamental violence, which was to emerge through the sense of survival and the trust in human dignity, located deep in themselves. . . . The typical anarchistic instinct of destruction, a weakness of the unorganized crowds in a rally but works a strong point at a certain stage of movement, erupted like an active volcano and people grew emboldened (Hwang Seog-yeong 1985, 51-52).

As far as the Gwangju uprising is concerned, this description does not seem to be an accurate explanation. In particular, it is not valid to describe the Gwangju uprising in a sweeping manner as the phenomenon of mass psychology, such as "instinct for destruction."

[48] According to a testimony, when the witness was eating breakfast at a restaurant on the morning of May 20, a man sitting next to him tossed down a glass of liquor and said, "I will kill the paratroopers." The witness goes on to testify: "He took out a knife from his chest and drove it into the table and let it stand. I asked the owner of the restaurant to give me a kitchen knife and plunged it into my table as a show of solidarity. As we tossed down our last cups and stood up, we saw a car full of demonstrators passing outside. They went from place to place appealing to citizens: 'We are fighting with the paratroopers in the Daein Market. Please join us.' Hearing it, we thought we would join other citizens, rather than waging a reckless fight of our own, and went to the Daein Market. . . . In front of the market, paratroopers were blocking the road with tanks, while merchants and citizens were fending off soldiers with large carts and portable display cases. Female merchants carried stones to the demonstrators, using their skirts gathered up in front of them" (ICKHD 1990A, 4011: 890).

[49] Kim Byeong-su, who walked along with the citizens to the downtown area around this time, testified that he "did not know why he went downtown," and at the time he "did not think about why we were doing it" (oral testimony).

[50] The description of the above scene is reconstructed from the accounts of Hwang Seog-yeong (1985, 82-83) and ICKHD (1990a, 42), and it has been confirmed by the testimony of Yi Jae-ui, who witnessed the scene at the site. Please refer to Kim Mun (1989, 36-39) as well.

[51] Although Hwang Seog-yeong (1985, 69) suggests that Jeon came forward on the afternoon of May 19, Jeon herself testified that she started working the crowd around midnight on May 19. In many testimonies based on memory, people remembered hearing her voice for the first time between the afternoon and evening of

May 20. Although Jeon began her activities on the night of May 19, it was only from this point forward that her clear voice left deep impressions and was etched in many people's memories.

[52] *Arirang* had similar effects in other places. According to the testimony of Bak Nam-seon, situations chief of the civilian militia, crowds were reading big-character wall posters near the intra-city bus terminal in Gwangju, although the exact time in his recollection is not clear. "One of the citizens reading the wall poster began to sing, 'Our Wish Is Reunification.' When it was followed by *Arirang*, the citizens, who began singing in voices tinged with tears, sobbed loudly and broke into loud wailing. The street suddenly turned into waves of weeping. . . . 'The murderer Chun Doo-hwan, step down!' 'The military, return to the 38th Parallel!' 'Bring my children back to life!' The slogans, amid loud wailing, began to fill the street . . ." (Bak Nam-seon 1988, 137).

[53] Kim Haeng-ju, a high school student at the time, testified as follows: "When we moved toward Hwangguem-dong, barmaids were lined along the street holding basins of water. Seeing them distributing water to demonstrators, I felt that all Gwangju citizens had become one. I used to think that these women were dirty and that they lived in a different world, but when I saw them share their sincere hearts, even if their help didn't amount to much, I was moved and felt that they were warm-hearted neighbors" (ICKHD 1990a, 2031: 464).

[54] According to a testimony, the scrimmages were so tight on the night of May 20 that citizens could not flee when paratroopers wielded riot sticks (ICKHD 1990a, 1045: 329). Forming scrimmage lines was a technique used by students in their demonstrations since the 1960 student uprising. The students, a pre-defined group, would gather on campus and take to the streets in scrimmage. It was the first time that the citizens, virtual strangers, had participated in a demonstration by forming a scrimmage in the streets.

[55] A riot policeman said in his testimony, "It appears that a sense of unity was instinctively formed among citizens. They took to the streets, shouting such slogans as, 'We must protect Gwangju.

With our own hands,' and the demonstrators running toward us from all directions were united in one, from grandfathers to children" (ICKHD 1990a, 8002: 1536). It is unlikely that the demonstrators shouted the exact slogan. He might have heard the impressive expression and felt as if they shouted it, as he witnessed the demonstrators' united front.

[56] While the citizens were in a sit-in on Geumnam Avenue, someone in the group revved a motorcycle, attracting a lot of attention. The man claimed that he, by himself, would push back the paratroopers, and raced toward the Provincial Hall, with a loud noise. All watched him with anxious eyes. When he had almost reached the hall, however, he swiftly turned his bike into an alley and disappeared. Citizens burst out laughing and clapped their hands. In Yim Cheol-u's fiction, when a vehicle demonstration slowly arrived at Geumnam Avenue, a cab veered out of line and disappeared into an alley. Citizens gathered around the taxi, lifted it up, and put it back where it had been in the queue. The citizens, laughing loudly along the street, clapped their hands and shouted, "Mr. Driver, hurrah!" (Yim Cheol-u 1997 III, 229).

[57] From the outset, the students put forth a large national flag in each demonstration. It is judged that the evening of May 20 was the first time that thousands of citizens demonstrated, waving small flags. It is not known where the flags came from. It is presumed that someone bought a bunch of flags at some stalls lining the street and distributed them. The demonstrators sang many songs at the time, but according to testimonies the song most frequently sung was the national anthem (ICKHD 1990a, 3071: 690).

[58] Kim Yeon-tae, who went to the Monopoly Bureau and obtained 10 boxes of cigarettes for the citizens, threatening to break the windows unless goods were handed over, talked about how he had felt at the time: "I didn't think I took cigarettes forcibly, and I didn't feel guilty. The goods at government and public offices belonged to Gwangju citizens, and it was natural that they would be used for our citizens. We shared among ourselves what government power failed to give us. To such an extent, we were confident and proud" (ICKHD 1990a, 3119: 813).

[59] A representative case may concern Bae Yong-ju, a bus driver. When he returned to his company after negotiating the messy traffic, an executive instructed him to follow other buses, and Bae unwittingly participated in a vehicle demonstration, but escaped when he was confronted with tear-gas bombs. He didn't realize while he was driving that his bus hit and killed four riot policemen. He was arrested and sentenced to death (ICKHD 1990a, 3056: 653-655). There may have been cases in which people lost their lives in a similar situation. The demonstrators transported citizens on trucks and buses. Whenever they spotted young people in the streets, they ordered them to jump in. Although such an act may be called a transportation service, from a different perspective it was conscription. Many citizens did not think twice when they boarded the buses, but they later found themselves in battle. Of course, in no case was physical force used to conscript citizens.

[60] A witness said that when his father discouraged him from going out on May 20, he talked back, saying, "Why? Do you think only your child is precious?" He left home after attaching a kitchen knife to the end of a long bamboo pole. (ICKHD 1990a, 1039: 301). This case shows that a spear was made at home with deliberation. Although many citizens found themselves holding wooden sticks, they often did not remember how they had gotten hold of them, and some specifically testified to this fact (ICKHD 1990a, 2015: 390 etc.).

[61] The Martial Law Command repeatedly showed these large-scale arsons on TV as evidence that the demonstrators were violent mobs. Although an argument has been raised that the fire at MBC was not started by citizens, they clearly demonstrated their intention by throwing Molotov cocktails. The situation in which fire was set to MBC was as follows: The demonstrators attempted to negotiate with the paratrooper unit confronting them on Jebong Avenue on the condition that they would carry out a peaceful demonstration. The negotiation was rejected, and when the representatives were turning back, the troops' armored vehicle revved up and charged toward the demonstrators at full speed. Many citizens jumped out of the way, but two children were run down and

died on the spot. The shocking scene rendered observers speech-less. Overcome with rage, the demonstrators are said to have at-tempted torching MBC (ICKHD 1990a, 3058: 661; refer to Yim Cheol-u 1997 III, 209-211 as well). Many testified, however, that it was not citizens who actually torched the MBC station.

[62] A witness said that he had heard it at the five-way rotary at Sansu-dong. Many heard it somewhere, though they did not re-member exactly where (ICKHD 1990a, 45; 1035: 283; 2009: 370). "The Martial Law Command's Daily Situation Journal" records: "According to intelligence, an all-out attack targeting the Provin-cial Hall is planned at 0100" (ICKHD 1990a, 52).

[63] The first attempt at negotiations took place at around 6:00 on the evening of May 20. Those calling themselves citizens' repre-sentatives said to the police, "We will carry out a do-or-die battle with the paratroopers, and we want the police to stay out of the way" (ICKHD 1990a, 43). Soon after, around 9:00 in the evening, citizens demanded negotiations with the paratroopers in front of MBC, asking the troops not to interfere because their demonstra-tion would be peaceful. The last attempt at negotiation took place in the Provincial Hall at around 10:00 on the morning of May 21; it ended with shooting.

[64] Carl Schmitt has said that determining the distinction between our side and the enemy is highly developed politics, and that this is a political act monopolized by a state (Schmitt 1976, 25-76). According to Schmitt's standards, Gwangju citizens' community existed as a state as long as it defined paratroopers as a negotia-tion partner, a departure from its initial definition of "devils."

[65] According to a witness, when a young man fell while running away, four paratroopers rushed to him and stabbed him several times, shouting, "If we don't kill them, they'll kill us!" (ICKHD 1990a, 2002: 352). This scene vividly reveals the paratroopers' psychology at the time. From this point on, the soldiers of the airborne unit fought for their lives. During an investigation pro-cess, Lieutenant Colonel An Bu-ung said that on the evening of May 20, the paratroopers, seized with fear, were in total disarray (*The Chosun Ilbo* 1999, 370-371).

[66] For example, on the morning of May 21, all over Gwangju, women lifted food to the demonstrators in vehicles. Some of them shouted the name of their neighborhood as they handed over the food. This act may be construed as a declaration in the vein of punching a time clock, implying "we are voluntarily fulfilling our duty."

[67] Yi Ji-hyeong, then a high school student, testified as follows: "The people who entered the tax office brought out the objects that had not been burned. There were all sorts of things, including clocks, electric calculators, staplers, office appliances, and radios. Each took away one or two with them. In a sense, it was stealing. Whenever I notice the lot where nothing stands now, I think, 'Yes, I did that.' Why did people set fire to the tax office and why did people take away property without guilt? People seemed to take it for granted. Although at the time I didn't know that it was the expression of anger over the brutality exhibited by the soldiers, who are expected to defend the country with the taxes paid by the general public . . ." (ICKHD 1990a, 3066: 677).

[68] According to Baek Haeng-ho's testimony, in a battle on the afternoon of May 20, 20-30 paratroopers were encircled by citizens near the wall of the Catholic Center. Some said they should beat the troopers to death, while others said, "Let's not kill them. Let's not harm them." All the paratroopers were allowed to leave toward the back of the East District Office. "It was a situation in which a disaster could have happened if the citizens pressed on with the fervor they had at the time. I think citizens were still naïve and not full of rage. Later, however, our side and the enemy's side were completely divided. Those bastards, who had been allowed to leave like that, betrayed the citizens and shot citizens in the chest" (ICKHD 1990a, 3104: 770). There are numerous cases in which citizens refrained from attacking the 31st Division and Combat Training and Doctrine Command troops, except the police and the paratroopers. A paratrooper was saved when he was taken to a hospital after citizens beat him.

[69] A witness described the situation: "We always had more than enough seaweed-rolled rice, pastries, milk, and soft drinks they had brought us. Everywhere we went, we didn't have to worry

about food. The saying—once you're away from home, you face difficulties—didn't apply here" (ICKHD 1990a, 2020: 409).

[70] Hwang Seog-yeong (1985) says that these machine guns spewed bullets on the Provincial Hall, where paratroopers were stationed, but in reality citizens did not use them, worried about injuring people with stray bullets. It is clear that a skilled machine gunner was a member of the civilian militia. Jo In-ho testified: "And there were two light machine guns. A man who was small in stature and looked about 27 said he had been a machine gunner during the Vietnam War, and fired three volleys toward the Provincial Hall. The sound of the gun was incredibly loud" (ICKHD 1990a, 2002: 352). Firing three volleys at a time is a typical way experienced gunners shoot.

[71] For example, when the Munhwa Broadcasting Station was in flames, "An electronic shop called Munhwa Company was in the building next to the broadcasting station. People were pulling out electronic goods in case the fire spread. I helped as well. We put them out near Jungang Elementary School, but no one stole or damaged them. . . . I heard later that an armored vehicle came from the Jang-dong Rotary and bulldozed the goods that the citizens had pulled out to protect from the fire" (ICKHD 1990a, 2015: 390).

[72] Pierre Bourdieu sees that social class is fundamentally decided by the distribution of material and social capital, not by the possession of assets or production means, and that the routine class struggle has the goal of depriving the target class of capital. Dignity is the key to capital, and the distribution of dignity is an inherent element in social class (Bourdieu, 1985). In this book, I use the concept of class on the basis of Bourdieu's theory, not Marx's. It is my opinion that as far as the class issue is concerned, Bourdieu's theory is much more elaborate and realistic.

[73] The citizens who participated in many rallies on May 20 and afterward often do not remember when, where, or how they fought, or even exactly what happened. Such examples abound among participants, but sometimes they are specifically mentioned in testimonies (for example, ICKHD 1990a, 2036: 486; 3109: 785 etc.).

[74] Yun Jae-geol also offered a similar argument: "Another unit was formed for those who had weapons, creating ranks. The organized ranks consisted mostly of people in their late teens and 20s. Their occupations were hard to know for sure, but most were workers, such as laborers and employees at bars and restaurants, shoeshine boys, scavengers, bar hostesses, day laborers, and vagabonds. Included were quite a few high school students in uniform" (Yun Jae-geol 1988, 93). There is no testimony anywhere, however, that "bar hostesses" or women took up guns. It is possible that the above quote was taken from Hwang's book. Yi Bong-hyeong, a high school student at the time, talks about what he felt while distributing guns after seizing them from Nampyeong Armory: "We distributed guns to all those who wanted one. Of those who took them, there were some who looked unpleasant, which made me wonder, 'What if they do something bad with the guns?' But we had to give them out anyway. It was fortunate that no serious incident happened afterward" (ICKHD 1990a, 2004: 356). Yun Seok-jin, who was preparing for his college entrance examinations after graduating from high school, said, "They distributed guns from heaps on the road, and they didn't look like students. From that day on, people who looked like university students disappeared" (ICKHD 1990a, 3102: 763).

[75] Kim Jeong-gi describes an interesting feeling after holding a gun in his hand: "Although the man taught me how to use the gun in a rudimentary manner, I listened to it perfunctorily. I was overwhelmed by fear that I was in possession of a gun that could kill people and at the same time by confidence that I could now fight paratroopers" (ICKHD 1990a, 2001: 350).

[76] At this point, the intellectuals centered on the Nokdu Bookstore had been frustrated after the paratroopers' shooting. They decided to take refuge and parted ways. Kim Sang-jip, one of those intellectuals, came across trucks laden with guns. He asked where they had taken the guns and counted the number of vehicles coming to the city. Judging that it was worth fighting from the unexpectedly large number of cars, he joined the battle again (ICKHD 1990a, 4011: 891). There could have been a considerable difference in feelings about armament between those who were deeply

156

involved in the absolute community and those who were observing on the sidelines. In fact, the students who had participated in the demonstrations all along broke away from the group at the time of armament; some said, "I cannot bring myself to hold a gun," while others said, "I am scared." The May 25 statement "Why Did We Have to Take Up Guns?" in the name of the civilian militia found the answer to be "all too simple. We could no longer watch extremely merciless atrocities, and we took up guns one by one and came forward" (Gwangju City 1997 II, 63). To the civilian militia, armament couldn't have been more logical and the answer could not have been simpler. At issue is why this particular question was raised four days after taking up arms, and why they felt compelled to answer it. The armed citizens must have felt they needed to issue this statement, due to the atmosphere of May 25, following the dispute over returning guns, and the occurrence of the poison needle scare that morning, in a bid to rally citizens again to their side.

[77] It is already known that affluent residential areas were empty and some wealthy people refused to donate their assets to demonstrators. Many members of the bourgeoisie—more broadly the middle class—were afraid of the mostly working-class makeup of the demonstrators. Jang Jong-pil, who was a store employee of Bokgae Arcade, testified as follows: "We closed shop early on May 20 because there was a rumor that the merchants at the arcade were not cooperating, and if they kept being uncooperative, the demonstrators would throw Molotov cocktails" (ICKHD 1990a, 3100: 756). From May 20, people took refuge in the wake of the rumor that demonstrators would set fire to some rich family's house (ICKHD 1990a, 7118: 1422-1423). Some vehicle owners tried to come up with an idea to hide their cars on the outskirts of the city to prevent the demonstrators from seizing them. A car was filled with four passengers to discourage demonstrators from asking for a ride, and to pass the demonstrators safely, they displayed the slogan, "Release Kim Dae-jung!" They were shot by the martial-law troops defending the outskirts of the city; some died and others were injured (ICKHD 1990a, 5031: 987-988).

[78] "Our Opinion on the Causes of the Gwangju Incident," a document officially presented to the citizens in liberated Gwangju by the Gwangju Situation Settlement Measures Committee on May 25, asserted that Gwangju should be designated as a holy place (Gwangju City 1997 II, 64). This assertion bears witness to the fact that Gwangju citizens already felt something sacred in their experience of the protest.

[79] Hannah Arendt simply defined the cause of fury leading to the use of violence: "When our sense of justice is offended we react with rage" (Arendt 1969, 63). I believe that Arendt's definition is inadequate because she didn't pursue and analyze rage in the depths of consciousness.

[80] Ferdinand Tönnies, distinguishing between "community" (*Gemeinschaft*) and "community of interests" (*Gesellschaft*) states: "The sharpest contrast, then, arises if affirmation of a social entity for its own sake is distinguished from an affirmation of such an entity because of an end, or purpose, which is extraneous to it. I call a will of the first kind *essential will*, and a will of the second kind *arbitrary will*" (Tönnies 1971, 65). Tönnies states the following regarding *Gemeinschaft*, "Likewise, a relationship which is affirmed through love or affection, or because it has become dear through custom and habit or in the line of duty, remains within the concept of *Gemeinschaft* (community)" (Tönnies 1971, 67). Tönnies has not used the term "absolute community." I am using this term to explain the special character of the Gwangju uprising. For Tönnies, love and affection are primary and more fundamental for a community than custom or mores. In the case of the Gwangju uprising, the community, as a social reality based on love and connected with life, pushes Tönnies' notion of the community to its furthest limits. To emphasize its exceptional purity, I use the term "absolute community."

[81] Nietzsche (1954; 1966). I do not mean that his philosophy in its entirety can be applied; it has sufficient room for misunderstanding. For example, Nietzsche regarded a community negatively as a way of primitive life. In addition, he did not think that supermen could form a community.

[82] I have invoked the concept of absolute war from Clausewitz (Clausewitz 1976). However, the unfolding of the Gwangju uprising is completely different from Clausewitz's absolute war, which he explains as an escalation by the participants. This concept may be useful to contrast Gwangju citizens' internal awareness and struggle with the wars between states.

Chapter Three

Life and Truth:
Agony in Liberated Gwangju

1. Fissure and Fragmentation of the Absolute Community

When the martial law troops withdrew on May 21 and the civilian militia occupied the Provincial Hall, the entire city exploded with gleeful shouts of victory. Vehicles carrying armed demonstrators, who chanted slogans and sang songs, sped through the streets, while citizens in the streets clapped their hands and shouted hurrahs. Citizens in the streets lifted food and beverages to demonstrators on trucks. The joy of victory and liberation belonged to all of the citizens who had fought by forming an absolute community. As early as this, however, cracks began to appear in the absolute community.

Some citizens were reborn as members of the civilian militia with guns in their hands; they covered part of their faces with kerchiefs, and the so-called "masked troops" emerged. Although masked demonstrators appeared from the morning of May 21 (ICKHD 1990a, 4013:905), it was when citizens began to arm themselves that they emerged in large numbers (ICKHD 1990a, 3021: 576; 3076: 701; 6004: 1029-1030; 6015: 1068 etc). The theory that they concealed their faces because they were afraid of the martial law troops' photographing them does not explain their emergence. If they had been afraid of being photographed, they could have gone home. When the absolute community was realized through struggle, the Gwangju citizens lost interest in their identities and those next to them, and soon their faces were unimportant. The masked troops were citizens who obliterated their faces and identities.[1]

At dawn on May 21, after the withdrawal of the 3rd Airborne Brigade, two terribly mutilated bodies were found at the Gwangju train station. The infuriated citizens did not ask who they were; they put them in a wagon, draped them with a national flag of Korea, and carried them all over the city, with their bloody ankles in full view, to display their horrible state. This action, of course, would be unthinkable in normal times.[2] On the afternoon of May 21, citizens carried people who had been shot to death on Geumnam Avenue to nearby cities to exhort the residents there to participate in the struggle. In a way, as members of the absolute community, even the dead lost their identities, attesting to the paratroopers' cruelty and inciting citizens to fight. The citizens in the absolute community, both dead and alive, were faceless warriors.

With the citizens' armament, visible changes came to the fore in the absolute community. First, although up to 5,000 citizens seized arms on the afternoon of May 21, at least a majority of the demonstrators, about 300,000 in number, who had participated in the rally in front of the Provincial Hall, did not.[3] Although many testified that women held kitchen knives, pokers, and coal pickers, there is no testimony that they were armed with guns. Many of the demonstrators were older people and children, and could not take up guns. However, in case of young and middle-aged men, when they decided not to hold guns, whether they felt afraid at the sight of weapons or for some other reason, it was not because guns were in short supply. Rather, they could not bring themselves to take up guns or they refused to do so. Many of them remained in the streets, applauding the civilian militiamen or watching them, but the rest must have gone home, feeling that they could no longer stay in the streets. In a situation where gunfights began, it was meaningless to fight with nothing in their hands or holding wooden poles.

The citizens who went home, refusing to arm themselves, could have participated in the rallies afterward from time to time, but only a handful joined the civilian militia after May 22, and a majority of those who joined at the time were mobilized university students.

In this way, the "general citizens" separated themselves from the civilian militia for the first time on the afternoon of May 21, and they were excluded from the struggle.[4] If all had been warriors in the absolute community before the citizens' armament, now a majority became general citizens. The civilian militia was an extension of citizens, but from the evening of May 18, they formed a group visibly different, with guns slung over their shoulders. The emergence of the masked troops began with the awareness that those who took up guns and those who did not could be differentiated by appearance. At this point, general citizens must have begun to ask, "Who are the masked troops?" The masked troops were the specters of the absolute community, and they must have struck the general citizens as frightening.[5]

The civilian militiamen, in turn, were unable to act as freely as they had done only a few hours before, when they had been members of the absolute community before the paratroopers opened fire. Efforts to organize the armed citizens were made in Gwangju Park and some other places. As soon as citizens took up arms, they could no longer come and go as they pleased, but had to learn how to handle guns from the reservists who were well-versed in military knowledge and experience. They had to organize themselves into teams, and move in sync for various reasons: to prevent misfiring, to protect one another from the martial law troops' shooting, and to wage street battles. Some formed commando units to attack from the Provincial Hall, while others were sent to the outskirts of the city to counter the paratroopers' re-entry. The citizens who had been to the army took such disciplines as a matter of course, and even those who had no military experience followed their examples. At night, they called out familiar, manly, nostalgic passwords from their military days, such as "cigarette glow, cigarette smoke." The struggle of the Gwangju community changed form in a flash.

On the evening of May 21, when the civilian militia looked like a real army at first glance, a rumor spread among its members that the person commanding them had been an airborne unit's captain (ICKHD 1990a, 77; 6015: 1070). In other words, citizens hoped that their leader would be braver and more skilled in tactics and strategies than their enemy, the paratroopers, and looked forward to victory under him. No testimonies mention a former captain of paratroopers who led the militants, however. In downtown Gwangju, brave citizens, stood at every alley and commanded other citizens, and no charismatic leader emerged from this bunch. It is possible that one of these leaders exaggerated his military background, and the story spread far and wide. Before the armament, all citizens felt they were great warriors and loved the brave look of their fellow fighters. As soon as they were organized with guns in hand, they might have dreamed of a leader on whom they could depend.

Among the Gwangju citizens who risked their lives to fight paratroopers, few openly revealed their names and identities. Announcing one's name to many people was no different from becoming a sniper's target. Shouting one's name to a crowd of people would have been equivalent to claiming to be their leader and asking them to follow. Jeon Ok-ju was the only person who revealed her identity to all the citizens.[6] Although she participated in a negotiation as one of four citizens' representatives on the morning of May 21, as a woman she was unable to become the leader. When citizens were armed and organized, some people began to shout their names. Toward the evening of May 21, when the citizens began to arm themselves, Mun Jang-u called out his name and identity in the square of Gwangju Park.

> Amid the confusion, a man who looked to be about 40 was teaching the citizens how to use light machine guns, using a megaphone. No one seemed to pay any attention to him. I had

led the seizure of weapons, and now I took the megaphone from him and stepped forward before the citizens. I thought order had to be introduced and we should work systematically. . . . I have a loud voice, but I shouted more loudly than usual. "I am Mun Jang-u, a Gwangju citizen living in Hagun-dong. I was discharged from the army as a sergeant several years ago, and I am now the reserve army head of Hagun-dong." Now everyone's eyes were on me (ICKHD 1990a, 2025: 435).

People looked at him in astonishment and followed his instructions. He taught the citizens how to use the guns, organized regional defense units, and went out to the bridge in Hagun-dong. At the time, it was out of the ordinary that a citizen disclosed his name and identity. Kim Won-gap was one of the first people whose names were known.[7] For some reason, however, this group of people did not make the list of the heroes of the Gwangju uprising. The citizens' expectations about the leaders appeared at a time when the warriors of the absolute community felt small after becoming mere members of an organization.

A majority of the militiamen had no interest in their comrades' identities. They knew that they were defending Gwangju risking their lives with guns in their hands backed by the absolute community's confirmation of their dignity. The majority of the citizens who did not take up arms also found the meaning of their existence from their experience in the absolute community. If they noticed people who looked like militiamen, they called out to them, spoke with them, and shared what food they had.[8] While standing guard at night, they introduced themselves, but they soon forgot each other's names. They were happy that the group they belonged to was made up of people from various walks of life. They forgot the names because they were not important; it was usual to know the others as "workers," "students," or "corporate employees." In later years, most militants did not remember the faces, names, and voices of those who had fought next to them to the end. Some members of the militia lied about their identities, but the identities were of no importance as long as they served as foot soldiers without asking for special positions.[9] Most of the organized ranks of the civilian militia had no leaders. Either the driver of a vehicle in which they moved around did as he pleased or the members reached a decision after a discussion. Relations among general citizens who did not take up guns were not greatly different. The memory of the struggle in the absolute community was represented as the civic spirit of the uprising.

The absolute community slowly began to lose its magic as citizens took up guns; the civilian militia was born, distinctions were made between general citizens and the citizens' army, and the civilian militia was organized like an army. The first sign that emerged on the evening of May 21 was the gradual return of fear of death, which citizens and militiamen had forgotten for some time. Mun Sun-tae, who was deputy editor of the *Jeonnam Maeil Sinmun*, recalled that night as follows:

> My house, located at the edge of Gwangju (on the ring road), became a sort of Maginot Line. Across the road, soldiers were gathered behind the tanks, and on the rooftop of my house, which stood in the direction of downtown, university students, who looked small and pale, fired endless blank shots at night. I approached the students holding guns and asked them why they kept firing when the soldiers were not approaching. I advised them to take a nap. One of them said, "We're so scared that we need to fire aimlessly to the sky to get through the night. We're so scared that we can't sleep" (Han Seung-won et al., 1987, 13).

The young members of the citizens' army fired blank shots toward the sky for various reasons: to test-fire, to amuse themselves, and to escape from fear. Some fired to destroy street lamps, afraid that they might be exposed to helicopters (ICKHD 1990a, 2031: 465). When gunshots rang out in the pitch-dark, the civilian militia fired to keep fear at bay. Citizens and the civilian militia amplified fear in each other. Hwang Seog-yeong described the night of May 21 as follows:

> The entire city was pitch-dark because the Gwangju citizens had turned off lights. Tracer shells of machine guns fired from outlying roads flitted across the dark night sky, as if they were fireworks. Outside, not a soul dared move around, except militia vehicles racing to relay secret passwords and troop transport cars going after the martial law troops (Hwang Seog-yeong 1985, 129).

An observer described that night, probably in exaggeration:

> Occasional gunshots, coming from all over the city and breaking the silence of the dark night, made weak-hearted citizens tremble with anxiety and fear. Although martial law troops were frightening, the armed civilian militia began to look like a scary enemy as well (Kim Yang-o 1988, 114).

Now, there was no knowing who would shoot citizens. On the night of May 21, someone was going around entreating on a PA system that people from all walks of life gather at the Provincial Hall, but most people were reluctant because "the situation outside was so out of hand that they could not bring themselves to enter the Provincial Hall" (Jo Bi-o 1994, 33).

In such a situation, the most politically important group was the armed civilian militia. Sufficient testimonies have not been gathered about who did what in the Provincial Hall following the paratroopers' withdrawal on the night of May 21. At the time, most armed citizens went out to defend many areas, fearing the martial law troops' re-entry. Some exchanged fire, and most stood guard to cope with the martial law troops' attacks. On the other hand, only a small number of armed citizens entered the Provincial Hall; it seemed rather quiet there.[10] In other words, there were few who thought they should take over the Provincial Hall to form an organization in a bid to control liberated Gwangju. Many citizens entered the Provincial Hall, but they went away for they felt either "it was not a place I belonged to" or "I was too frightened" and joined other militiamen to defend the city.[11] With the disappearance of the enemy, many citizens, who had fought with all they had, were overcome with fatigue and fell asleep.[12] On the night of May 21, no students were present in the Provincial Hall; there were some civilian militiamen, but they were not many in number. What is odd is that the activities of these people did not continue into May 22 and thereafter.[13]

Against this backdrop, political groups secretly began their activities from the evening of May 21 to control liberated Gwangju. Some Catholic priests and well-known dissidents, who had been active in the democratization movement, gathered at Nam-dong Catholic Church to discuss the situation that evening and agreed to get together the next day.[14] On the other hand, the Martial Law Command made many phone calls during the night to discuss measures of settlement and to prepare for organization and operations.[15]

Some of them had been leaders before the uprising, and others considered themselves social leaders, though politically alienated. In other words, social and political elites in Gwangju braced themselves for a new political conflict in the transition period, on the general expectation that the absolute community would break down soon and they had to return to the existing social system, and also fearing various problems in the process of such change. However, the armed civilian militia, which had emerged in the struggle of the absolute community, was not sensitive to political conflict. The elite groups scrambled to come up with necessary measures for exerting influence on the civilian militia. The absolute community found itself in a revolutionary situation—in other words, the world had turned upside down, and the civilian militia was a class that was socially so far from the existing ruling classes that it was unable to communicate or cooperate with them.

The question raised with the collapse of the absolute community was the issue of identity between individuals and groups. On the one hand, it was an issue of power, and on the other hand, it was a matter of class. The questions that had never been asked in the absolute community—"Who are you?" and "What are you?"—were now heard everywhere, and the expected answers were always about social status and class. Some were able to give an answer more readily, while others were unable to come up with satisfying replies.

2. Politics and Class

Downtown Gwangju on the morning of May 22 was still reminiscent of a battlefield. Around 7 o'clock, someone went around shouting through a loudspeaker, "Armed citizens, please gather at Gwangju Park." Others said through bullhorns, "Let's clean up the streets" and "Let's maintain order." Nothing much is known of who these people were. At around 7 o'clock in the Gwangju Park square, young men centered on Kim Won-gap put vehicles under his control, for they were the most important weapons for the civilian militia; they registered cars, gave them numbers, and assigned duties. They designated gas stations to secure necessary fuel. Around 9 o'clock, almost 1,000 militiamen were gathered at the square, smacking of a field army headquarters. Piled high in one corner were weapons. The youths distributed them, taught the rudiments of handling firearms, and sent the armed men to the areas in confrontation with the martial law troops. Earlier, at around 6 a.m., hundreds of citizens drove into the gates of the Provincial Hall to occupy it (ICKHD 1990a, 1029: 263). The civilian militia used the General Affairs Department on the first floor, calling it the "Situation Room"—a modest name for the civilian militia command—

169

and started to tighten the organization and check on the equipment abandoned by the martial law troops.

The first organized action to take control of liberated Gwangju was a meeting held around 8 o'clock that morning involving the deputy governor, high-ranking officials, and some employees of the Provincial Hall. The governor intended to come to the office, but high-ranking officials discouraged him from doing so (Kim Yeong-taek 1996, 128). Soon after, Deputy Governor Jeong Si-chae phoned influential Gwangju figures, representing all walks of life, and dissidents, asking them to participate in a settlement committee. Some people moved around the city in vehicles, asking through a P.A. system that "representatives from all walks of life" gather at the Provincial Hall. Dozens of influential figures gathered in the deputy governor's office, but few well-known dissidents made an appearance.[16] At 11 o'clock in the morning, a Chonnam National University professors' meeting was convened in the Boy Scouts Office in the Provincial Hall, and this seemed to have a similar goal as the aforementioned meeting. It was a failure, however, because only seven or eight professors showed up (ICKHD 1990a, 1002: 133-134). In the deputy governor's office, there were too many people who talked about unrelated subjects, preventing the meeting from proceeding smoothly. Archbishop Yun Gong-hui suggested that a settlement committee be organized with a limited number of people, with each sector selecting one person. He left after asking Father Jo Bi-o to represent the Catholics. Representatives were selected, and the settlement committee was launched around noon with the lawyer Yi Jong-gi as chairman. In the meeting, the members agreed on seven points of demand and went to Sangmudae to negotiate with the martial law troops. It was around 1:30 in the afternoon when they sat across from the negotiation team of the martial law troops headed by Kim Gi-seok, deputy commander of the Combat Training and Doctrine Command.

Meanwhile, at Nam-dong Catholic Church, where Kim Seong-yong was head priest, about 10 of the so-called dissidents, who had a collective sense of their experience as democracy fighters but were reluctant to attend the gathering to form a settlement committee in the Provincial Hall, got together as they had promised the evening before.[17] They were commonly called the Nam-dong Catholic Church faction. Judging that there were few trustworthy people in the settlement committee, they planned to participate in it cautiously, keeping a certain distance. They took note of what was going on in the settlement committee through Father Jo Bi-o. On May 23 , they drafted "eight points" and attempted through the police chief to hold an independent negotiation with the Martial Law Command (Yun Gong-hui 1989, 54). These dissidents participated in the settlement committee as a group after most of its members left the Provincial Hall on May 25 after Bak Nam-seon, head of the Situation Room of the civilian militia, entered the committee meeting and threatened them in the wake of the "poison-needle scare." The dissidents seized control of the settlement committee and expressed a stance that was more hard-line.

Meanwhile, in the Nokdu Bookstore, located near Jang-dong Rotary, was another group centered on Yun Sang-won, an experienced activist. Throughout the resistance period, members of this group manufactured Molotov cocktails, collected information, participated in the struggle with enthusiasm, and printed leaflets, including the *Fighters' Bulletin*. On the early morning of May 22, these young men discussed the actions they would take.[18] They were often called the Nokdu Bookstore team, and after they moved their headquarters to the YWCA, they were referred to as the "YWCA team." Their first activity was to distribute about 2,000 black ribbons to the citizens in front of the Provincial Hall. Yun Sang-won entered the Provincial Hall at around 11 o'clock on the morning of May 22, met Kim Chang-gil, who was the de facto student representative, and grasped the movement in the Provincial Hall through his younger acquaintances.

In this way, he acted quickly to urge further resistance.[19] The key constituents of this organization were the Wild Fire Night School Team, the Clown team, Songbae Society, and the Institute for Contemporary Issues. To secure mobility and equipment for public address in the streets, they forcibly took a Chonnam National University school bus and obtained a P.A. system on board. In the evening, they gathered university students to seize control of the Student Settlement Committee that was to be organized in the Provincial Hall, but it came to nothing because of a glitch in timing. Only a few participated at the outset (ICKHD 1990a, 4011: 892).[20] They brought all public relations and planning organizations to the YWCA on May 23.

On May 22, the first day of liberation, the armed civilian militia almost monopolized the means of violence, but it was unable to carry out political activities, such as controlling various organizations. The reason seems to be that the militia was busy participating in various battles that took place on the afternoon and evening of May 21 and the whole day of May 22 on the outskirts of the city, and had little presence of mind to pay attention to the Provincial Hall and its environs. From around 6:00 on the morning of May 22, armed troops in many vehicles advanced into the Provincial Hall from Gwangju Park, but for some reason they seized only the Office of General Affairs on the first floor and did not touch high-ranking officials' rooms on the second and third floors. They were antagonistic toward the members of the settlement committee and the work of "settling," but they did not dare overwhelm them; each side coexisted, preoccupied with its own workload. Those who entered the Provincial Hall from various sectors were diverse people. In the Situation Room, a fierce battle of nerves took place; those present were wary of each other, threatened with guns at the drop of a hat, fired blank shots, and brandished hand grenades.[21] On the morning of May 22, many people were vigilant about the spies and snitches who might have been sent by the Martial Law Command. Contrary to an orderly picture created by

Gwangju citizens downtown, tempers flared in the Provincial Hall. On May 22, the civilian militia kept distributing weapons and organizing groups at Gwangju Park, while masked troops raced around the entire city all day long, urging the citizens to participate in the struggle.

Bak Nam-seon, who would later seize control of the civilian militia's Situation Room, gave orders to the militants to carry out guard duties before he briefly stopped by the Provincial Hall on the morning of May 22. He finally settled into the Provincial Hall in the afternoon after making rounds of regional defense units.[22] Upon arriving at the Provincial Hall, he clashed on several occasions with other members of the civilian militia. It was only around 11 o'clock at night that he secured his position and formed an official organization called the Situation Room, where he worked in earnest as the head. On May 23, he began to exert control over the Situation Room by issuing passes (Bak Nam-seon 1988, 41). At the time, he had little interest in the activities of the Citizens' Settlement Committee and the Student Settlement Committee, which met upstairs (Bak Nam-seon 1988, 166-167). It was partly because he was busy with a lot of things to do, but also because he did not seem to have the political acumen to judge that he needed to seize control of the entire Provincial Hall. It was on May 23 when Yun Sang-won, who was vying for a chance to control the Provincial Hall, learned about Bak Nam-seon, and they met for the first time on the afternoon of May 24.

Throughout the period of liberated Gwangju, the Citizens' Settlement Committee was a very unstable organization. A considerable number of its members did not make an appearance at the Provincial Hall, while others resigned. The committee had to be reorganized frequently.[23] In addition, the composition of this committee drew suspicion that its members were pro-government. Most committee members were dismissive of the argument that paratroopers had used excessive suppression in the clashes before May 21 (Yun Gong-hui 1989, 176; ICKHD 1990a,

1003: 138). According to many testimonies, some of them seemed to speak for the Martial Law Command.[24] What the settlement committee members considered of utmost importance was negotiations with the Martial Law Command. As soon as the Citizens' Settlement Committee was formed around noon on May 22, its members left to negotiate with the Martial Law Command, believing that this was the only way to cut losses. It was not a homogeneous group, however, with each individual evaluation differing about the negotiation objectives.[25]

Meanwhile, citizens who were eager to know what was going on and those who were looking for their family members who had failed to come home began to gather in the morning. Around 9 o'clock in the morning, someone toured the city in a car, urging people, via a P.A. system, to gather in front of the Provincial Hall (ICKHD 1990a, 82).[26] Many citizens, having heard that Acting Prime Minister Bak Chung-hun would come to Gwangju, went to the Provincial Hall with high expectations. By noon, the crowd had reached 70,000-80,000. When they heard that the prime minister would not come, they vented anger. Soon, a flag at half-staff was raised at the rooftop of the Provincial Hall, the national anthem rang out, and a rally took place as a matter of course.[27] In the afternoon, corpses from many hospitals were moved to the fountain in the Provincial Hall square. Citizens prayed in silence and held a solemn rally. Around 5 o'clock in the afternoon, settlement committee members returned from a negotiation with the Martial Law Command and reported the results to the citizens. The crowd seemed to accept their explanations at first, but they rejected the idea when Jang Hyu-dong said that the situation had to be settled by collecting and submitting arms to the Martial Law Command. Jeers arose, some members of the civilian militia fired blank shots, and several young men jumped up to the podium. Kim Jong-bae, a Chosun University student, took the mike away and shouted, "Hey! You bastards who want to rise in the world by selling Gwangju citizens' blood! We don't need you! Go away, all of you!" (ICKHD 1990a, 1014: 204). The settlement committee members went away, and soon the rally turned into a tool for denouncing the committee.

The young men in activist circles, including Yun Sang-won, worked hard to get support from the Gwangju citizens, in particular the crowd gathered at the Provincial Hall. Getting an idea from the voluntary citizens' gathering on the afternoon of May 22, they decided to hold a "citizens' rally to defend democracy" the next day, and they were busy with preparations that evening. They soon mobilized students to the YWCA through the groups that were affiliated with various activist circles. On May 23, when some of the young activists who had fled returned, they were put to work. That day, they moved their headquarters from the Nokdu Bookstore to the YWCA, located near the Provincial Hall, and began to manage a large-scale organization. The leadership of the organization paid attention to security; to discuss important issues, the leaders got together at an office in Honam-dong, away from the eyes of the others.

The last political group organized in the first day of liberation was the Student Settlement Committee. However, this committee cannot be viewed as an independent political force or organization; rather, it must be understood as one of the organs created by diverse political elements for a certain need. The Student Settlement Committee was the arena of conflict at the center of politics. Unlike the elders in the Citizens' Settlement Committee, university students were young and they could serve on a committee and at the same time fight physically; they were comrades-in-arms and at the same time rivals of the most important members of the civilian militia—workers and the downtrodden who were of the same age group. Although the students were targets of criticism that they had run away after triggering the uprising, they were the only group that could link the armed civilian militia with the Citizens' Settlement Committee, for they had participated in the uprising from the outset.

They occupied a place in the Provincial Hall on May 22 by creating the Student Settlement Committee; it reflects the identity and the social class status of the group. This is vividly revealed in a confrontation between Kim Chang-gil, a Chonnam National University student, and Kim Won-gap, a high school graduate preparing for college entrance examinations, on the morning of May 22 at the Provincial Hall. Kim Won-gap was a brave fighter who had fought at the forefront of the citizens on the afternoon of May 21 and organized the civilian militia on the morning of May 22, whereas Kim Chang-gil, head of events of Chonnam National University student clubs, came to the Provincial Hall on the morning of May 22 after lying low at his cousin's house throughout the struggle. The following is Kim Chang-gil's testimony:

> At the Provincial Hall, I showed them my student ID and demanded that I be let in. After entering the building, I looked for the commander. A young man came out. I asked him what his name was and which university he went to. At first, he said he was a student at Korea University, and then changed his story and said he went to Chonnam National University. I kept asking questions until he confessed that he was a repeater for university examinations. He was Kim Won-gap. "This issue cannot be resolved with a repeater for university admission at the forefront. University students started rallies for democratization and this situation can be viewed as an extension. How can you, a repeater, take charge and settle the matter? I will take over until the student leadership is formally formed." I tried to persuade him after telling him who I was, but Kim Won-gap refused to step back. At the time, the Citizens' Settlement Committee happened to be formed on the second floor, and its members were discussing which direction to take (ICKHD 1990a, 1013: 203).

"University students" were a class whose status both sides recognized. Kim Won-gap tried to lie that he was a student of Korea University, the legendary bastion for the 1960 Student Uprising, before he claimed that he attended Chonnam National University. When his bluff was called, he found himself on the defensive. He himself admitted that even if he was a warrior of the civilian militia, it would be difficult to maintain the status of youth leadership as a repeated candidate for university.

Jang Hyu-dong wrote a will at home in the early morning of May 22 before he went to the Provincial Hall and joined the Citizens' Settlement Committee at the time of its formation. He quickly realized the political importance of university students; he attempted to form an organization with Kim Chang-gil as its head and Hwang Geum-seon as general affairs' head. He entrusted Kim Chang-gil with the chairmanship upon the evaluation that he appeared "strong and trustworthy," while his appointment of Hwang Geum-seon was on the fact that he spoke logically (ICKHD 1990a, 1009: 184). Jang Hyu-dong introduced the student committee, which he had organized based on his instinct, to the settlement committee, and had Kim Chang-gil accompany him to a meeting with the Martial Law Command. The formal organization of university students, however, was attempted by Professors Myeong No-geun and Song Gi-suk around 5 o'clock in the afternoon as the citizens' rally was being wrapped up. Professor Myeong felt the necessity of organizing university students because citizens were nervous about the situation in which anonymous, menacing people ran around with guns in hand.[28] Using a portable microphone, Professor Myeong urged that university students gather at Namdo Arts Hall, and some 100 students came. The two professors selected about 10 Chonnam National and Chosun University students among those gathered and went to the Provincial Hall with them.

The civilian militia stationed in the Provincial Hall had a vague understanding of the university organization's political meaning. Accordingly, the working-class militia in the Situation Room balked, immediately souring the atmosphere. The militia threatened Professor Song, brandishing a hand grenade. They protested against the word "settlement," claiming that a combat headquarters had to be established instead. Then, they balked at the university students' prominent role. In response, Professor Song Gi-suk used the logic that the civilian militia lacked organization and therefore order had to be introduced before it put up a fight. His argument for university students was as follows:

> "You make sense as well, but who will come forward when there is no knowing who's who? If those who fought with guns stand at the forefront, even the members of the civilian militia wouldn't trust them because they don't know who they are. Then how can such people display leadership? It is only students whom everyone can trust." The man failed to come up with a counterargument, but he didn't seem to be convinced (ICKHD 1990a, 1007: 162).

His argument was that it was not simply his personal opinion that students were those "whom everyone could trust" while the workers in the civilian militia were unknown people; it was a general belief in Gwangju. The civilian militia had no choice but to accept the student organization. After several bouts of dispute with the civilian militia, Professor Song formed the Student Settlement Committee around 10 o'clock in the evening on the condition that the committee would be handed over to officers of the Chonnam National University Student Association upon their return. For chairman, Kim Chang-gil was chosen because he had been to the Martial Law Command for a negotiation. Kim Jong-bae, who had jumped to the podium during the rally, shouting his objections, became vice chairman. The civilian militia in the Situation Room, which had antipathy toward university students, bowed to the dissident professor's courage and logical arguments.[29]

Although the civilian militia criticized university students for backing away after triggering the uprising, some citizens asserted that the students had to take full responsibility since they had started it. This argument, the class-oriented discourse, was

178

built on the logic that university students were trustworthy and also more organized than workers. The explanation that university students were trustworthy revealed class prejudice against armed civilian soldiers of unknown identity, who were believed to be untrustworthy, lacking organizational power, and unreliable in possession of guns. This prejudice, of course, does have objective grounds. University students belong to official organizations—universities—part of a giant mesh of students who went to school before them or after them; it is a group in which each individual can be placed. In a word, unlike workers, university students could readily give answers to the questions, "Who are you?" and "What are you?"

At the time, it was impossible for the Citizens' Settlement Committee members and the civilian militia to sit together for discussion; only the university students' organization could bridge and exert influence on the two groups. Although the absolute community was slowly losing power, it still existed. In a transitional period in which the existing community was coming back, the two classes that could not sit together in normal times confronted each other. The university students came to the fore both as ruling classes in the existing community and as warriors in the absolute community. The argument of the university students' responsibility summed up their complex status as a social class. When a group asserted its own social, political accountability or another group imposed responsibility on this group, it was an act of confirming its class-oriented status. Young activists, for their part, used the Student Settlement Committee as a channel through which they could approach the civilian militia, the new entity of authority.

Most political conflicts in liberated Gwangju took place within the Student Settlement Committee. Some of the members, who had participated in the protest with their lives on the line, held the position that they had to fight to reclaim the "price of blood," but the majority did not go through the resistance and maintained the stance that they could not allow more losses.

179

Such a situation was troubling for all, and many left the Provincial Hall on several occasions, saying that they were resigning. Every time, however, the elders dissuaded them by saying, "If the students leave, the rogues with guns will rule. What will happen to Gwangju then?" The students would reluctantly return to the Student Settlement Committee (Kim Yeong-taek 1996, 178-179). The participation of the elders of Gwangju, the well-known figures of the existing community, and the armed citizens' status were the given conditions. These two groups could not communicate, for they were poles apart socially. In this situation, students, regardless of their intentions, had no choice but to bridge the two groups and resolve their conflict. The students themselves were viscerally aware of their difficult position.

In liberated Gwangju, the movement of political elements within the Provincial Hall took place as the conflict among social classes and in the framework of hegemony. Ordinary citizens hoped to return to the everyday life of the community preceding the absolute community, and for this reason they imposed their class prejudices on the organization in the Provincial Hall in many forms. By contrast, the civilian militia with workers' background stood toe to toe with the ruling classes for the first time in the revolutionary situation of the absolute community. The ruling classes acknowledged, at least a minimum level, the status claimed by the civilian militia made up of the working classes on account of the logic of the struggle at the time. The limitations of this group's political capabilities were exposed in the early hours of liberated Gwangju. This situation pushed university students to emerge as the most important group in liberated Gwangju, and their presence was constantly demanded.[30]

3. Return to Everyday Life

With citizens' armament on May 21, the absolute community experienced an outward change, soon followed by gradual internal fissures. Various forces intending to return to the existing community infiltrated into the absolute community, whereas the civilian militia, hoping to remain in it, was intent on maintaining it. Most citizens had to admit to two conflicting ideals—the existing community versus the absolute community and the struggle to restore order versus the fight to recover honor—and all those concerned were in agony.

In the process of the existing community's restoration and the absolute community's breaking down, different logic and emotions came to the fore. First, the issue of individual identity and class emerged. Second, emotions and obligations of family—the key system in the existing community—found their ways back. And finally, the preciousness of individual life was highlighted as individuals re-emerged. Those who had not experienced the struggle and came to the Provincial Hall after liberation put forth the preciousness of individual life as the ultimate value, and this position gained persuasive power as the fervor for struggle cooled down. Although the logic of reducing human losses coincided with the demand of the Martial Law Command that weapons be returned, this universal value was an ideology that could not be refuted. For the citizens who had personally participated in the struggle for the community's life, the value of individual life was subordinate. It was a confusing experience for everyone to see a clash between the concepts of life and death. In liberated Gwangju, it was vividly shown that the value of individual identity and life was logically inseparable from power and rule.

Professor Song Gi-suk recalled his thoughts as he was forced to embrace the retrieval and return of weapons, though he felt torn.

> For the sake of activism, 2,000 deaths were sufficient. I believed that even if 1,000 or 2,000 more died, the meaning would not grow in proportion to numbers (ICKHD 1990a, 1007: 162).

Here, life and death are manifested as an event in which numbers could be counted at an individual level. Compared with the concept of death in light of individualism and communitarianism, death experienced as a community in the absolute community's struggle was not the end of life, but the continuance of life and the extension of struggle. The warriors who defended the community's life were beings who with their dead bodies encouraged citizens to a continued battle. However, the aspects of individualism and wholeness of life were natural to all people concerned; by nature, the conflict and contradictions between the two could not be resolved with discussion. Therefore, the conflict between the settlement and pro-resistance factions within the Provincial Hall inevitably had to move in a confrontational direction, with the militants brandishing guns at the slightest provocation.

At the dawn of liberation, the Gwangju citizens' foremost interest was to locate their family members who had gone out and had not been heard from since. Many citizens flocked to general hospitals in the city, and the first duty of service for the settlement committee and the Provincial Hall executives was to help them. On the afternoon of May 22, the corpses from all hospitals' morgues were transported to the square in front of the Provincial Hall, and citizens performed official rites for their dead colleagues. In the evening, the identified bodies were moved to Sangmu Gymnasium, while the unidentified ones were transported to the front yard of the Provincial Hall. Individual homecoming started with the dead. Although the bodies still belonged to the public, it was the privilege of family to display sorrow and weep in abandon. The mangled bodies and the keening of families reinforced hostility against paratroopers among the civilian militia, but also pulled at the heartstrings of the militants; they remembered their parents and family members whom they had forgotten for several days. The old community called family was an irresistible force that surreptitiously made its way into the absolute community.

On the surface, the biggest conflict in liberated Gwangju was the issue of recovering weapons. It is generally known that the primary reason for this conflict was the Martial Law Command's threat and the citizens' hope to reduce human losses at the time of the troops' re-entry. The Martial Law Command maintained that unless weapons were returned before a specified time, sophisticated heavy arms, such as tanks, armored vehicles, and helicopters, would be mobilized for suppression. This induced immense fear in those who had witnessed the airborne unit's atrocities. The Martial Law Command reiterated this threat several times during negotiations with the settlement committee. One day, the settlement committee members were shown tanks and helicopters lined up on the parade ground. If soldiers re-entered, heavy firearms would be mobilized; it was difficult to imagine how many innocent people would be sacrificed, not to mention armed citizens, and the settlement committee members, including Father Jo Bi-o, and the elders who did not personally go through the revolt felt that they had to disarm as many people as possible to prevent more human losses, despite their misgivings about the Martial Law Command's arm-twisting. However, most of those who were involved in the struggle did not accept this view.

From the military's stance, the best solution of the Gwangju issue might have been to make all citizens disarm and return weapons, and to occupy the city bloodlessly as soon as possible. If that solution worked out, the military could pretend that all the shameful things during the uprising had not happened, and it could push forward with the argument of "rioters," as long as the Gwangju citizens expressed regret over their deeds. The logic of the pro-resistance faction, whose members believed that they had to fight to the end to achieve goals such as recovering honor, held that they could never allow the military to stick to this "best" solution. For the Gwangju citizens to survive, they felt that the truth of the struggle had to be defended, and this was life to the citizens. The settlement committee, rather than speaking for the

183

Martial Law Command's stance, must have been faithful to its own stance, but the front line of conflict over the concepts of life and death was drawn here. In liberated Gwangju, life and truth became contradictory themes. It was impossible to be engaged in a philosophical dispute in an urgent situation at the time, for the two values would yield opposite results. Although it was undeniable that individual life is a humanitarian value, hopefully to be protected by those who loved the Gwangju citizens, this in reality coincided with the military's political strategy of branding the Gwangju citizens as rioters forever. From the pro-resistance faction's viewpoint, it was no different from "selling the blood" of the Gwangju citizens.

It appeared that the Martial Law Command used negotiations with the settlement committee to disarm the civilian militia. While pressuring the committee members to step up the recovery of weapons, the command tried to defend the committee's stance in front of the citizens. During negotiations, especially when the members brought collected arms, the command released some arrested people as a reward. On May 22, it released 848 and on May 23, 34 people. Those who were released returned to the Provincial Hall with the committee members and received applause from the citizens in rallies. These events were staged to drive the pro-resistance faction to a corner.

On the first day of liberation, most Gwangju citizens were for the retrieval of weapons; on the morning of May 22, weapons were distributed in one corner, while in another arms were being collected.[31] Other than reducing losses at the time of the martial law troops' re-entry, citizens had another reason for agreeing to collect weapons. On May 22, citizens gathered of their own accord and started a rally, where they agreed to recover weapons. After a while, crowds jeered at a settlement committee member who was reporting on the negotiation with the Martial Law Command, and people jumped up to the podium and seized the microphone, turning the mood of the rally into a

184

confrontation. Kim Tae-jong, leader of the theater group Clown and master of ceremony in the rallies the next day, testified to the atmosphere of the May 22 gathering as follows:

> Then the negotiation report meeting was held. When the settlement committee members said that we should recover arms and maintain peace, all citizens agreed. Then the committee members seemed to go overboard to settle the situation; they went on to say that rather than escalating tension, we should disarm as soon as possible and wait for the government's apology. When they made such makeshift, lukewarm, and humiliating remarks, the Gwangju citizens were enraged. Some of the citizens rushed up to the podium, took away the microphone, and shooed away the settlement committee members. While watching it, I came to understand what the Gwangju citizens truly wanted (Gwangju City 1997 V, 353).

On the first day, citizens agreed to retrieve weapons and restore order, but they were strongly against the idea of ending the fight by recovering and returning weapons to the Martial Law Command so that its soldiers could enter without having to use arms. Although they agreed to the act of collecting weapons, citizens reacted sensitively to its purpose and to what would happen next. The recovery of weapons in liberated Gwangju did not begin with the Martial Law Command's coercion. Citizens began to collect them to restore order before they sat down for negotiations with the Martial Law Command.[32] Citizens wanted both order through recovery of weapons and the continued struggle with the military authorities—in a word, they hoped to kill two birds with one stone. They wanted to save their lives and at the same time to fight with their lives on the line.

From the first day of distributing guns on May 21, middle and high school students posed a problem. Some of them received guns when the situation was deemed urgent, although others were turned away. In some places, guns were distributed to high school students as young as sophomores, along with the instructions on how to handle them. On the afternoon of May 21, when armed citizens attacked the Provincial Hall, middle school students were organized as commando units to take part in assaulting the hall (ICKHD 1990a, 2014: 386-387). In liberated Gwangju, however, chills went down the spines of those who watched high school students, and sometimes middle school boys, go around holding guns or with grenades hanging from their clothes. As soon as the troops withdrew, middle and high school students were the primary targets for the surrender of guns. It was dangerous for teenagers to go around with guns, and some caused trouble here and there (ICKHD 1990a, 4002: 836). High school students, however, were not completely excluded from the civilian militia. On the evening of May 26 when the final resistance was being prepared, some high school students insisted on staying even after they were urged to return home; they remained as the defending militia of the Provincial Hall to the end, and some of them were organized as the mobile strike unit. High school students, as a group, took the heaviest toll in the uprising.

As long as guns were in circulation, the danger of crime existed. An opinion was strongly raised that general citizens must be protected from armed citizens. Since the Martial Law Command disparaged Gwangju as a "lawless land" where "rioters" were teeming, citizens wanted to prove that this allegation was untrue. From the first day of liberation, the Provincial Hall Situation Room dispatched armed guards at all government offices, major buildings, financial institutions, and even the houses of the police chiefs and the very rich in order to protect citizens' assets. On the morning of May 22 , some regional defense teams were sent out to prevent crimes.[33] When an unorganized man or two moved around the city with guns, their weapons were forcibly taken away (Bak Nam-seon 1988, 44-45). Individual armed militiamen could no longer exist except in organized groups, including the units that guarded the Provincial Hall, defended local areas, moved around for patrol, and those in Gwangju Park.

The problem of crime was the most sensitive issue for the leaders of the civilian militia in liberated Gwangju. It was sensitive because a considerable number of the members of the civilian militia defending Gwangju belonged to the classes of workers and the downtrodden, who had been in proximity with the criminal world. The leaders in the Provincial Hall believed that the danger of riots still existed downtown, and those who were active in the hall feared, probably in view of the militia's rough behavior and speech, that they might be shot to death by civilian militiamen who were at the bottom of the social hierarchy.[34] Many militiamen took up arms swept by a feeling of righteousness, but returned them because they did not feel like going around with the "rogues" in the civilian militia.[35] Throughout the uprising period, the bourgeoisie were afraid of those at the bottom of the social hierarchy who did not carry guns, not to mention the civilian militia, and busy protecting their lives and assets (ICKHD 1990a, 7118: 1422). Some bourgeois citizens were unnaturally polite or acted in a servile manner to the downtrodden and those who had taken up guns. The world seemed to have turned upside down with the emergence of the absolute community and there was no knowing what would happen next. In such a situation, they might have felt it would be best to be on the good side of the people they used to treat roughly.[36] Needless to say, the civilian militia had a sense of mission and acted as exemplary democratic citizens, but many middle-class citizens were nervous about the militia composed of workers and the downtrodden.

May 23 was the first beautiful, peaceful day in a long while. Archbishop Yun Gong-hui recalled that morning's freshness as follows:

> The scene from my window, as I looked with a relieved heart, was more beautiful than ever. There was a truck that carried people who went around cleaning up. The blue New Village Movement caps on their heads looked so peaceful. . . (Yun Gong-hui 1989, 17).

187

From 6 o'clock in the morning, about 700 middle and high school students swept the streets, restoring the clean state of the past. The number of the militia's vehicles that rushed around the city began to decrease that afternoon. The excitement of the absolute community was still strong among general citizens who did not take up guns, expressed as an unprecedented awareness of order. From that morning, the Nokdu Bookstore team put up big-character wall posters and hung placards to mobilize citizens to the "First Citizens' Rally To Defend Democracy," slated at noon in the Provincial Hall square. The members of the Council of Artists for Free Gwangju put up a large number of placards and wall posters. In other words, young activists embarked on a campaign to mobilize general citizens. In the hands of the citizens who participated in the rally were pickets indicating their neighborhoods. The scenes of May 23 revealed glimpses of an important political change.

From that day, the word "civilian militia" was adopted as an official term. The biggest change that day, however, was that the general citizens who did not take up arms emerged as a central political category. As can be seen above, they were the targets to be mobilized at political rallies. The mobilization was not for the struggle, as it had been until then, but for the simple political act of getting together. The Provincial Hall settlement committee members and the YWCA team agreed that general citizens should return to their daily routine of making a living and issued an official recommendation. The four-point General Principles of Democratic Citizens, composed by the YWCA and put up on the front of the Jeonil Building, urged citizens to "return to daily life."[37] From May 23, both the pro-resistance group and the settlement faction officially recognized that the general citizens were the targets of political mobilization and expressed the understanding that order was an urgent issue and the individual citizens wanted to return to the existing order. These notifications were no different from declaring that the emergency or the "full mobilization" system was over. Such an official stance was to put the citizens at ease and gain their political support, but it resulted in cooling the atmosphere of struggle among citizens. In the same context, the *Fighters' Bulletin* was changed to *Democratic Citizens' Bulletin* on May 26. This decision was based on the judgment that the struggle might turn into a long-term affair and that the major readers of their discourse should be general citizens.[38]

When Gwangju recovered its calm, the absolute community and the existing community, which was recovering its shape, exposed the line of confrontation. Kim Hyeon-chae, a militiaman, recalled the morning of May 23 as follows:

> As we approached the park, I saw that some grandfathers were sitting at the lion statue on the right side of the stairs leading to the park. I spotted my father among the group. I told In-su that my father was sitting over there and hid myself among those who were with me. Until we entered the restaurant, I observed my father, hidden among my group. . . .
>
> I looked up at the stairs as I left the restaurant, and my father was still sitting there. When he looked in our direction, I hid myself behind my comrades. As I watched my father from the window of the car, I felt like crying for some reason and I clamped my teeth. I couldn't take my eyes off of him. My father didn't seem to have seen me, because he was now talking to someone next to him.
>
> Since I came down from Seoul, I hadn't stopped by my parents' house. My father couldn't have imagined that I was in Gwangju. I had plunged into the fight after I was severely beaten on the train by paratroopers. I couldn't tolerate a sense of guilt that I hadn't thought of my family until then. At the same time, I hated myself for not being able to confidently tell my father in front of the civilian militia's Special Weapons and Tactics (SWAT) Team that I would fight to the death to defend Gwangju. My heart was torn at the thought of my father, who

wouldn't worry about me, thinking his youngest was safely in
Seoul . . . .

If my father had spotted me, he would have grabbed me
to take home. If I died, however, he might understand me
because he had seen the miserable reality in which all citizens
had to become one to fight. He might be proud of me in
front of the others that his son had died while fighting for
freedom and justice (The Association of Comrades of the
May 18 Gwangju Uprising 1987, 107-108).

On the other hand, Yi Jae-ui, who had participated in the struggle
from the beginning and busied himself from May 22 to organize ranks in the Provincial Hall, stopped by his home on the
night of May 23 to take a rest. His family forced him to leave
Gwangju (ICKHD 1990a, 1045: 333).

When the intoxication of being in the struggle wore off a
little, the family, the central unit in the traditional community,
began to awaken guilt in the individuals of the civilian militia.
Many tried to avoid the eyes of their families as they went around;
when they ran across their siblings, they lied that they would
come home soon or asked them to lie to their parents. To the
civilian militia, there was no way to resolve the conflict between
the loyalty to the struggle and their sense of obligation to their
families. For this reason, many laid down guns and went home.[39]
The following account by Yeom Gyeong-tae could not have been
an exceptional case.

I was busy going back and forth between the Provincial Hall
and downtown. By accident, I caught sight of myself in a mirror attached to a wall in the Provincial Hall. I was shocked to
see how scruffy I looked. Not to mention my pants, which I
had had custom made only a while ago, my shirt was tattered,
torn here and there. My hair had grown long and my face,
which I hadn't washed for several days, was too dirty to take a
long look. Until then, I had had no presence of mind to pay

attention to my appearance. I wanted to wash my face, but there was nowhere to do so. It was only then that I thought I had better go home. That day was May 25 (ICKHD 1990a, 2015: 391).

Literally, it was the magic of the mirror. A militiaman, who caught sight of himself in the mirror, turned into Narcissus and could no longer be a warrior. The face he saw in the mirror was not just his own, but also that of home and family. Thinking of home and family was tantamount to being selfish, which ran counter to the loyalty to his colleagues and the Gwangju community. Tears welled up in the eyes of the civilian militiamen with the sudden remembrance of their parents. Some of them carried in their pockets pieces of paper bearing their names and addresses. This could have been a gesture of filial piety in an ironic sense, hoping that they would be delivered to their family if they died from a barrage of gunshots.

The only valid relationship that was carried over from the existing community to the absolute community was friendship. When armed citizens came across their friends, they were overjoyed and fought with redoubled courage. School and hometown ties provided strength during the struggle in the absolute community. The special character of friendship, often lauded by the East and the West in the past and present, manifested itself. The only relationship that did not change no matter how the world changed was friendship, and the civilian militia took advantage of friendships in its organization.[40] In such a situation, militiamen from the bottom of the social hierarchy, whose life revolved entirely around friendships, with few family members to rely on, showed exemplary loyalty and they wanted to remain in the militia to the end.

The civilian militia at the time was vulnerable to such a change in atmosphere because of its organizational weakness. On May 21 and 22, ROK Army reservists organized units in Gwangju Park and assigned them regions to patrol and defend, but they fell out of control and most dispersed (ICKHD 1990a, 2015: 390 etc.). Some armed citizens ran around as they pleased, often caused accidents, and inflicted losses on the troops of the civilian militia.[41] When the weapons-collection team came, some civilian militia readily handed their guns over and went home, and would never rejoin the organization. At the time of organizing the civilian militia in Gwangju Park and downtown in the wake of the paratroopers' shooting on May 21, people moved in an orderly manner. From May 22, with the enemy out of sight, they gradually relaxed and began to worry about their families. Since the citizens joined the militia voluntarily from the beginning, no one had control over their behavior.

The atmosphere of May 22 turned menacing as some brandished guns; one side argued for settlement while the other side insisted on continued struggle. On May 23, however, the settlement faction took the higher ground in the Provincial Hall, and activist circles expressed their opposition in rallies. Although the pro-resistance faction was set against returning weapons to the Martial Law Command, they had no choice but to agree to recover arms as a way to keep order, given the atmosphere of May 23. They decided to cooperate with the recovery of weapons on the condition that in contingencies the citizens would be rearmed with recovered guns.[42] It was on the afternoon of May 23 that the settlement committee officially decided on the recovery of arms, but a considerable number of the civilian militiamen already had voluntarily returned their guns and gone home. From that afternoon, the weapons-collection team of the settlement committee began to work vigorously, visiting the civilian militia on the outskirts of the city. Many people returned weapons on May 23. Kim Chang-gil returned 200 guns to the Martial Law Command and received wild applause from the citizens in a rally, where there were 34 who had been released in return for the submission of guns. The fervor for struggle died down quickly, and the number of the civilian militia dropped drastically after many armed citizens went away upon returning their weapons.[43] The settlement faction and the pro-resistance group began to clash on May 23 over the issue of returning arms to the Martial Law Command. Kim Chang-gil said that he would return 100 guns to the Martial Law Command to see how the military authorities would react, but he secretly took 200. The pro-resistance group was angered and began to view him with suspicion. Immediately, Bak Nam-seon issued an order that weapons should not be allowed to be taken out. Among the soldiers of the civilian militia, discontent and a sense of crisis were rising.[44] The confrontation between Kim Jong-bae, vice chairman of the Student Settlement Committee and the head of the pro-resistance group, and Kim Chang-gil, the head of the settlement faction, rushed headlong into a situation where each felt danger to his person.[45]

The weapons-collection team actively retrieved arms by approaching the organized civilian militia, including regional defense teams. The workers, especially the downtrodden in the militia, began to harbor blatant class hostility toward those who went around retrieving weapons, the learned, affluent people. Kim Hyeon-chae, a restaurant employee, who worked as a civilian SWAT Team member, testified as follows:

> I don't know exactly what day it was, but while I was patrolling in a SWAT Team vehicle, I saw people in a sedan who said they were collecting weapons. I wanted to shoot them in the head. We had to defend Gwangju and fight no matter what happened. I thought recovering weapons was no different from blowing ourselves up (ICKHD 1990 a, 2041: 509-510).

To a restaurant employee, the "people in a sedan" had a meaning that was all too clear. Since the recovery of weapons for the sake of order began with class prejudice, his response was natural. The gun-collection team went beyond recovering citizens' weapons in the name of order, however, and began to approach organized regional defense teams with tenacity. Open conflicts,

193

including brandishing arms, occurred between those who attempted to take guns away and civilian militiamen; many attempts ended in failure.

Based on their experience of collecting guns on May 23, from the early morning hours of May 24, religious leaders in the settlement committee started recovering arms in earnest to save lives, going around from one regional defense team to another that stood in confrontation with the martial law troops. Since it was no easy feat to retrieve arms from the civilian militia aiming guns at the martial law troops, the collectors had carefully prepared an argument to persuade armed citizens.[46] The settlement committee members mostly argued that they needed to protect citizens' lives. Those who had taken up arms for the community had already given up on their lives, but they were weakened by the assertion that other Gwangju citizens' lives had to be protected.[47] In some cases, they talked to the armed citizens while providing food, given that food delivery was not going smoothly and some had missed several meals (Jo Bi-o 1994, 40). When they approached the downtrodden in the militia to disarm them, they exploited their class weaknesses.[48] They even collected money to disarm the downtrodden in the militia (Jo Bi-o 1994, 153-154; Gwangju City 1997 V, 294).

When the fervor for struggle cooled down and most citizens began to think about returning to their normal lives, the civilian militia was confronted with various problems. At the beginning, local residents voluntarily took care of all supplies, including meals to all regional defense units. From May 23, however, the system was changed to delivering food by car from the Provincial Hall. With weak organization, problems began to occur in distributing meals to outlying regional defense units.[49] The gun recovery unit of the settlement committee recognized and exploited this vulnerability of the organized militia. In particular, the recovery team members took advantage of human, organizational weaknesses; they prostrated themselves and offered bows to the downtrodden, they fell to their knees as they cajoled them, supplied food, lightly slapped them on the back for encouragement, and persuaded them that they should return arms to save all Gwangju citizens' lives.

As a result of tenacious effort to collect weapons, a total of 4,000 guns and over 1,000 grenades were retrieved on May 24. Only a few hundred weapons held by the militiamen remained at large. Most of the militia organizations that had been voluntarily formed on the morning of May 22, for example the SWAT Team, were disbanded around May 24. The remaining troops amounted to the guard unit at the Provincial Hall, part of the mobile patrol unit, and those who had been disarmed but hung around the Provincial Hall, helping out and biding their time to take up arms again after the militia's reorganization.[50] There were some signs of agitation in the Situation Room of the Provincial Hall (Bak Nam-seon 1988, 187). In the aftermath of the "poison-needle scare," more armed citizens laid down arms and went home, while almost all regional defense teams were disarmed on the morning of May 25.[51] The gun-collection team, as quoted above, went around, pleading that arms had to be returned for everyone to survive, in the belief that retrieving one more firearm meant saving one more life. Now, the settlement faction and the pro-resistance group began to fight over the issue of weapons collection and both sides felt danger to their persons.[52]

Following the formation of the pro-resistance leadership on the evening of May 25, the conflict within the Provincial Hall was acute between those who insisted that weapons should be redistributed to reorganize the civilian militia and those who were against this idea (ICKHD 1990a, 2028: 452). From this point on, the recovery of weapons was out of the question. On May 26, too, the settlement committee and the pro-resistance faction co-existed; all day long, squabbles broke out. In one corner weapons were collected while in another corner people shouted their opposition and wielded weapons (ICKHD 1990a, 1038: 297; 1039: 303). During the last meeting on the evening of May 26, the point of contention was whether they should lay down arms, disarm the organization, and vacate the Provincial Hall for the martial law troops or whether those who intended to fight to the end should stay there and fight. Throughout the liberated period in Gwangju, justifications in the conflict between the settlement faction and the pro-resistance group were not fixed, but changed continuously. Their conflict did not revolve around principles expressed in certain words and arguments but was related to the concepts of life and death, which were impossible to express in words.

The civilian militia shrank with the recovery of weapons, and those who considered resistance against the martial law troops were worried about the loss of troops. Neither the leadership in the Provincial Hall nor the head of the Situation Room had the authority to mobilize the civilian militia. Mobilizing reservists was an unrealized dream by the resistance leadership in the Provincial Hall. The only way to counter the subdued atmosphere was to turn the civilian militia into a disciplined organization that could be manned by trustworthy citizens. From May 24, attempts were made to reinforce the mobile patrol unit. The Situation Room considered compiling a list of the militia members, but did not do so, afraid of the ramifications for the future. The militia leaders were simply thankful for those who fought with them.[53] The only way to control the ranks and files of the civilian militia was to cook meals at the Provincial Hall and deliver them in time as best as they could, and commanders appealed for their loyalty with moving speeches from time to time.

The only solution was to mobilize university students, and this was the direction embraced by Bak Nam-seon, chief of the Situation Room. The only people who could introduce discipline were university students. They belonged to universities, and each university had alumni networks. Relying on these relations, commanders could order them around and create discipline by training them with commands such as, "Stand! Sit!" The leadership stationed in the Provincial Hall and the YWCA appealed to university students for their participation every day via P.A. systems in vehicles or microphones after rallies. The leadership, including the Situation Room head, made efforts to replace workers guarding the Provincial Hall with university students as much as possible during the last period of resistance. The reasons were that "university students were trustworthy" and they could "greatly raise the level of control" (Jeong Sang-yong et al. 1990, 302). On the evening of May 22, Kim Chang-gil mentioned the issue of TNT in the hall's basement. He said, "If it is exploded by impure elements, Gwangju citizens will be killed. At present, those who guard the explosives do not know each other and no commanding system is in place. We cannot ignore the situation. There are a number of pastors and priests among the settlement committee. Please bring your flocks to replace the guards" (Jo Bi-o 1994, 45). What he referred to were acquaintances or those whose identities were verifiable, and for this reason they believed that important duties should be assigned to students and churchgoers. The priests put the word out and summoned young Christians in a hurry. On the evening of May 25, however, the guarding troops in the Provincial Hall already had been replaced with armed university students, brought by Yun Sang-won from the YWCA. In a sense, they were coup d'état troops for Yun. What must be pointed out here is that the justification to replace guards in the Provincial Hall with university students was identical.[54]

Liberated Gwangju went through a process in which the absolute community was being broken down and the return to everyday life was under way. For Gwangju citizens, it was inconceivable to return weapons to the Martial Law Command and let the troops enter the city bloodlessly. Most citizens, however, wanted to return to order and normal life; for this reason, they were for collecting a limited number of weapons. Class prejudices were inevitably involved in recovering weapons in the name of keeping order. However, the Martial Law Command's threat and, more importantly, the emergence of the value of individual

life pushed the retrieval of weapons to the militia's overall dis-
armament. With the re-emergence of individual identity and family obligations, fear of death and re-evaluation of individual lives
led to the absolute community's collapse. The gun-collection
team of the settlement committee went beyond the level of keeping order; it devoted itself to recovering arms to save general
citizens' lives. The Gwangju citizens hoped to return to normal
life under control, but this was difficult to realize. After May 24,
it was clear that the conflict between the settlement and pro-
resistance factions was impossible to resolve with rational discussion. It was not because Kim Chang-gil or Kim Jong-bae, the
heads of each group, lacked reason. The pending issue—the
conflict of different concepts of life and death—was not something to be compromised through rational discussion. There was
an aspect they could not comprehend in each other, and this was
what could not be compromised.

What the Gwangju citizens wanted from the first day of
liberation were two goals that could not be achieved together—
life and the struggle against the unforgivable military. In reality,
the only way for them to kill two birds with one stone was with
outside assistance; in other words, uprisings in other regions and
support from the United States. The Gwangju citizens were isolated and they strongly hoped for the United States' support or
the US ambassador's mediation.[55] After the "poison-needle
scare" of May 25, most middle-class people lost patience over
the continuing crisis. Some openly said that they hoped that the
martial law troops would enter and put an end to the situation.[56]

4. Final Resistance and the Meaning of Death

The martial law troops were getting ready for a crackdown operation. On May 21, they completely cut off Gwangju to prevent the rebellion from spreading. On May 24, airborne units
were summoned to Songjeong-ri to establish a concrete plan
and stage a dry run. Finally at 11:49 on May 25, the martial law

198

commander delivered the guidelines to all subordinate units, stating that the suppression operation would be carried out according to orders after 0001 on May 27. President Choi Kyu-hah's visit to Gwangju was a gesture of appeasement in a scenario in which the suppression operation was already in place. In the early morning hours of May 26, tanks and units were sent to the city to test the citizens' will to fight and to secure supply and transport routes for the operation. As expected, the citizens' enthusiasm had dissipated. With the troops' open expression of intention, many members of the civilian militia deserted their troops. While the citizens' representatives, who had just finished the "parade of death," started to negotiate with the deputy commander of the Combat Training and Doctrine Command at 10 o'clock, the head of this command summoned the chiefs of the 3rd, 7th, and 11th Airborne Brigades, the Infantry School, the Artillery School, and the Armored School and held a commanders' meeting at 10:30 in preparation for the operation. On the afternoon of May 26, paratroopers succeeded in kidnapping Jeon Ok-ju, who was judged to be a dangerous person at the time of quelling. At 4:40 in the afternoon, the new military junta secured agreement for the operation from the head of the ROK-US Combined Command. That afternoon, US Ambassador William Gleysteen received a phone call from the armed citizens in the Gwangju Provincial Hall, requesting his mediation, but he refused.[57]

From the beginning, the activist group centered on Yun Sang-won maintained the stance that citizens should fight to the end in liberated Gwangju and carefully forged an alliance with other citizens who favored resistance. They approached the Provincial Hall via the Student Settlement Committee. After winning Bak Nam-seon, the de facto commander-in-chief of the civilian militia, over to their side, they took steps to seize control of the settlement committee. During the May 24 rally, they drove the settlement committee into a difficult position through careful preparations and by burning an effigy of Chun Doo-hwan. The settlement committee members, nervous about Yun's group, tried to prevent the rally from being staged by cutting off power to the amplifier, but those who prepared for the gathering pressed ahead with the meeting by using the equipment in a police pepper-fog vehicle. Their criticism of the settlement committee was carefully planned out. Harsh critiques of the Citizens' Settlement Committee poured out during a meeting that started at around 3 o'clock in the afternoon. When Yun's group exposed the Provincial Hall executives' attempts to hinder the rally, citizens expressed fury.[58] The citizens in the rally were roused by the burning of Chun Doo-hwan's effigy. Despite rain, they stayed until the end of the rally, which continued in heated atmosphere until 7 p.m., without opening umbrellas.

As the rally was being wrapped up, Yun Sang-won met Bak Nam-seon for the first time in the Situation Room. They soon agreed on the nature of the situation and the direction of action (Bak Nam-seon 1988, 189). Bak Nam-seon was exhausted by the situation, which was unfolding in a complicated manner, and Yun Sang-won renewed his will to fight.[59] Yun Sang-won envisioned the final showdown with conviction, and the leadership of the YWCA team convened a secret meeting at Boseong Company at 7:30 in the evening. The settlement committee meeting in the Provincial Hall was held in a hostile atmosphere and the pro-resistance members declared that they would leave. However, they soon rejoined to form a new organization. With the compromise between the pro-resistance group and the settlement faction, Kim Chang-gil was retained as chairman, but university students and the civilian militia were merged into the same organization, and the Student Settlement Committee was disbanded on the evening of May 24. At 10 o'clock on the morning of May 25, Yun Sang-won and Jeong Sang-yeong asked dissident elders to come to the second floor of the YWCA and obtained their approval about the pro-resistance faction's advance into the Provincial Hall. In fact, only a few dissidents supported their stance, while the rest kept silent. The older dissidents did not accept the young people's request that they stand on the podium during a rally, but they granted tacit approval of the younger activists' intention to play a leading role in the Provincial Hall—in other words, defending the Provincial Hall to the end.

The Martial Law Command grasped the atmosphere and staged the so-called "poison-needle scare" at 8 o'clock on the morning of May 25. Not only at the Provincial Hall, but the atmosphere throughout the city was chilled. Those who led the resistance had to fight against the agitated atmosphere in the Provincial Hall in the aftermath of the scare. The head of the Situation Room read a manifesto "Why did we have to take up guns?" to state the civilian militia's stance during the afternoon rally. Immediately the Citizens' Settlement Committee passed a resolution about the unconditional submission of weapons. Hearing this, Bak Nam-seon put armed guards on alert, jumped into the room where the meeting was being held, and drove committee members out by brandishing a gun.[60] At the time, Bak Nam-seon was conscious of his status and active in assisting Yun Sang-won's plan.[61] Around 2 o'clock in the afternoon, with almost all the existing settlement committee members gone, the Nam-dong Catholic Church group joined the settlement committee at the earnest request of young activists and students, thus the committee was reorganized. Father Kim Seong-yong, who soon became the group's spokesman, put forth four-point demands, and they were passed unanimously. The weapon-returning ceremony slated at a rally that day was scrapped, and the mood of the rally was consistently in favor of continued fight. From that day, Bak Nam-seon put various departments of the Provincial Hall under his control, relying on the arms he controlled.

At around 7 o'clock in the evening, Yun Sang-won entered the Provincial Hall from the YWCA, with 70 university students in tow. Bak Nam-seon armed 100 university students, adding the new crop to the 30 who already had been in the Provincial

Hall, and replaced the guards at the Hall with these students. He held a meeting with the Student Settlement Committee members in the Industry Promotion Bureau on the third floor and passed a resolution that a new executive committee should be formed. This big decision was made while Kim Chang-gil was out of the Provincial Hall for a negotiation with the Martial Law Command.[62] Kim Chang-gil resigned around 9 o'clock in the evening. A new enforcement committee was launched in the anteroom of the Internal Affairs Bureau at 10 o'clock in the name of the Democratic Citizens' Struggle Committee, thus officially announcing a new struggle line. This was how the Student Settlement Committee was disbanded and the resistance leadership was born. The Democratic Citizens' Struggle Committee was generally called the resistance leadership. With the establishment of the new leadership and Kim Chang-gil's resignation, the cooking team left the building. The new leadership was compelled to revamp all the organizations of the Provincial Hall. The reorganization of the resistance leadership came as a coup, which signified an immense political change. As soon as the resistance leadership was born, nationwide television evening news announced that a hard-line faction had ascended in the Provincial Hall. It is evident that the military authorities were carefully collecting intelligence. At this point, the military had already decided on an entry operation. At dawn the next day, the authorities turned up the pressure by driving tanks into the city. All of the 17 settlement committee members, who had remained in the Provincial Hall, suggested that they walk out to block the tanks with their bodies, which led to the so-called "parade of death."

The new resistance leadership's main duties consisted of preparing for the final battle against the army, reducing inconveniences in citizens' everyday life, and biding time until the final showdown. On the morning of May 26, they put up a wall poster announcing that a US aircraft carrier had arrived in South Korean waters. Many citizens expected that the carrier might help them, but Yun Sang-won was well aware that it had not come to assist Gwangju. At a rally around noon, the resistance leadership officially revealed its political stance by adopting the "Resolution of 800,000 Gwangju Citizens." The resolution called for the government to push for democratization, not just recover their honor, and pledged to fight to the end unless such demands were accepted. The leaders knew that the new military junta could never accept their demands. The resolution was the expression of their intention to fight until all of them died, and was their last statement to the general public. The leaders did not forget to add a political gesture befitting civilized people, saying that they would attempt a peaceful resolution until the end. While the rally was going on, from the sky a helicopter dropped fliers that said, "The military will soon embark on a crackdown." During the rally, reliable intelligence arrived that the martial law troops would enter the city early next morning, and the resistance leaders agonized over whether to make it public. They decided to inform the citizens and did so via a microphone. A sudden silence descended on the crowd. In such an atmosphere, the leaders could only say, "Those who want to fight to the end, please remain with us, and the rest of you, please go home." Some 500 citizens vowed that they would fight to the end.

The most important thing in preparing for the final showdown was to reorganize the civilian militia. Most regional defense units had collapsed with the collection of arms, and many armed citizens had gone home. From May 25, the leadership and the civilian militia felt the shortage of troops. They made attempts to mobilize their friends and urged anyone they came across to join them.[63] It had been a failure to deploy the university students who had been brought from the YWCA on May 25; a considerable number of them had disappeared. Around noon on May 26, Bak Nam-seon organized the mobile strike unit, with Yun Seok-nu as its head and Yi Jae-ho as deputy head, at the Industry Promotion Bureau Chief's Office on the second floor. This was the most organized, well-armed organization among the groups of the civilian militia during the uprising. This organization was tiny. It was made of seven teams of six or seven persons each.[64] The resistance leadership had already set up a plan to mobilize local reservists (ICKHD 1990a, 4011: 894). However, it never had the time to put it into practice.

On the evening of May 26, the last meeting took place in the Provincial Hall; Kim Chang-gil, who had resigned the day before, attended. The settlement faction put forth a proposal for a resolution that the militia lay down arms and disband the organization. Debate ensued. Although a majority voted for the return of weapons and the dissolution of the organization, Yun Sang-won called on Bak Nam-seon and Yun Seok-nu to drive away the settlement faction by threatening them with guns (1990a, 1013: 205).[65] After leaving the meeting, Kim Chang-gil and Hwang Geum-seon went around the Provincial Hall, pleading with the students and young men in the building that they could live if only they abandoned guns and went home. Bak Nam-seon, outraged, fired a gun to threaten them and drove them out of the building. A considerable number of students and the civilian militia left along with them. It was a little before 9 o'clock in the evening.

A novel depicts what Yun Sang-won said in the last meeting, where the Provincial Hall executives were present.

> Of course, we will be defeated tonight. We are likely to die. But all of us cannot throw away guns and hand over this place without putting up resistance. The fight for the past several days was too heated and tragic for that. The Provincial Hall will be a place where we will put a period to this battle. Some-one must defend this place to the end in order to complete the citizens' hot resistance and not to nullify the meaning of noble sacrifices. I will stay here until the very end. Others, of course, should make their own decisions (Yim Cheol-u 1997 V, 391).[66]

Bak Nam-seon later remembered his feelings at the time.

> Most of the Citizens' Settlement Committee members, except
> a few, argued that we should return the weapons and disperse,
> so that all of us could survive. Everyone had the right to choose
> a path at a crossroads of life and death, but in Gwangju it was
> not possible. The path to live was to defend Gwangju and
> fight to the end, and the path to die was to give up on Gwangju.
> We had to defend the Provincial Hall to the death and resist to
> the end in order to defend Gwangju (Bak Nam-seon, 1988:
> 214).[67]

Needless to say, this is not the way people think in normal times.
Many people who were at the Provincial Hall at the time, those
who had not experienced the salvation of the absolute community achieved with a bloody fight, did not think in this vein, either.

Some Provincial Hall executives and the civilian militia, after being notified that the martial law troops would attack, had
a solemn "last supper" in their own ways. Some ate pastries delivered from bakeries, while others drank liquor and nibbled on
bread, reflecting on their feelings toward food and life, in keeping with Leonardo da Vinci's reflection on feelings toward life
and food. The old artistic inspiration put their lives and deaths
in a meaningful, beautiful light. Most young people knew that
the final moment was approaching; they said goodbye to each
other and exchanged encouragement and kept guard over the
Provincial Hall and Gwangju, which they could never defend
physically, until the small hours. It is impossible to know how
many people were ready to die. Some might have been unable
to leave the Provincial Hall, held back by loyalty, while others
could have been swept into the excitement of the moment. Many
of them could have truly believed that they would live if they
stood their ground until dawn. Although it is impossible to know
what they really thought, they refused the advice that they should
go home if they wanted to live, for the sake of the Gwangju

205

citizens or the country's democracy, and opted for the path of death.

Father Jo Bi-o, who had done everything in his power to recover weapons and mediate between the two conflicting factions, participated in the last meeting on the evening of May 26. He remembered leaving the Provincial Hall to perform a mass celebrating the parish fete at Gyerim-dong Catholic Church, where he was presiding priest.

> As a priest, I believed that the citizens' losses had to be reduced as much as possible, and frankly I was more sympathetic to the moderates' opinion, for it was crystal clear that everyone would have to die. I hinted that they would never withstand the elite special airborne unit, equipped with immense firepower, no matter how many troops citizens reinforced, but I couldn't change the hard-liners' minds.

> In principle, the hard-liners' argument was right. Rather than avoiding a destiny that was bound to bring tragedy, they were resolved to face it head-on. This spirit was fitting for the young men of Gwangju, who were brave and admirable, and whose losses would be missed. Amid tension and fear, the two sides' opinions clashed head-on, but there was no fight. . . . The moderates judged that they could never win a battle and left the Provincial Hall that evening. Now the hall was controlled by the members of the civilian militia, who had passed a hard-line resolution. While 200 citizens with arms were getting ready, I received a message from the faithful of Gyerim-dong Church. I told those around me that I had no choice but to leave for the church, and exited through the front gate. It was around 8:45 in the evening.

> As I left the gate, tears began to stream down my face, because I felt I was leaving like a coward to survive alone, and I thought that it might be a fateful night in which so many

young men could lose their lives. No matter how many times I wiped them, tears kept coming (Jo bi-o 1994, 47-48).

Father Jo Bi-o had moved around the city retrieving guns to save lives until he developed blisters on his feet. However, on the final night, he only "hinted" to those who stuck to the hard-line stance that they could never win and that they must lay down weapons if they desired to live. Whatever stance he had held prior to this moment, by this point Father Jo was deeply aware that someone had to fight there, though he did not say it, even if they were defeated and had to die honorably. Contrary to what he said, he was not "more sympathetic to the moderates' opinion." At heart, he was a hard-liner. He acted to save individual lives as a conscientious priest, in view of clerical status that mandated protecting lives. Tears kept flowing because of the conflict between two consciences—value of life vs. death for the sake of truth—and because he was turning away after dedicating great young men to the altar of sacrifice for the sake of the truth. Father Jo Bi-o had two minds, two consciences, and it might have been the same for Father Kim Seong-yong (ICKHD 1990a, 1008: 177). Neither of their two consciences was hypocritical. That night, Father Jo Bi-o delivered the following sermon.

In the aftermath of Abel's innocent blood, Cain was punished by God and wandered around the wilderness. The tragedy of killing the same ethnic people — the soldiers cultivated with taxpayers' money killing innocent citizens—will not simply end as misery. The lives of the citizens who died without knowing why they had to die and the blood of young people who protested against injustice will become righteous blood that may rescue our country's history from distress. The wronged, grief-stricken deaths of the righteous people and their blood will rise to the sky and God will surely listen to our heartfelt wish (Jo Bi-o 1994, 48-49).

He prayed to God for revenge as he thought of the young men's impending deaths. He prayed for everyone's salvation at the expense of their sacrifices and sought punishment of the evil beings that robbed them of their lives. In the early morning hours of May 27, a young, anxious woman's voice shrieked from a loudspeaker, "We will fight to the end. Please don't forget us!" With this cry, Gwangju citizens, along with Father Jo Bi-o, felt guilty about sacrificing the youth in exchange for their lives, dreamed of revenge for their sakes, and harbored a heartfelt wish for their salvation.

At dawn on May 27, a stream of martial law troops flooded into the city from all directions. Soon gunshots rang out, and the militia's mobile strike teams on the outskirts returned to the Provincial Hall one after another. With searchlights focused on the front of the Provincial Hall, the martial law troops opened fire in unison. While all the civilian militia returned fire, the 3rd Airborne Commando Squad climbed over the back fence, stole into the building, sprayed bullets, and threw grenades here and there. They even fired to make sure that the wounded would die instantly (ICKHD 1990a, 1044: 323). Many members of the civilian militia saw the entry of the commando unit, but could not bring themselves to pull the triggers of their guns. Some surviving militiamen raised their hands to surrender. They were roped together "like dried fish" and taken to the military jail at the Combat Training and Doctrine Command in four buses. No one knows exactly how many died at the Provincial Hall that dawn.[68]

5. Conclusion

In some ways, liberated Gwangju had a tragic ending without even the chance of putting up a good fight, and too many young talents were sacrificed unnecessarily. Though it may sound cruel, both the pro-resistance and settlement factions did what they had to do. Those who wanted to live did, and about half of those who were determined to die survived. The final show-down came to an end without much of a battle, but the young people's bloody resistance defended the truth of Gwangju. They knew that the only way to communicate with the world in an island cut off from the rest of the world was in the realm of time. They turned themselves into black fossils, but are now eloquently telling the truth, reincarnated as freedom at a time when their oppressors turned into ashes. If they had opted for a different path—for example, mobilized thousands of reservists—or vacated the Provincial Hall in a bid to survive, the heritage of the May 18 Gwangju uprising could not have amounted to what we have now.

The complicated development of the situation in liberated Gwangju vividly shows that no one—the minjung, students, activists, or workers—had any intention of starting a revolution. When armed citizens occupied the Provincial Hall, they placed themselves on the building's first floor, where it was easy to come and go, and they did not go up to the second floor to the executives' offices and meeting halls except when they attended meetings, their presence was requested, or they were ordered to do so. In addition, they called the headquarters of the civilian militia the "Situation Room" and the militia's commander "director of the Situation Room," settling on modest terms. Even if their modesty was not praiseworthy, they did not negate the existence of the settlement committee composed of influential personages of Gwangju when the world appeared to have turned upside down. Although armed citizens did not like the settlement committee members, they did not try to do away with the committee itself.

Young activists and dissidents believed that the political rulers had to be changed, but all agreed that general citizens had to return to daily economic activities, and all made efforts to protect their assets. In other words, they did not deny the economy and the community. Although citizens and influential figures were suspicious, wary, and afraid of the revolutionary intention of the civilian militia manned by those on the lowest rung of society, the civilian militia was simply proud of taking up guns to protect the Gwangju citizens. The absolute community formed by the armed citizens was a form of life organized voluntarily without asking the reason for its existence, coming from rage over the enemy, individual courage of the citizens who overcame fear, and love for other courageous citizens. Their absolute love may have been made possible in the face of the common enemy. Insomuch as their absolute community was pure, they did not see why they had to defend it at all costs and accordingly they could not find why the absolute community had to be prevented from being fragmented into individuals.

The most notable political event in liberated Gwangju was citizens' rallies, which took place once a day—and twice on May 26, a spectacle created by an enormous crowd near the fountain in front of the Provincial Hall. Many Gwangju citizens participated in these demonstrations, voicing their opinions, displaying enthusiasm, letting out boos, and expressing complaints. These demonstrations sprouted from a unique political situation; it is wrong to take them as a direct democratic system as in ancient Greece. The gathering on May 22, the first day of liberation, was a voluntary meeting of citizens, although in the morning someone had gone around the town with a loudspeaker urging them to gather and there was a rumor that the acting prime minister was coming to Gwangju. Following a mourning rite for the dead, the focus of this gathering was the issue of negotiations being conducted by the Citizens' Settlement Committee. The rally was not where citizens made important decisions. Rather, the focal point was criticism of the settlement committee's activities. Previously, rallies had begun with fury and denunciations of martial law troops; in this sense, they were dependent on the existence of the enemy, the martial law troops.[69]

The demonstrations after May 23 were reminiscent of a theater staged by university students centered on young activists, with the disarmed general citizens as their audience. The masters of ceremony were like leading actors, and the representatives from all walks of life on the podium were known actors (ICKHD 1990a, 4001: 834). The intentions of the majority of citizens were not reflected, but this particular rally was a political activity to reproduce citizens' intentions as voluntarily expressed on May 22, and to shape public opinion. In a nutshell, rallies were political activities with the goal of continuing the struggle by arousing the spirit of fight among citizens and pressuring the settlement committee. The settlement committee was well aware of this fact. The rallies were also acts to prevent the general citizens' fighting will from sagging after their return to daily activities. On May 24, eye-catching scenes were staged, such as burning Chun Doo-hwan's effigy. Seizing this opportunity, the activists embarked on the work of seizing control of the Provincial Hall, as they turned up the pressure on the settlement committee.

These rallies followed a pre-planned script, but citizens remembered the absolute community's atmosphere and sometimes volunteered to stand on the podium to pour out their bitterness. From May 24, theatrical factors became more refined, and with the creation of spectacles, such as burning effigies, citizens enjoyed the rallies as a carnival, reproducing some of the experience and mood of the struggle.[70] The carnival elements were in full splendor on the evening of May 26. The leaders knew that the martial law troops would enter that night, and after long consideration, they announced the news to the citizens. The noisy crowd began to murmur among themselves, and soon silence fell as if cold water had been splashed over them. Hwang Seog-yeong describes this situation as follows:

> The heightened atmosphere in the rally site suddenly turned chilly and heavy silence descended on the square. *So it is finally coming.* Instead of looking each other in the face, people seemed to be pensive. Tears welled up in the eyes of the silent citizens (Hwang Seog-yeong 1985, 204).

The citizens were jolted as if they had fallen from a virtual world into reality. In the rallies, the citizens did not discuss common reality with rational consciousness; they vented their resentment, enjoying their eyes and ears and freedom of speech, by creating another world to lessen their torment and loneliness. The rallies were not where rational discussions took place to solve problems in reality, but where they comforted each other and soothed each other's wounds.

They were not in a situation where they could make democratic decisions. Although they knew that only the fatherland's democratization would prevent a tragedy of such magnitude, this would come only in the future. In Yun Sang-won's case, what he had to do at the moment was to stage a coup with armed university students and kick out the settlement faction from the Provincial Hall. If they had laid down weapons according to the majority's decision and vacated the Provincial Hall, the call for democratization in June 1987 would not have happened and South Koreans would be still under the rule of Chun Doo-hwan's Sixth Republic. In realistic terms, South Korea's democracy was made possible through undemocratic acts, including mass agitation in rallies, Yun Sang-won's coup, and Bak Nam-seon's threat with guns.

The settlement committee, which was criticized by the citizens gathered in rallies, determined the fate of liberated Gwangju. As soon as the battle was over on Geumnam Avenue on May 21, an attempt was made to organize this type of committee. No matter who manned it, the settlement committee was where representatives from all walks of life congregated, and this very constitution of the committee—the principle that had to be accepted by everyone—foreshadowed the dismantlement of the absolute community. The absolute community was the absolute singular, while the representatives from all walks of life consisted of plurals: in other words, the reproduction of the existing community divided by class. Restoring order, which meant dissolving the absolute community, was the grand proposition that was accepted by everyone. Everyone knew that the absolute community was possible for only a short period of time, and that they were fated to return to daily lives, where plural classes existed. Although daily lives were not a fixed entity, there was not much room for choice. They did not believe that the settlement committee members, dissidents, and activists could shape everyday life independently, and they did not imagine daily lives beyond those known to general citizens. The civilian militiamen were against the word "settlement" and hoped for a "struggle," but they were doomed; it was a matter of time before they would be subdued. Those who wanted to keep fighting did not envision a new routine, and they failed to refute the theme called "settlement."

Alongside the settlement committee appeared family authority and affection. To armed citizens, the neatly cleaned streets on a bright spring day, suddenly looking unfamiliar, brought back memories of their parents and siblings, whom they had forgotten until then. Although the Gwangju citizens called for struggle in the rallies, they did not mean a struggle for their own benefit; they could have remembered the truth they had realized several days earlier, and they could have also envisioned democratization that they would achieve in the coming struggle. The young people who could never forget the truth of struggle had to fight against the thought of their families and the fear of death that had returned.

All—the settlement committee members, activist circles, dissidents, and civilian militia—converged on the Provincial Hall, following the demonstrators' slogans. The Provincial Hall was the new seat of authority, into which the past had already infiltrated and a battle had begun. This is where politics, which had been suspended until then, resumed, and this is where individuals, whose identities had been on hold in the absolute community, had to reveal who they were. Residential cards, names, occupations, and ages were demanded at the Provincial Hall. This was a place where behind-the-scenes maneuvers between martial law troops' spies and impure elements were expected. It was also a place where new political power was supposed to disclose its identity. While fighters were finding their places as democratic citizens in an affectionate atmosphere all over the city, the Provincial Hall was redolent of hostility; each side regarded the other side with suspicion, guns and grenades were brandished, and blank shots were fired at the ceiling. The Provincial Hall was where Gwangju's internal strife took place.

Those who tried to do away with this menacing strife were none other than religious people, who attempted to save individual lives. What they wanted to save was the individual's physical life, not spiritual life. Another symbol they put forth was the lives of "all Gwangju citizens," an entity that had been fragmented as soon as citizens armed themselves. What they intended to save was neither collective lives nor permanent life, but aggregated lives of secular individuals. As idealistic members of the settlement committee, they came forward to protect Gwangju, which had been already split into all walks of life, into existing classes, as well as individual lives and assets within the city. They aspired for a peaceful settlement by recovering weapons to protect the safety and assets of disarmed general citizens. Their argument was a civilized ideal that could not be rejected. Even those who were not eager to save their own lives could not find any justification to reject it. The lives they attempted to save were not the religious. Father Kim Seong-yong had already stated that only "the blood of the righteous" could save everyone.

Many Gwangju citizens came to pay respects to the dead and waited in long lines to burn incense sticks. Numerous citizens looked at unidentified bodies to search for their family members. Jeong Sang-hyeon, who was preparing for college examinations after graduating from high school, described his feelings at the time.

A rally was held in a solemn atmosphere with the caskets of the dead placed in front of the Provincial Hall. When new caskets were taken down from trucks draped in white mourning cloth, we sang the national anthem in unison. What was really strange was that after seeing so many deaths at the same time, one's feelings for death soon were dulled, although one normally feels so sad after an acquaintance dies (ICKHD 1990a, 3073: 696).[71]

Near the Provincial Hall, if the students and militiamen had nothing special to do, they often helped take care of managing bodies. Many warriors, for example Kim Jong-bae, volunteered to look after the corpses. Handling the bodies that were miserably mangled and mutilated, and enduring the stench amid sorrow and fury, they may have wanted to ruminate over why they had seized guns. In addition, taking care of the bodies may have been an effort to confront and tame the encroaching fear of death. As they fought the malodor, they might have wanted to reduce the shock of their imminent deaths and tell themselves that death was nothing out of the ordinary. To them, death was the extension of struggle, and therefore the logic of the absolute community—life and death were a strategic choice of struggle without much difference between them—pushed them to fight against an ever-growing interest in themselves in liberated Gwangju and the consequent fear of death.

However, fighting against death could be successful only when the warriors depended on authority, going beyond the individual level, and they needed God and an organization made of god-like leaders and colleagues. They wanted a leader whom they could obey. The Gwangju citizens looked for a charismatic leader at a time when the citizens imposed constraints on themselves, as they grew small with fear of death.[72] The Gwangju citizens had no absolute leader at the time. Bak Nam-seon, the head of the Situation Room, was merely a candidate for such a leader and he hadn't been tested yet.[73] The duty of the militiamen's leader was to organize the militia, lead them in fighting, and win the battle. The militiamen with working-class backgrounds had a weakness in organizational power, and on the first day of liberation, this seemed to be an inherent problem that was impossible to overcome. University students advanced into the Provincial Hall to compensate for the militia's weakness. A younger acquaintance of Yun Sang-won, who worked in the Situation Room without revealing his student identity, had opportunities to observe at close quarters the militiamen who were from the bottom of the social hierarchy. He commented on them as follows:

> During that May, I learned a lot. I was surprised by the minjung's explosive power, which I had been unable to understand by studying the theories of social science. I hadn't realized how immense their power was—forged in daily labor sites as they threw abusive remarks, vented anger, and fought—that power described in the phrase, "all they've got are their own bodies." They might have lagged in organizational capability, but they were creating rational, flexible organizations (ICKHD 1990a, 1046: 338).

The civilian militia was mainly organized at Gwangju Park on the afternoon of May 21 and the morning of May 22. Dozens of reservists in their 30s, including Mun Jang-u and others who did not disclose their names, taught the recruits how to use guns, divided them into teams, assigned vehicles and weapons, and imposed duties. They began by organizing and sending off commando teams to attack the Provincial Hall, and in the evening, most were sent to regional defense teams that were in confrontation with martial law troops. Some were given patrol duties; they were ordered to patrol designated areas and make reports if something unusual happened. Most commandos fought bravely and were shot to death or wounded, and the organization disappeared that day. From the patrol teams, there are few testimonies that indicate that people were assigned to be in charge of them. In most cases, drivers set out in any direction as they saw fit or made decisions after consulting with other members of the teams. These hastily formed organizations, lacking internal discipline, did not last long. Most of them seemed to have been disbanded that very day or the next day.

After the civilian militia occupied the Provincial Hall, the Situation Room was almost entirely responsible for managing the militiamen. On the first day of liberation, armed citizens seemed to have no organization and moved all over the city in groups; they were gathered inside and outside the Provincial Hall or slept in parked cars. When they heard that a battle was taking place on the outskirts of the city, everyone who was carrying guns boarded vehicles to rush over to the battle site. Guarding various spots—such as the front gate and inside the Provincial Hall, major government offices, major buildings, and the powder keg in the Provincial Hall basement—started voluntarily. For some strategic points and buildings, armed citizens organized their own groups to take on the guard duty. For example, a group of militiamen voluntarily started guarding the Jeonil Building. If some of them laid down guns and went home, others took up the slack. If the Citizens' Settlement Committee or the Student Settlement Committee asked them for help, acquaintances among the militiamen volunteered (ICKHD 1990a, 2021: 414-415 etc.). On the other hand, from the first day, it appears that the Situation Room controlled vehicles; drivers were assigned to vehicles, their range of duties was specified, and when they went out, they were required to inform the Situation Room and receive a vehicle pass.

It was only after May 25 that the Situation Room managed to establish a minimum level of organization. Bak Nam-seon appointed his friends and younger school friends as vice director, controller, and head of the guard unit. With the issuance of passes, they maintained a minimum level of security (Bak Nam-seon 1988, 178). However, the inherent problem of reining in the wild warriors of the absolute community could not be solved in a day or two. The organizational problem for all the militiamen centered on the Provincial Hall was that it was impossible to grasp who belonged to which group, and therefore individual movement was impossible to control. From the start, the militiamen joined voluntarily in the spirit of the absolute community; therefore, they did not know who the others were, and they simply communicated with people who looked familiar but whose names they did not know.[74] They entertained the idea of making a roster of militiamen, but they decided not to, fearful of future ramifications. Since it was impossible to control the organization while the militiamen had to be wary of the martial law troops' spies, the organization itself was the target of mistrust. In a nutshell, the militiamen in the Situation Room and around the Provincial Hall were troops hastily put together on the basis of affinity shared by strangers during a short period of time.

Regional defense teams were the first troops organized in Gwangju Park, other than commando units. At the outset, they confronted the martial law troops in seven areas, and it appears that these areas were guarded by local reservists and the militiamen dispatched from downtown, complete with commanders and team heads. The regional defense unit with detailed records was the Hagun-dong Regional Defense Unit, organized and commanded by Mun Jang-u. On the evening of May 21, he ordered a group of militiamen to board 11-passenger Mercedes-Benz buses, and they went to Hagun-dong's Baegopeun Bridge. The armed citizens were organized into six 12-member teams, later expanded to 12 teams, including the headquarters. In this defense unit, the commander was the platoon chief; he had an aide, and each team had a chief. In the small hours of May 23, a shootout began and the unit captured two spies from the martial law troops. Despite its considerable fighting power, it was disbanded on the afternoon of May 23 after returning guns to the gun-collecting team from the Provincial Hall (ICKHD 1990a, 2025: 435-438). All the other regional defense units were disbanded around May 24.

The mobile patrol unit might cut a typical picture of the militia organization. It was an organization that carried out the roles of both police and military. From the first day of liberation, these teams went out in vehicles whenever policing problems occurred in the city or battles took place in the areas of confrontation, and when necessary, they transported goods. The unit lacked a unified organization or any formalized apparatus; a vehicle and a radio were all each team possessed. Members joined or returned home voluntarily (ICKHD 1990a, 2038: 496). On the afternoon of May 22, Kim Hwa-seong gathered together 20-30 young men. He ordered that five of them board each of five cars, and gave each team a radio. He provided all members with riot policemen's caps and rain gear before asking them to patrol the city. This was how the mobile patrol unit was formed. (ICKHD 1990a, 2039: 501). More were recruited on May 23, but there were no formal procedures. It appears, however, that after May 24, the Situation Room attempted to restructure the mobile patrol unit. An unidentified man recruited 50-60 men in the Provincial Hall lobby, and acted as their commander (ICKHD 1990a, 2037: 492).[75] On May 26, applicants were accepted; at this time they were allowed to join after a simple interview (ICKHD 1990a, 2035: 483).

Nevertheless, there is no testimony as to the mobile patrol unit's general commanding system and it is not known how many teams there were in total. Some mobile patrol teams went around collecting weapons, whereas others openly resisted the settlement committee, destroyed office appliances, and aimed guns at the settlement committee members (ICKHD 1990a, 2038: 496). In a word, there was no unified organizational system. Still, citizens welcomed them by clapping and waving hands when a car with the "mobile patrol unit" written on it passed. Many people believed that the mobile strike unit was organized on May 26 due to many organizational problems in the mobile patrol unit. However, not all mobile patrol teams were absorbed into the mobile strike unit; some patrol teams continued to be active (ICKHD 1990a, 2027: 448).

Of the armed citizens organized during liberated Gwangju, there were people who were called the SWAT Team. Its members were organized into 12-14 teams and moved in a 24-passenger minibus. The team was organized on the afternoon of May 21 with volunteers. This private organization was not under the control of the Provincial Hall; rather, it was an independent civilian unit that maintained a close cooperative relationship with the Provincial Hall.[76] The name "SWAT" was adopted from a foreign television series aired in Korea at the time. The word "SWAT" was painted on both sides of the bus in large letters (ICKHD 1990a, 2041: 509). The identities of the leaders are unknown, but there were two; one was a former marine and the other knew how to use a radio. The members boarded the bus after pledging that they were ready to die. Some members had been friends before they got on the bus, while others did not know each other's name to the end. The members carried their own rifles and live ammunition, and in the car there were two boxes of TNT, a machine gun (50-caliber or LMG), many grenades, and loaded cartridges. On May 23, they went to Asia Motors, obtained steel sheets, and turned the bus into an armored vehicle. The team members toured the areas where martial law troops and civil militiamen were in confrontation, and when they learned of an ongoing battle via radio, they rushed over to assist. The members were proud of their activities and felt a strong sense of camaraderie. They carried pieces of paper bearing their names and addresses in their pockets, for they did not know when they were going to die (ICKHD 1990a, 2038: 497). They ate in the Provincial Hall and they slept in cars or in inns. Most of them were disarmed on May 24 or May 26 (testimonies vary) for some unspecified reason. Some stayed around the Provincial Hall and joined the mobile strike unit (ICKHD 1990a, 2040: 505).

The symbol of the civilian militia during the Gwangju uprising was unquestionably the mobile strike unit organized on May 26. The unit was the only civilian militia organization officially formed by the leadership stationed in the Provincial Hall. The Situation Room head organized it by appointing Yun Seoknu its head and Yi Jae-ho deputy chief (Bak Nam-seon 1988, 54). The unit attempted a new organizational method with the unique situation of liberated Gwangju in mind, and this seemed to be envisioned by the deputy chief Yi Jae-ho. The mobile strike unit was an official unit to wage a battle with the martial law troops, and had the leaders of teams under the chief and vice chief appointed by the Situation Room head. This unit made it clear that it was not a target of gun collection. At the founding of the unit, a formal ceremony was held and the members were sworn in, instilling in them a sense of belonging and pride. They were issued membership cards, and they were made to wear clean uniforms, all in riot police outfits and protection headgear. Some team heads wore berets of the airborne unit. The team aspired to homogeneity; it was made up of young men around 20 years old with working-class backgrounds. It appears that university students were assigned to the Provincial Hall guard unit. Each team of the mobile strike unit had a small number of members—six or seven—so that it could move in a vehicle and keep an eye on other team members. Solidarity was promoted by assigning friends or acquaintances to the same group. The unit created the members' individual identities in a unique way. In the absolute community, they did not know others' names, and names had little significance. They were encouraged to come up with their own nicknames, such as Steamed Bun, White Bear, and Tiger, which were easy to remember and made them feel closer to each other. Written on each protection headgear was the team number and each one's nickname, for example, "Team 1 White Bear" (ICKHD 1990a, 2032: 474; 2036: 489; 2038: 497).

With this, for the first time after liberation, on the fifth day, a new type of organization was formed with individuals as official entities. It was a dramatic development for a civilian militia organization that had its starting point from the absolute community in which individuals were dissolved. By nature, discipline in an organization does not automatically appear in individuals who are physically under control, but begins with the control of various attributes, history, social status, and social relations of each individual. In liberated Gwangju, it was impossible to create an organization complete with rules without shaping individuals in a unique way. At the time, individuals had departed from previous social relations. Although they did not know who the others were, they got acquainted with each other and were friendly while fighting side by side. The nicknames were created based on individual characteristics, which appeared naturally in the militiamen's community. After individuals became an official system itself, the members could not leave the team as they pleased or change teams. More than anything else, the chief and deputy chief of the unit—in particular, Deputy Chief Yi Jae-ho who envisioned the organization—enjoyed the respect of the members.

Although the mobile strike unit came up with a new method of organization on the last day of liberation, it had neither enough members to fight to the fullest nor the time to expand and develop. Probably thanks to this new organizational method, none of the unit members broke away from the group despite the urgent situation on the night of May 26 (ICKHD 1990a, 2032: 474).[77] What is notable is that the members would be proud of their memberships in later years, and they knew about their colleagues at the time, and would remember and cherish them for a long time. They continued to be proud of their identity formed in the organization.[78] Time was running out for the Gwangju citizens and the militiamen. Needless to say, the military authorities wouldn't give them sufficient time.

Although the mobile strike unit and young students in the Provincial Hall fought in their own way, they could not defeat the martial law troops. They defended the truth of Gwangju, the truth of struggle, with their deaths. During the last meeting in the Provincial Hall, the pro-resistance group, including Yun Sang-won, asserted that morning would come if they stood their ground that night. Few, however, believed that they would survive, as can be seen by the "last supper" partaken of by all the young people in the Provincial Hall that night. Yun Sang-won's assertion might have been a gesture by those who knew the truth to earn recognition for freedom to fight to the end, from those who had not experienced the truth of the absolute community's struggle. They may have wanted to say that they were no fanatics, no irrational human beings addicted to fighting. What they knew for sure was that they did not want to hand over the Provincial Hall to enemies to let them destroy the truth permanently and bury all Gwangju citizens alive as "rioters." They wanted to bury the truth of the struggle in the ground and make it a fossil so that some day it would be taken out before the general public and be resurrected as the truth.

In the small hours that day, the Gwangju citizens heard a young female student scream via a loudspeaker, urging them to come out. They did not go out because they were afraid and they wanted to save their lives. The Gwangju citizens offered their youths on the altar of sacrifice to save their own skins. They rushed into their caves without throwing a backward glance and trembled there throughout the fearful night. The young people's deaths constituted the only path to protect their image from the days of their human being and their fight as human beings. They pledged to avenge the deaths of the youths, just as the young female student shrieked, "Please do not forget us!" The Gwangju citizens could never forget their pledge of revenge for their children, who had to die to protect their humanity. As people who were guilty of sacrificing their children, it is possible that they could carry on with the pledge of revenge.

The Gwangju citizens have never died. During the night of May 31 and June 1, after the martial law troops withdrew, the curse "Bloodthirsty Killer Chun Doo-hwan" in red letters appeared on all the electric poles on the streets in front of *The Jeonnam Maeil Sinmun* and the Jisan-dong judicial court. On June 2, the next day, *The Jeonnam Maeil Sinmun* reminded that the heady

10 days had not been a dream by publishing the poet Kim Juntae's "Ah, Ah Gwangju! Cross of our Nation!" *The Gwangju Jeonnam Ilbo* staged a silent protest by printing "Mt. Mudeung Knows" in an extra-large font. The blood of Gwangju has not been erased. Atop the altar of that sacrifice, South Korean history resumed.

ENDNOTES

[1] Kim Sang-jip began to wear a mask on the afternoon of May 21. He explained this as follows: "Until then, activist circles had not come to the fore. That is why I wore a mask and pulled a cap to my face; only my eyes showed. We did not know who the others were, but I plunged into the situation with a trusting heart" (ICKHD 1990a, 4011 891). It is not easy to fathom what he really means.

[2] On the morning of May 20, a day earlier, a body was discovered at the Jeonnam Brewery. At the time, citizens did not carry it around to show it to other citizens in a bid to encourage them to join the protest. This body was identified as Kim An-bu, but the identities of the two bodies found at the dawn of May 21 remain unknown.

[3] According to the Martial Law Command, about 5,400 rifles were taken by the citizens.

[4] The expression "general citizens" has not been officially used. However, the term "civilian militia" was sometimes used from May 21, and became official on May 23. The student activists working at the YWCA penned the "Democratic Citizens' General Principles" and in a meeting decided to use the expression "civilian militia" as an official term (Seo Cheong-won, "Aah, Gwangju! Weeping of Dark History," Journalists Association of Korea et al. 1997, 277).

[5] Many people, for example Kim Yeong-taek, suspected that they were spies sent by the Martial Law Command to agitate the citizens. Most of them went around exhorting citizens to fight to the end (Kim Yeong-taek 1996, 156-157). However, the nature of the absolute community is a struggle. It is impossible to take the masked troops' radical words and actions as odd.

[6] Kim Chung-geun, a reporter of the *Donga Ilbo*, testified to what transpired when he met her at the time: "She said that she ate, slept, and even relieved herself in her clothes among the demonstrators because she was nervous that military spies could be creeping in and she could be shot by a sniper or arrested if she stepped

away from the ranks. She was wearing overalls. She told me to touch them at the back. I did; they were damp and her excrement seemed congealed in a half solid state. Her mouth and hair smelled bad, because she hadn't brushed her teeth or washed her face for several days" (Kim Chung-geun, "Arirang on Geumnam Avenue," Journalists Association of Korea, et. al., 1997, 217-218).

[7] Regarding the situation on the afternoon of May 21, Kim Sang-jip testified as follows: "After I heard that people would gather at Gwangju Park at six o'clock, I went there. In one corner of the park, chaotic with a throng of people, weapons were being distributed. A young man suggested that we choose a leader. When no one volunteered, this young man came forward to assume leadership, together with another youth. Their names were Kim Hwa-seong and Kim Won-gap" (ICKHD, 1990a, 4011: 891). Little is known about Kim Hwa-seong. According to Kim Yeong-taek, "Kim Won-gap spent the night at the Provincial Hall. At around 7 o'clock in the morning, he commanded about 500 civilian militants, putting up barricades in many parts of the city, establishing temporary outposts in seven places—Dolgogae, the correctional facility, Baegun-dong, Unam-dong, Jiwon-dong, Gwangcheon-dong, and the access road to the expressway. He dispatched some 600 militiamen to observe the martial law troops' movements. He also assigned some militiamen to major downtown buildings" (Kim Yeong-taek 1996: 127). No other testimony of his activities exists. Many citizens witnessed that Kim Won-gap gave orders to register and control vehicles at the square of Gwangju Park. According to Yi Jae-ui, Kim Won-gap handled a lot of matters with outstanding competence, and he asked Yi to help organize the civilian militia (ICKHD 1990a, 1045: 332). Kim Won-gap appears in various testimonies during the May 22 situation, but little is known about him afterward.

[8] Sin Man-sik reminisced as follows: "As I was passing the old City Hall intersection, I stopped by the bar I frequented. Several citizens carrying arms were drinking and welcomed me heartily. 'Comrade, join us.' Without feeling any awkwardness, I drank with them, offering and accepting liquor. Afterward, I went to the Provincial Hall with them. No special security precaution was in place. As

226

long as people were not soldiers, we regarded them as our side and worked together without exchanging our names. However, Bak Nam-seon, Kim Hwa-seong, and Yun Seok-nu went around introducing themselves. While we were at the Provincial Hall, we got to know their names" (ICKHD 1990a, 1044; 322).

[9] In Mun Sun-tae's short story, a man talks about how he came across a friend in Gwangju: "I took that fool to the corner of a bank and told him that he would be able to live only if he laid down the gun and slung his shoeshine box around his shoulder again. That fool pretended he didn't hear me. He tilted his chin toward a member of his group and said, 'You had better not tell that guy Thomas that I am a shoeshine boy. He thinks I'm a university student, so he calls me Older Brother. I'm not ashamed of being a shoeshine boy. It's just that if he knows I'm not a university student, he will look down on me and stop trusting and following me. He's scared, so he follows me around all the time'" (Mun Sun-tae, "Rising Land," Han Seung-won, et al., 1987, 31).

[10] The residents who lived behind the Provincial Hall testified that the government building was quiet and "empty." However, it is judged that it looked empty, though it was not completely deserted.

[11] Kim Yong-gyun testified as follows: "I circled the fountain at the Provincial Hall and entered the building with firm resolve. Surprisingly, the building was empty. The martial law troops, which had been defending it in a steel-strong manner only moments ago, had disappeared without a trace. Instead, only heavy silence weighed down. It didn't feel real that we had seized the Provincial Hall. The building exuded coldness in the dark. Afraid of staying there any longer, I fled as if chased by something" (ICKHD 1990a, 2021: 414). Kim Tae-hyeon also testified: " . . . the civilian militia let out a sigh of relief after taking over the Provincial Hall, but soon had to find something more important to do. It occurred to me that I couldn't be optimistic about the unfolding situation. If the situation escalated, I would lack confidence because I was so young. . . . Determined to continue with the struggle, I left the Provincial Hall. My staying there didn't seem to be fitting. I lost

confidence, for I knew few people and I knew so little. I thought that I belonged to the battlefield against the martial troops" (Young Comrades Society 1987, 237).

[12] Kim Sang-jip testified: "When I entered the Provincial Hall at around 8 o'clock, the martial law troops had already withdrawn toward the hill of Chosun University, and there were only corpses in the flower garden. We dug them out to identify them. . . . Afterward, I got out of the Provincial Hall and went to my friend No Hyeon-jun's sister's house. After telling her what he was doing, I fell asleep" (ICKHD 1990a, 4011: 891). Kim Jong-bae, who later stuck to a hard-line stance as the vice chairman of the Student Settlement Committee, went home to sleep before he came out again (ICKHD 1990a, 1014: 206).

[13] During a National Assembly hearing in 1988, Rep. Kim In-gon pointed out: "What I mean is that a suspicion is raised by the fact that those who occupied the Provincial Hall from the afternoon of May 21 to the morning of May 22 were neither students nor radicals. . . . Regarding the situation in which the Provincial Hall was guarded by the self-described civilian militia, two men stood guard at the entrance. They didn't eat from the evening of May 21 to 11 o'clock on the morning of May 22. They asked a Provincial Hall employee to provide a meal. When the employee asked them who ordered them to stand sentry, they answered that a man in his 30s told them to do so. In the General Affairs Department of the Provincial Hall, Eom Mun-nam, who was 35 years old at the time, was supervising the situation, and he had grown up in an orphanage in Hak-dong. In the Regional Department, there were about 15 people, who called themselves security personnel, and they all had walkie-talkies and they were skilled at using them. Professor O Byeong-mun of Chonnam National University visited the building, for the first time as an outsider, and stayed there for 30-40 minutes to grasp the situation, but nobody recognized him. At the time, students did not carry weapons, but the young men in the Provincial Hall did and deliberately controlled citizens' access. In other words, there is a suspicion that they were neither students nor demonstrators. They disappeared when conscientious citizens' representatives and students came forward. They haven't been

seen in Gwangju and South Jeolla Province since" (Gwangju City 1997 IV, 236-237).

[14] Father Kim Seong-yong testified as follows about the situation of May 21: "As for Nam-dong, I arrived home using various alleyways in light rain at about 5 o'clock, after the gathering at Honamdong came to nothing. About 10 people were waiting for me, including the YWCA people and lawyer Hong Nam-sun. They were so-called dissidents. It was already late then, so we agreed to get together at 10 o'clock next morning. This was the first meeting. At the time, the participants included Fathers Jang Ji-gwon and Jeong Gyu-wan" ("Round-Table Talks," Yun Gong-hui 1989, 176).

[15] Kim Yeong-taek, a journalist who had gathered news in the city, received a phone call from a Kim, a lieutenant colonel and an intelligence chief of the South Jeolla Regional Security Corps, at home around 11 o'clock in the evening. It was after Bak Gi-jeong, a Security Command officer stationed in the Provincial Hall, informed the journalist at around 10 o'clock that the lieutenant colonel would call him at 11 o'clock (Gwangju City 1997 IV, 651-652).

[16] Catholic priest Jeong Gyu-wan, who went to the deputy governor's office on the second floor on the morning of May 22, said the following: "I expected that I would see those whom I had often met to discuss the political situation and work together for democratization as I entered the deputy governor's office on the second floor, but none of them was there. I saw only strangers. Deputy Governor Jeong was working hard along with some employees, but I felt viscerally that in a security vacuum it is necessary to have a leader who can exercise special commanding authority to reassure and lead the crowd" (Jeong Gyu-wan, "A Small Participation in Big Pain," Yun Gong-hui 1989, 124).

[17] The fact that these people had a collective sense is revealed in various accounts, such as testimonies of Jo A-ra, a church elder, and professor Song Gi-suk (ICKHD 1990a, 1003: 1007). Regarding the Nam-dong Catholic Church faction among the settlement committee members, Jang Hyu-dong testified as follows: "At some point, Gwangju dissidents made their presence known in the Pro-

vincial Hall. Those who had gathered at Nam-dong Catholic Church, including Father Kim Seong-yong, came over. When I first announced the agreement and the members passed a resolution, Father Jo Bi-o and Jo A-ra were there. But later they came with other dissidents and claimed that the existing settlement committee was a thorough mouthpiece for the government. They made it sound as if they had to be the mainstay of the committee. Furthermore, the contents of their proposal had little difference from the already suggested seven points" (ICKHD 1990a, 1010: 185). According to this testimony, the Nam-dong Catholic Church faction had no other purpose than seizing control of the settlement committee.

[18] Kim Sang-yun, who managed the Nokdu Bookstore, had been arrested in a preliminary roundup. That was how Yun Sang-won (born in 1950), who was a year younger than Kim Sang-yun, played the leader. The participants in the morning included Yun Sang-won, Kim Yeong-cheol, Kim Sang-jip, Jeong Yu-a, and Yi Haeng-ja (ICKHD 1990a, 4100: 891). Only some members of the group were present because it had been decided to take refuge since the troops had opened fire on the previous evening. The rest returned on the afternoon of May 23. At the time, the *Fighters' Bulletin* was made at Gwangcheon-dong, and Yun Sang-won was in command of these two places, in addition to various rally sites in the city. The *Fighters' Bulletin* team moved to the YWCA only on May 25.

[19] Jeong Sang-yong testified on the Nokdu Bookstore team's stance as follows: "At the time the most urgent matter was to remove the faction promoting a quick settlement in the Citizens' Settlement Measures Committee within the Provincial Hall. This faction rejected the opinion of the pro-resistance faction, which urged the return of weapons, and this settlement faction was larger than the pro-resistance group" (ICKHD 1990a, 1015: 210).

[20] Yun Sang-won dispatched Son Nam-seung to the Situation Room through Yi Jae-ui. Son worked there, keeping it a secret that he was a student. He sometimes stopped by the Nokdu Bookstore to inform on the situation, and soon introduced Yun Sang-won to Bak Nam-seon, head of the Situation Room (ICKHD 1990a, 1046: 335).

230

[21] Yi Jae-ui, who entered the Provincial Hall on the morning of May 22, testified as follows: "More and more people moved in and out of the Situation Room in the Provincial Hall, and it was impossible to control them. It was highly likely that intelligence or operation agents from the martial law troops could sneak in, so we couldn't trust people. In particular, two men in their 40s, who led investigations, gave off the strong impression that they were police inspectors with their close-cropped hair and sharp eyes. Their behavior was odd, and it was not just one or two things that made us suspect them; they handled the people arrested by the civilian militia as they pleased. . . . In the end, together with a friend I came up with a scheme to drive them out. With a loaded rifle in one hand and a grenade in the other, I climbed a desk and shouted. . . . Now all moved in single file, but the person who had headed the investigation stayed in his seat, showing displeasure on his face. I pressed the grenade below his chin. 'You don't mind you and me dying with this grenade, do you?' He must have felt he didn't have a chance, because he stood up and left the room. . . . One of the investigation heads later said, 'If you really feel that way, I will leave. But organize reservists as soon as possible.' I demanded, 'Why don't you do it yourself?' He said, 'I'm just telling you what to do' (ICKHD 1990a, 1045: 331-332).

[22] Bak Nam-seon, eavesdropping on a seized radio, heard that military troops would converge at the Gwangju Stream. Fearing that troops might attack from that side, he waited in ambush with other citizens. There he spent the night shooting, an exchange triggered by mistaken firing (Bak Nam-seon 1988, 153-157).

[23] In a National Assembly hearing, Yu Yeong-gyu, who worked as a settlement committee member said the following: "Any number of people—dozens and hundreds were settlement committee members" (Gwangju City 1997 V, 291).

[24] Yun Yeong-gyu said the following in a National Assembly hearing: "On May 22, I joined the settlement committee, in which the lawyer Yi Jong-gi participated. The members there kept arguing that weapons should be collected and submitted, in other words, to settle the situation as soon as possible. . . . They pushed the

conversation in that direction. I thought it would be useless if I opposed it alone, and Father Jo Bi-o sometimes expressed strong opposition for some points, but it didn't seem to work because everyone was busy and we couldn't find the time to talk. I went to the YWCA and there I found older people, the so-called dissident elders in Gwangju, such as the lawyer Hong Nam-sun, Jo A-ra, and Yi Seong-hak. I urged the elders to hurry and come to the Provincial Hall and form a settlement committee, and said that the incumbent committee couldn't resolve the Gwangju issue. While I was trying to persuade people, the Nam-dong Settlement Committee, including Father Jo Bi-o, was formed. In the end, the Nam-dong side, the government side, called us a hard-line faction . . . " (Gwangju City 1997 V, 293). The Catholic priest Kim Seong-yong testified as follows: "I visited the Provincial Hall in the morning to help the settlement committee, which was trying to retrieve weapons. I had the impression that a Rev. Jang and another Mr. Jang seemed to act like the authorities' pawns, for they were on the phone all the time to receive instructions. The representatives of students and citizens kept coming in and requested that elders settle the situation as soon as possible, asking what good it would do to collect weapons" (Kim Seong-yong, "Sorrow Rather Than Fury," Yun Gong-hui 1989, 54).

[25] The evaluation of the first negotiation was mixed. Archbishop Yun Gong-hui recollected: "From the time the settlement committee members left for Sangmudae, I had three phone conversations with the governor. During the first conversation, I heard that the negotiation had gone well, and that the martial law troops would not be sent. Regarding the second conversation, I called to verify the rumor that armored vehicles were coming toward downtown from Sangmudae, and I heard that the negotiation had not gone well. The third conversation took place in the evening after the South Korean acting prime minister (Bak Chung-hun) issued a statement. At the time I heard that the settlement was impossible" (Yun Gong-hui 1989, 16-17). Jo Bi-o, the Catholic priest, suggested that records of the negotiation be left with the use of tapes or shorthand, but the proposal was not accepted, for no one supported his position (Jo Bi-o 1994, 36). As far as he understood,

the military made no concession, but some committee members seemed to be happy, thinking that the negotiation had gone well. In fact, according to the "Report on the Negotiation Results With the Martial Law Command," drafted and distributed by the settlement committee on May 24, the representative of the Martial Law Command admitted to "excessive suppression." This does not appear to be true; this seems to be how the committee members defended their position in front of the citizens.

[26] Kim Nak-gil, who was employed at a bar, testified that he voluntarily went around the city in an armored broadcast car and urged via a microphone, "Gwangju citizens! Let us gather in front of the Provincial Hall" (ICKHD 1990a, 4005: 863).

[27] It is known that Kim Yeong-cheol, age 32, who worked at the YWCA Credit Cooperative, raised the flag at half-staff (ICKHD 1990a, 1595). He was active at the Nokdu Bookstore, and on the night of May 25, he became planning head of the resistance leadership. He was arrested at dawn of May 27 while defending the Provincial Hall to the end. He died recently, after suffering many years of mental illness as a result of torture.

[28] According to Professor Myeong's testimony, when he was about to enter the Provincial Hall, "A young acquaintance who had gone to Chonnam National University held onto me. He said, 'We have to instill some order into this anarchy. Please mobilize the students and settle the situation. I will concentrate on mobilizing them, so please persuade them.' I readily agreed to his idea" (ICKHD 1990a, 1012: 200-2-1). Of his remarks, we need to ruminate over the meanings of "young acquaintance who went to Chonnam National University," "anarchy," "instill some order," and "students."

[29] After the meeting, Professor Song asked for car service. The civilian militia immediately brought a car and gave him a ride to his house, complete with an armed escort.

[30] Hwang Seog-yeong describes it this way: "The students' position was rather delicate. General citizens' trust in them was huge because teenagers brandished weapons as they pleased, and because citizens were worried that the armed elements might be-

come radical and hamper their safety, for a majority of armed elements was from the lumpen class at the bottom of the social hierarchy" (Hwang Seog-yeong 1985, 191-192).

[31] Hwang Geum-seon toured the city in a vehicle in the morning, pleading via a P.A. system for the return of arms. He felt that weapons had to be collected after hearing people talk in the Provincial Hall earlier in the morning, and he independently went around the city to urge the citizens to turn them in (ICKHD 1990a, 1021: 239).

[32] This issue will become clearer when Mokpo is used as an example. There was no coercion from the Martial Law Command in this city, but citizens began to feel nervous about their armed colleagues on May 21. The leaders of the demonstration recovered arms between noon and 3 o'clock on the afternoon of May 22.

[33] Regarding the Gwangju Park situation on the morning of May 22, Jo Cheol-ung testified: "In one corner, duties to defend the outskirts of the city were assigned by numbering vehicles. I got on a Jeep after one older man asked us to defend an outlying area because delinquents might be rampant there" (ICKHD 1990a, 2018: 398).

[34] Regarding the so-called "parade of death" at dawn on May 26, Jang Sa-nam, who was a member of the settlement committee, testified as follows: "As I walked with the settlement committee members, I was seized with a melancholy thought. 'Ah, I will die now. I can be killed by a shot fired by the martial law troops or by the armed civilian militia.' It occurred to me that it would be most adequate to call our parade the 'parade of death,' and I was the first to name it as such" (ICKHD 1990a, 1006: 152). At the order of the parish office on the afternoon of May 26, Father Kim Seong-yong left for Seoul. According to Archbishop Yun Gong-hui's testimony, Kim desired to leave, saying on the afternoon of May 26 that he felt the danger of being shot by either side, and Yun accommodated Kim by officially ordering him to go to Seoul (Yun Gong-hui 1989, 22). It appears that Father Kim left feeling guilty after returning from a negotiation with the Martial Law Command, which took place after the "parade of death," with nothing but the

command's final crackdown notification, and his life seemed in danger, for he was not trusted by either side. Father Kim himself, however, testified that he had gone to Seoul at the order of the archbishop.

[35] Song Tae-heon testified as follows: "I was asked to become the head of the Situation Room because I knew the city very well and I was good at handling firearms, but I declined because I was not educated and my handwriting was so bad. . . . At this point anyone, even those without a drivers' license, drove cars. I heard that a man fell from a car and died in a traffic accident in front of the Gwangju train station, a result of reckless driving. Somehow I didn't like to see shoeshine boys and rag-pickers move around arrogantly with guns in hand. . . . Such acts are beautified as the will for democratization or citizens' united action, but at the time it was just a means to survive" (ICKHD 1990a, 2029: 457). He returned his weapon on May 22 and went home.

[36] A road sweeper named Kim Gwang-yeong was beaten by paratroopers on May 19. He was treated at a clinic and since he had virtually no clothes on him, he asked the doctor to lend him some old clothes. The following is his testimony: "The doctor snapped, 'I've treated you. Isn't that enough? Do you expect me to give you clothes, too?' I was embarrassed and sad. I walked toward the Call Box intersection barefoot and with no shirt on. Some citizens came over and took off their shirts and slippers for me. . . . On May 22 after the martial law troops' withdrawal, I went back to the clinic and the doctor said, 'Mister, I was going to give you my clothes, but you left before I could.' I muttered to myself, 'When the world has changed, doctors have changed, too. He is now calling me mister.' Yet, the doctor didn't forget to collect money after the treatment" (ICKHD 1990a, 3083: 717). On the other hand, Wi Seong-sam testified as follows: "On the morning of May 22, I found a lot of people gathered in the street. They were happy that the civilian militia had taken over the Provincial Hall. One of the men said we had gone through so much and told us to come to his home for a meal. His house was an affluent household in the neighborhood, and it looked like he was doing something on the off

chance that we would do something against him" (ICKHD 1990a, 1038: 297).

[37] This document was the first to officially use the term, "civilian militia." The General Principles of Democratic Citizens consisted of the following four points: 1) Citizens must trust the civilian militia and cooperate actively. 2) Let us be vigilant about disguised martial law troops and impure elements. 3) Let us make efforts to recover order. 4) Let us return to our normal lives. "You, Democratic Citizens," which was written by a self-described citizens' representative, seems to have been read aloud in a rally, saying, "The doors to the stores are closed. We have just received the news that the voluntarily organized civilian militia will protect all of us. Please do not worry and let us engage ourselves in our livelihoods" (Gwangju City 1997 II, 47).

[38] Regarding this, Hwang Seog-yeong explained as follows: "As there were signs that the protest might turn into a long-term affair, the title was changed to overcome the existing focus of raising consciousness and suggesting the direction of struggle, and to make it more systematic, and in terms of content, it intended to pay more attention to the general masses, rather than the vanguards of the struggle. In addition, it planned to argue for the continuity of the protest among the masses by switching the tone into an editorializing one to illuminate the inevitability of the rebellion. The creation of the press geared for the minjung and the operation with a tone of propaganda during the uprising reflected the voices of the minjung and contributed a great deal to the unity of citizens' actions. . . . It is notable that the *Democratic Citizens' Bulletin* used the medium itself as a weapon of struggle" (Hwang Seog-yeong 1985, 154). Of course, we need to understand that the decision of this change was made soon after the "poison-needle scare" of May 25.

[39] Yu Seung-gyu's case was typical. "On the morning of May 25, while I was standing guard at the front gate of the Provincial Hall, my grandmother, who lived with me at Sansu-dong, came to see me. She urged me to come home, telling me that my father had arrived from the countryside. I handed my gun to a friend standing next to me and went home" (ICKHD 1990a, 1035: 284).

[40] Bak Nam-seon organized the Situation Room mostly with his friends and younger acquaintances (Bak Nam-seon 1988, 167).

[41] Kim Tae-heon, who acted as a member of the civilian militia's patrol unit, testified: "The driver stopped the car in front of the YWCA main gate. He took out two detonators from the car. He said, 'I hear that there are two martial law soldiers on the Jeonil Building rooftop. I will blow them up.' I was sitting next to the driver and tried to dissuade him from going out, but he wouldn't listen to me. As he tried to enter the building, he discovered that all the doors were locked. He kicked them several times before he gave up and returned to the car. . . . Some middle-aged women were walking briskly along an alley, probably hoping to get away from Gwangju. The driver spotted them and turned the car with great difficulty into the alley where the women were walking. I told him that we were departing from the area assigned to us, but he didn't pay the slightest attention to me." A shot was fired, followed by a combat exchange, and the witness was shot in the eye and would lose his sight (Young Comrades Society 1987, 242-244).

[42] Regarding the settlement committee members' recovery of arms, Bak Nam-seon said: "When I went outside, there were well-known Gwangju personages, including pastors, priests, professors, and lawyers. They said that a citizens' settlement committee should be organized to prepare for measures and go to the Martial Law Command Substation for negotiations. I thought that keeping order among armed citizens was more urgent than settling the situation. I told the armed citizens and the leading figures in front of the Provincial Hall that negotiations could take place after a command system would be imposed on the civilian army and measures for contingencies would be in place. They nodded in agreement, because what I said was most needed" (Bak Nam-seon 1988, 165). Kim Jong-bae, who stuck to the pro-resistance faction's position to the end at the Provincial Hall, explained his stance: "Although we were against returning weapons, almost everyone agreed that we should collect arms from citizens. As they went all over the city carrying guns after the soldiers' withdrawal, citizens were

nervous about it and also there was a big burden of risk" (ICKHD 1990a, 1014: 206).

[43] The representative case was the regional defense unit of Hagun-dong, organized and led by Mun Jang-u. On the evening of May 21, he organized 140 as militiamen. On the afternoon of May 23, he was requested to return the arms and he did. He went to the Provincial Hall to find out what was going on. Feeling that something was wrong, he fled to Naju. He had played a leading role in seizing arms and announced his name in front of many people (ICKHD 1990a, 2025: 436-438). Mun Jang-u decided to return the weapons because he believed the promise that the Provincial Hall would collect arms and then reissue them after organizing a striking unit (ICKHD 1990a, 2024: 431).

[44] Some members of the civilian militia criticized Father Jo Bi-o, who went around collecting weapons, calling him "the government puppet" to his face. There were many cases in which individual militiamen threatened settlement committee members (ICKHD 1990a, 1011: 192).

[45] Jang Hyu-dong described the situation at the time: "I carried guns on my belt because I felt danger to my person. Young people would aim pistols at me and threaten me inside the Provincial Hall because I intended to return the guns and settle the situation. This wasn't all. I couldn't go home. I slept in an inn because citizens kept calling me at home to complain and threaten. My family couldn't sleep at home, either. They moved around from one relative's house to another. At night, I couldn't fall asleep with so much to think of" (ICKHD 1990a, 1010: 186). Kim Chang-gil also said: "The more days passed, the more menacing it became inside the Provincial Hall. Instead of people with different opinions sitting together to express their thoughts and carry on discussion, they brandished pistols to threaten each other" (ICKHD 1990a, 1013: 104).

[46] Father Jo Bi-o recalls the meeting on the evening of May 23: "At the request of Jang Se-gyun and Kim Chang-gil, I spent the night with Yi Jong-gi, Jang Se-gyun, Sin Yong-sun, Kim Jae-il, and Father Nam Jae-hui at the Health Affairs Bureau Director's Office in

the Provincial Hall on May 23, and persuaded Kim Chang-gil, the representative of students, to actively cooperate with our settlement committee members on recovering and retuning weapons, instead of being swayed by other arguments. At Jang Se-gyun's suggestion, we also discussed how to recover arms. First, we would get acquainted with the militiamen while distributing snacks and beverages at 4 o'clock in the morning of May 24. Second, on our second visit, we would recover arms. If they didn't respond, we would persuade them one-on-one" (Jo Bi-o 1994, 152-153).

[47] Father Jo Bi-o persuaded armed citizens as follows: "The martial law troops are planning to press ahead with an armed suppression after a certain period. If collecting weapons is delayed, huge human tolls will result, not only among the civilian militia that holds guns with loyalty and passion but also from general citizens. To prevent more human losses and bigger tragedy and misfortune, weapons must be collected" (Jo Bi-o 1994, 39-40).

[48] Yun Yeong-gyu, a settlement committee member, later testified in a National Assembly hearing about the situation in which he pleaded with some 30 armed citizens, who had stayed in a rehabilitation facility. "I told them in a solicitous tone, 'All Gwangju citizens will be branded rioters because of you. If you just disarm, the problem will be solved.' One of the young men said, 'Hey, are you the only patriot here? Let us be patriots, too.' I was shocked. I took it as a joke or a ridicule that seemed to mean, 'Are only educated people like you patriots? People like us, who are ignorant, can be patriots and we will love our country, too'" (Gwangju City 1997 V, 293-294). The witness played up vulnerable class aspects as he tried to take the initiative in the discussion. A young man stood toe-to-toe and struck back, squarely seeing through his interlocutor's intention. In the young man's nonsensical words, the witness took note of his personal guilt about the resentment of a weaker class toward the ruling class. Before the dialogue, both sides expected class conflict and friction between the educated and the uneducated.

[49] After May 25, food was in short supply in the Provincial Hall, and in some cases, it had to be solicited from citizens in the down-

town area (ICKHD 19901, 1042: 314; 2032: 474). On May 26, the resistance leadership attempted to solve the food shortage by officially requesting the City Hall to supply rice.

[50] Kim Hyeon-chae, who was disarmed while working for a special mobile unit, recollected as follows: "After returning all weapons, I felt empty and there didn't seem to be anything left to do. I got into a car parked at the guard post and took a nap. After the nap, I couldn't find anything to do. I stayed around the Provincial Hall and then went to Sangmu Gymnasium. . . . With In-su, I helped the citizens who came to burn incense and those who wanted to see the bodies to find out whether those of their family members were there. I also kept order around the place." (Young Comrades' Society 1987, 112-113). He waited until May 26, joined the mobile strike unit, and fought to the end. Needless to say, most militiamen must have gone home in this process (ICKHD 1990a, 2027: 448).

[51] Father Jo Bi-o testified about the number of the civilian militiamen outside the Provincial Hall: "Some of them (those disarmed by Jo at the entrance of the industrial complex) left the Provincial Hall, and 70-80 participated in defending the Provincial Hall. Since most in the Provincial Hall were university students, they could have eventually gone to the park. Before they returned guns, the number of civilian troops guarding the outskirts of the city was big. There were about 150-200 at Gwangju Park, 50-60 at Seobang, and troops in the size of one military company or so stood guard at the Baegun-dong railway, the Hagun-dong bridge, the road toward the correctional facility, and along the expressway, respectively. I remember details because I supplied food to them" (Jo Bi-o 1994, 42). Except for Gwangju Park, the areas mentioned above were where Jo disarmed the civilian militia with other settlement members. There are few testimonies about what happened to those at the park.

[52] The priest Jeong Gyu-wan talked about the atmosphere of the settlement committee in the aftermath of the "poison-needle scare": "Due to the incident, we couldn't bring up the matter of recovering guns. Deputy Governor Jeong and his people, who had

been present until the day before, didn't show up and the atmosphere was chilly. It appeared that a big commotion had taken place in the morning because of the poison-needle scare. Afterward, the settlement committee members and those who had worried about the situation didn't appear. In this situation, settlement committee members who had gathered at Nam-dong Catholic Church naturally gathered in the Provincial Hall to listen to what the students had to say" (Jeong Gyu-wan, "Small Participation in Big Pain," Yun Gong-hui 1989, 127).

[53] Bak Nam-seon, head of the civilian militia Situation Room, testified: "The troops following me were not a unified, well-trained, organized army. Even most of the executives and staff members who helped me in close quarters were those whom I had met only five or six days earlier. It was literally a combat army hastily put together. I was never disappointed that it was not a well-trained, organized army. I was proud of our civilian militiamen who fought with no supplies and risked their lives, but on the other hand I couldn't dispel worry and anxiety about their lives" (Bak Nam-seon 1988: 33).

[54] Kim Gil-sik, who worked for the YWCA Trust Cooperative, went to the YWCA on the morning of May 25 and stayed there the whole day. He said, "At 7 o'clock in the evening, about 100 students gathered for a meeting to settle the situation and then went to the Provincial Hall. During the meeting, the prevalent argument was that students had to recover order in view of the bad impression created by the fact that in the Provincial Hall people who looked like rioters were in control of guns" (ICKHD 1990a, 1039: 303). In addition, Kim Han-jung testified about the situation at the YWCA on the evening of May 25 as follows: "A citizen from the Provincial Hall came and gathered us together. He said, 'Now Gwangju is being ruled by vagabonds. The situation is not effectively being settled because their nerves are frayed. Now is the time that they should be replaced with university students.' At midnight, we went to the Provincial Hall, in the rain without umbrellas. The atmosphere in the Deputy Governor's Office on the second floor was hostile. I had no idea about what was going on in the settlement committee. I heard a long speech delivered by a

priest and slept there" (ICKHD 1990a, 1041: 310). There was a concern that the militiamen would resist while being replaced. An instruction was issued that the replacements should say politely, "You must be tired from missing sleep for several days. We will take a turn" (Hwang Seog-yeong 1985, 194).

[55] Father Cornelius Cleary remembered that when he went out to the streets and talked with the citizens at the time, they always asked him to inform the US President of what was happening (Father Cornelius Cleary, "I am from Gwangju, too," Yun Gong-hui 1989, 112).

[56] Many citizens phoned a number of settlement committee members or those who testified afterward (Kim Yeong-taek 1996, 225). Father Jeong Gyu-wan remembered as follows: "Around Whitsunday (May 25), those with vested rights, such as intellectuals and people with good social positions, seemed to feel nervous. They wondered how long such an abnormal state would continue. Those whose statuses were guaranteed in normal times cautiously expressed their concern. A good friend of mine called me and complained, "How long will it go on? Shouldn't it be ended in one way or another at this point?" ("Roundtable Talks," Yun Gong-hui 1989, 185). Yim Chun-sik, who ran a gallery and was active in demonstrations, testified as follows: "At the rally, however, I got the impression that the atmosphere had subdued a great deal. Despite being an 'anarchical situation,' no shameful incident happened and I knew that it was a fierce struggle for what was right, but I had a feeling it would not do if this situation dragged on" (ICKHD 1990a, 3082: 714).

[57] The reason of his refusal was revealed as follows: "Such a role was not suitable for the US ambassador, and he believed that the South Korean authorities would not accept it" (Jeong Sang-yong et al. 1990, 297).

[58] Father Kim Seong-yong watched the meeting as he stood next to the podium. He was shocked by the citizens' deep mistrust of the settlement committee. He remembered, "I thought it would not do. It is the end for the settlement committee, for it has lost trust to such an extent. With this judgment, I entered the Provin-

cial Hall. I stressed the fact that demanding the blood of the righteous people was the fundamental way to settle the situation" (Father Kim Seong-yong, "Sorrow Rather Than Fury," Yun Gong-hui 1989, 55).

[59] On the evening of May 23, Bak Nam-seon held a meeting with the Student Settlement Committee members, led by the settlement faction. He dozed off and left early. After he met Yun Sangwon on the afternoon of May 24, however, he was a different man. During the extended meeting with settlement committee members and the militia's leadership at 8 o'clock in the evening, he said, "Pent-up discontent over the settlement committee exploded. I jumped up and threw a chair. I shouted that if they decided to return the weapons, I would rather blow up the Provincial Hall and fight with the bastards to the end. Some left the room with scared expression on their faces, while others looked nervous, as they couldn't make a decision. In the end, only those who agreed with me remained. We held a meeting of our own, agreed that we would be together in solving all the problems that had occurred in Gwangju and setting a direction for the future, and would revamp the organization" (Bak Nam-seon 1988, 190).

[60] Regarding the situation at the time, Bak Nam-seon said, "I jumped up and went to the second floor with some 20 armed troops. I stationed the men armed with M16s in the hallway and at the door of the Deputy Governor's Office, and ordered that they kill everyone unconditionally if I gave the order. I entered by kicking the door with my boot. In the deputy governor's room were well-known personages, including Choe Han-yeong, a former anti-Japanese independence fighter and the head of the settlement committee, and Deputy Governor Jeong Si-chae. I pulled out my pistol from the holster on my belt, aimed it at the ceiling, and then slowly lowered it to them. I yelled, 'Which bastards passed a resolution to return weapons as they see fit?' I then warned as I aimed my gun at one of them, 'I will kill all of you if you babble such nonsense, betraying the blood of the people who have died'" (Bak Nam-seon 1988, 198).

[61] Bak Nam-seon said as follows: "The atmosphere in the Provincial Hall until then was that no matter what kind of decisions the settlement committee made, nothing would come of it if I, the one who controlled armed troops, did not agree" (Bak Nam-seon 1988, 199).

[62] Kim Chang-gil talked about his feelings at the time: "I went to the Martial Law Command on May 25 following Father Kim's advice. After returning to the Provincial Hall, I saw that Jeong Sang-yong, Yun Sang-won, and their ilk were walking around the building with Kim Jong-bae, sporting armbands. I thought it was all over now" (ICKHD 1990a, 1013: 204).

[63] Cheon Sun-nam, a woodworker, took a look at the corpses in the Provincial Hall on May 25. After getting a free meal there, he was leaving when he was approached. He testified: "After finishing the meal, I walked down to the front gate of the Provincial Hall. Bak Nam-seon, who introduced himself as the Situation Room chief, asked me to show him my residential card. After checking my identity, he asked me whether I could handle weapons. I answered I could not. But he gave me an M1 and a clip of live ammunition, saying that it was necessary to arm more people. Bak Nam-seon ordered six of us holding guns to board a police bus and transport people. He explained that food was running short, and put a red piece of cloth that said 'Food Supply Vehicle' on our bus. He then told us to ask citizens to give us some food." Cheon Sun-nam stayed with the group until the early morning of May 27 when he was captured by the martial law troops (ICKHD 1990a, 1042: 314). Na Il-seong met a friend who was in the civilian militia on the afternoon of May 26 and applied for the mobile patrol unit at his urging. After a simple interview at the Provincial Hall, he became a member. The mobile patrol unit was soon reorganized as the mobile strike unit (ICKHD 1990a, 2035: 483). Kim Tae-chan heard that a mobile strike unit was being organized. He "gathered together some guys" and joined the unit as its last team (ICKHD 1990a, 2032: 474).

[64] In many books, the unit is said to have been composed of 13 teams, but this seems to be merely the initial plan. According to

testimonies of the mobile strike unit, the seventh team was the last reserve team of the mobile strike unit (ICKHD 1990a, 2032: 474; 2036: 489 etc).

[65] Kim Han-jung was working at the YWCA on the evening of May 26. He said, "At night Jeong Sang-yong came. He looked troubled as he said, 'There has been a meeting at the Provincial Hall. The moderates, including Kim Chang-gil, are stronger and it looks like we have to lay down weapons.' Someone shouted, 'We cannot forget the price of the blood of our comrades, the price of the blood of Gwangju citizens. I can never put down our weapons!' Jeong said, 'I understand what you want,' before he returned to the Provincial Hall. We renewed our resolve that we would never lay down arms. After a while, Kim Jong-bae, a hard-liner, came and said, 'An agreement has been reached to maintain peace, overwhelmed by the moderates, so please go home.' Some put down guns. I lost my temper and shouted, 'When was it when we said we should defend Gwangju with our lives? Why are we already talking about returning weapons? I cannot follow the opinion of the settlement committee members because it is not what the citizens want. How can we compromise with the martial law troops? You go and reverse the settlement committee decision.' Some concurred. Kim said he understood and returned to the Provincial Hall. Some time later, a message came via radio: 'Now the hard-liners' opinion has been accepted.' We gladly took up guns" (ICKHD 1990a, 1041: 310).

[66] In Yun Sang-won's critical biography, he is supposed to have said: "We must fight against them to the end. If we hand over the empty Provincial Hall, the struggle we have waged so far will become wasted effort, and we will be guilty before history and the numerous souls of those who have died. Let us not be afraid of death. Let us face the struggle. Even though we are killed by their bullets, we will live forever that way. We must be united and fight to the end for this country's democracy. By doing so, let us leave a proud record that all of us fought to the end against injustice. If we go through this dawn, morning will definitely arrive" (JSRI 1991, 321).

[67] During a National Assembly hearing, he talked about his thoughts at the time: "So, we tried to defend the Provincial Hall to the end after making the firm resolve and decision that we couldn't at least lay down guns unless our demands were accepted, and even if we had to die, we should leave the record in history that we Gwangju citizens resisted to the end without flinching, if nothing else, and we couldn't simply step back as it was" (Gwangju City 1997 V, 316).

[68] A Hong, a sergeant of the commando unit of the airborne unit at the time, stated as follows in an interview with a member of the Gwangju Special Committee: "After entering the Provincial Hall, I shot everyone in sight. It was a situation in which surrender was impossible. We couldn't just tell people who came out with raised hands to stay put. Bodies were strewn here and there. There were three or four in every room, and I am sure that there were more than 17 in all. The infantry unit (20th Division) was pulling out corpses, and bodies were stretched out in every room" (Jeong Sang-yong et al. 1990, 312). Bak Nam-seon, the head of the civilian militia Situation Room, who had been in control of the situation, said that there were 500-600 people within the Provincial Hall, while General So Jun-yeol, who commanded the quelling operation as head of the Martial Law Command Substation, testified that there were about 360 there (Gwangju City 1997 IV, 240). These numbers must have been based on their own concrete information. Those who were arrested at the Provincial Hall at dawn were about 200; they were taken away in four buses. This number is precise; therefore those who died must be between 160 and 400.

[69] Bak Nam-seon, who watched the rally on May 22, recalled his feelings afterward: "Citizens had their own ideas on how to solve the tragic incident, but they lacked organizational acumen to converge them into a unified opinion. Therefore it was a sort of venting individual fury and resentment over the martial law authorities that had brought about the situation at hand" (Bak Nam-seon 1988, 164).

[70] Refer to Bakhtin (1984) for the concept of carnival.

[71] Bak Hae-il, who had been released after being beaten by the paratroopers, relayed his mother's experience as she went all over the city looking at bodies: "She went to the morgue in every hospital. After seeing many bodies, she soon got used to them. The bodies that hadn't been claimed by kin were scattered around, and they looked like dried fish in a fishing ground, rather than human bodies. My mother looked for her son as she weaved through those gruesome bodies teeming with maggots and reeking with rotting stench" (ICKHD 1990a, 7139: 1461).

[72] Max Weber employed the identical logic in grasping the situation and a leader's emergence, saying that charismatic domination appears in "an unusual, in particular political, economic situation" (Weber 1978, 1121). However, in an extremely unusual situation, like the Gwangju uprising, it is possible to say that the situation calls for no special authority. In other words, an absolute community existed, and the demand for charismatic authority appeared only at the time of its disintegration.

[73] Son Nam-seung, who worked in the Situation Room after lying that he was a student, described the Situation Room chief as follows: "Bak Nam-seon showed a rather favorable response to students. He introduced himself as a former heavy equipment driver and a former member of a special airborne unit. Since he was experienced in actual battle, he was excellent at grasping the situation, he had a loud voice, and he was articulate. I would wonder whether he would make the type of hero who appears during a revolution" (ICKHD 1990a, 1046: 336).

[74] Bak Nam-seon described such a situation positively by saying, "All organizations were formed naturally in the Provincial Hall" (Bak Nam-seon 1988, 168). Wi Seong-sam, age 26 and a university student, went to the YWCA after hearing an announcement after the rally on May 25 that university students should gather there. He testified: "When I arrived at the YWCA, a long-haired woman (I don't know her name) and a student named Yi Yeon asked that I show them my student ID, and I did. About 30 students gathered. A curly-haired young man suggested that we go to the Provincial Hall. Five representatives were chosen. I was one

of them and we went to the Provincial Hall. On the second floor
of the building, the settlement committee was in session. It was
said that control over the Situation Room and the Investigation
Department was difficult during meetings, and it was decided that
I would take on the responsibility for overall security within the
Provincial Hall. I said that weapons should be under control, and
the militiamen should wear clean clothes so that citizens would
not feel nervous about them" (ICKHD 1990a, 1038: 297). Giving
a new arrival such a responsibility may be evidence that the organization was not structured at the time.

[75] It is said that IDs and passes were issued to them, but there is no
testimony as to when and how they received them.

[76] Kim Yeo-su testified that he boarded a minibus on the afternoon of May 21 (ICKHD 1990a, 2040: 505), whereas Kim Hyeon-
chae got on the bus in the afternoon (ICKHD 1990a, 2041: 508).
The team had only one bus, and the above mentioned two witnesses knew each other by name and they later joined the mobile
strike unit. According to testimonies, four members from the SWAT
joined the mobile strike unit.

[77] Team 2 was mobilized during the night and was delayed after a
traffic accident. It stayed at an inn and couldn't fight at the Provincial Hall. The members were captured by martial law troops on
the morning of May 27 (ICKHD 1990a, 2036: 489). Team 5 stayed
at an inn on the night of May 26 after being sent to the joint bus
terminal rotary, and did not participate in the battle on the early
morning of May 27 (ICKHD 1990a, 2039: 502).

[78] Na Il-seong, who was a member of Team 6 at the time, testified
as follows: "At the time of the martial law troops' raid, those who
were with me were eight in all, six of my team members and two
high school students who had joined us later. Bak In-su, the head
of our team, was shot in the neck, and I met the other three in the
military police jail at Sangmudae. The whereabouts of the other
three are unknown. If they had been wounded, their names should
have been on the list of the injured, and they should have been
buried in Mangwol-dong if they had died. I tried hard to locate
them, but they are nowhere. Then what happened to them?"

(ICKHD 1990a, 2035: 485). It is clear that the members knew each other's names and addresses, but this is an exceptional case in a civilian militia organization. According to testimonies, members in Team 6 were friends or acquaintances (ICKHD 1990a, 2041: 510). Yeom Dong-yu, who belonged to Team 3, testified that he didn't know the names of his team members except one person (ICKHD 1990a, 2037: 493). On the other hand, all members of Team 1 were friends and hometown acquaintances; they prided themselves on their great solidarity (ICKHD 1990a, 2038-497).

Chapter Four

Attempts at Interpretation
and Theoretical Problems

1. Character of Violence

Until May 18, 1985, political rallies were the privilege of university students in South Korea. This privilege was granted to university students—even those who did not study at all—because of the social definition that they were "intellectuals" and on the ideological premise that, as members of the bourgeois class, they could not negate the social system. Most citizens felt that they could not join even when they agreed with the demonstrators' slogans. In particular, workers and merchants in the streets did not dare participate in rallies, conscious of their shabby appearance. On the other hand, many citizens dismissed university students, who were born to affluent families and did not "study as they were supposed to" while their parents paid their tuition.

Doubtlessly, university students used violence as much as riot police did. In this sense, the two sides' use of force constituted a game of symbolic violence. Violence exercised by university students and police was the target of criticism, but was tolerated by Korean society. Students threw stones at faceless riot policemen clad in protective gear and broke the police bus windows, while riot policemen threw tear gas bombs and wielded sticks, sometimes cracking the students' heads open. Such scenes were painful to watch for citizens, but they considered them inevitable and watched on the sidelines. Political violence became part of the social fabric after the 1960 student uprising, and routine violence was one of the stated reasons for the 1961 military coup. The Park Chung-hee regime, which took power with the coup, however, was unable to undo this fabric because South Korean society tolerated university students' demonstrations as a reasonable form of political criticism and recognized them as part of democracy.

The Park Chung-hee regime managed to interrupt the game of violence between university students and police with the dictatorship geared for economic development. When students' demonstrations went beyond a certain level, martial law was declared and troops, behind the tanks, were sent to big cities to stop the game for some time. Korean citizens knew that martial law was illegal, but tolerated both the privileges of university students and the dictatorship's focus on economic development. The regime's revision of the constitution to allow the president a third term in 1969 was a declaration of dictatorship, which could not be tolerated by intellectuals and the general public. The Park regime intended to permanently reverse the balance of violence with the perception that it would be impossible to tackle the situation with the usual political game. In 1971, the regime issued an executive order to send the Capital Security Command troops to universities, which resulted in the beating and arresting of students. From this point on, the regime arrested and tortured students who led demonstrations and the intellectuals who supported them. Their torture, however, was not violence inflicted to obtain information from them, but an inhuman political act to break the political will and to deprive the victims of dignity and the spirit of resistance.

From this point, the conflict between the Park regime and the intellectuals who defined it as a military dictatorship and called for democratization escalated. After the 1972 adoption of the Yusin Constitution, the regime made a serious attempt to create a situation in which student demonstrations were impossible. All the government organs with intelligence functions focused on watching and oppressing university students and intellectuals who were against the regime. In the late 1970s, the regime began to systematically train troops, in particular those that could be politically used, to crack down on demonstrations. The Busan-Masan incident immediately before President Park's assassination in October 1979 was a testing ground for a new plan. At a glance, the result was a resounding success. An airborne unit trained to clamp down on demonstrations quelled the situation that had been triggered by students. This incident, however, convinced the Korean Central Intelligence Agency chief that the state could no longer exercise its legitimate authority and prompted him to assassinate Park. The Busan-Masan incident and the paratroopers' suppression gave birth to contradicting interpretations.

The state organ's violence displayed in the Busan-Masan incident went beyond the usual exercise of state power. Using paratroopers, instead of police, to quell demonstration was not simply the employment of stronger means of suppression. This went beyond putting the military drill book into practice. Paratroopers, stressed out with arduous training and burdened with an inferiority complex, typical feelings harbored by professional soldiers, and who were filled with class hostility toward the "bastards who paid expensive tuitions to attend university," reacted like wild animals when unleashed. They beat anyone on any part of the body as they saw fit, and the officers and commanders knew that it was impossible to control their subordinates after sending them to big cities with an order of suppression. The commanders were well aware that the paratroopers had received highly intensive training to prepare for the duty of infiltrating into enemy territory and that they always had their lives on the line. No matter how much training they received in suppressing demonstrators, this duty was a sort of excursion or an occasion to release tensions. The code of operation to quell the Gwangju uprising—the "glorious vacation"—vividly reveals the structural relations between the paratroopers and the suppression of demonstration. After the Busan-Masan incident, the paratroopers' crackdown on demonstrations was not only the purposeful, official use of state violence but also a carnival of cruelty in which personal bitterness was freely vented with violence.

The first months of 1980 were an exceptional period in the history of political violence. The traditional game of violence between students and riot police was resumed. Since the president had declared democratization as the task of the times, the regime could no longer repeat the Busan-Masan incident. Rather, the new military junta, planning to seize power, looked for excuses to buck the trend of democratization by inducing a dramatic scene, and it encouraged students to stage traditional demonstrations. In Seoul, a riot policeman was run over by a bus during a student demonstration. This was what the military authorities had hoped for. They must have been shocked by the picture created in Gwangju, however, when the police gave up cracking down on demonstrators, as citizens and students joined forces to stage a peaceful rally. If student demonstrations cut a picture of harmony, not chaos, there was no room to maneuver. They were confronted with a crisis, should nothing come of their plan to manipulate the media with the excuse of violent demonstrations. The hard-line crackdown on demonstrators in Seoul on May 17 was a declaration that politics would return to the normal track of history with the end of the exceptional period, the so-called "spring in Seoul." The new military authorities had prepared for the situation from early in the year by training paratroopers to quell demonstrations.

Early on May 18, Yim Yeong-nam, a student of Gwangju National University of Education, was on his way to play tennis at school. He saw about 10 paratroopers at the front gate, but he did not take it seriously and walked on. The following scene displays the character of prepared violence at a time when no one imagined the enormity of the Gwangju uprising.

There was about a 12-meter distance between them and myself when soldiers called out to me gently as if they were talking to an acquaintance. "Hey, Student, will you come here for a minute?" I was heading toward them, thinking nothing bad would happen. The woman at the supermarket urged me not to go, so I stood there facing the soldiers. Then I thought they wouldn't do anything because I hadn't participated in demonstrations, so I crossed the street. When I approached within 2-3 meters of them, they rushed over and took hold of me. A chubby sergeant took me to a tea field to the left of the guard post. He was a paratrooper with a parachute emblem on the chest of his uniform. After dragging me to the field, he didn't say anything but kicked me with his boot. I fell, and he kicked me on the stomach and beat me in the shoulders and back with a round-end black club. I was beaten for a while in the confusion of the moment before I shouted. "Why are you beating me?" He said, "You're a student, right?" I answered, "Yes, I'm a student of this school." He retorted, "We couldn't eat for three days because of the students like you. Why are you demonstrating? What do you know, anyway? You deserve it. I could kill several of you and wouldn't be guilty." He hit me some more before he pulled out a dagger and tried to stab me. At this moment, the school guard, who had been looking on at a loss for what to do since I was forcibly taken to the school, approached us. . . . The guard pleaded, "Mr. Soldier, this student does not join demonstrators. He devotes himself to sports. Please take my word." A second lieutenant, who had been watching us, said, "Now, that's enough." The sergeant looked unhappy as he said, "We couldn't eat for three days because of the likes of him. How can I leave him alone?" The second lieutenant answered, "To me, he looks like a good student who doesn't get involved in demonstrations, and it seems to be true after listening to the guard. Let him go." Then he addressed me, "You should study. Don't think of participating in demonstrations. And you shouldn't come near the school." He then let me go. . . . As I was passing by the supermarket, the woman said sympathetically, "I told you. I told you not to go. I was right, wasn't I?" (ICKHD 1990a, 6001: 1023)

The soldiers of the airborne unit were determined to get a hold of students and beat them to a pulp. The fact that they "called out gently as if they were talking to an acquaintance" demonstrates that they harbored malicious intent from the outset. At the time, kicking, punching, and beating the shoulders and back with a stick were tolerable violence in the eyes of the guard, although he felt bad for the student. It was the kind of violence that was not shocking in Korean society. Korean society's penchant for violence is partly responsible for the violence used during the Gwangju uprising.

When the sergeant pulled out a dagger, the guard rushed over and discouraged him. In other words, he felt that things had gone too far when the sergeant brandished a dagger. The officer was not surprised but gently intervened, saying, "That's enough." He did not think much of such violence exercised by his sergeants and enlisted men and expected them to act the way they did. The sergeant of course did not beat the student to carry out an order; he intended to vent class resentment and bitterness about his hard military life, rather than to lash out at students' political stance or actions. The officer took it as a matter of course that his men would behave the way they did. Although the officer intervened when the sergeant pulled out a dagger, he was not surprised, unlike the guard. When the officer told the sergeant to stop, it was not an order. Then the sergeant complained, citing his own resentment as the justification of his violence. In response to the sergeant's complaint, the officer spoke for the student in an odd way, saying that there are some good students, and the sergeant acquiesced to save the officer's pride. The officer also seemed to indicate that most students could be the targets for harsher violence.

The officer gave a piece of advice to the student. At the time, he seemed to think that his troop would withdraw after some time. His advice that the students should not come to school was a warning that his subordinates would use worse violence. On the eve of the Gwangju uprising, the paratroopers arrived in the city with the firm resolve to beat up anyone who fell into their hands. To the sergeant, it was no big deal to pull out a dagger and stab a student. This scene vividly shows that the officers came to Gwangju with their subordinates in tow with the belief that they had no choice but to vent their resentment by exercising violence on citizens and that they were willing to do so. The paratroopers' violence during the Gwangju uprising was far from the result of escalation between soldiers and demonstrators, triggered by particular on-site incidents.

The following is a dialogue in the novel *Spring Day*, carried out between the airborne unit's soldiers who were being mobilized to Gwangju. Although this is a fictional account, there must be a factual base; the soldiers' thoughts are clearly revealed:

> "I wonder if we'd end up being like in the Busan-Masan incident."
> "Fuck, I couldn't hope for more. I'm mad as hell anyway, and I want to vent my anger. If the student bastards didn't act up like that, we wouldn't have to suffer until our balls fall off. Those fucking sons-of-bitches."
> "Anyway, life's unfair. Some guys are lucky so their parents send them to the university, but they're not happy and demonstrate day in and day out, while we eat bad army grub and get trained until we are dizzy and suffer so much, going here and there to clean up their mess." (Yim Cheol-u 1997 II, 9-10)

In this dialogue, the soldiers express the intention that they would use as much violence as they could on anyone in Gwangju if they had the chance. They made up their mind to express their class resentment against university students and their bitterness about their harsh military life and the arduous life they found themselves in during the state of emergency. What is notable is that the soldiers knew very well about the Busan-Masan incident and expressed the willingness to vent resentment to that extent when a similar opportunity presented itself. The Busan-Masan incident, about which they had heard in the barracks, was a factor that prepared them to use more brutal violence in Gwangju, having tasted the pleasure of using violence on civilians. Although the airborne unit's soldiers during the Gwangju uprising did not take hallucinogens, they were imagining more "exciting" violence.

The paratroopers who were sent to downtown Gwangju on the afternoon of May 18 began to use mind-boggling violence. There was no difference among officers, sergeants, and enlisted men. It was like an event for amusement, like a party in which all of them took turns having fun.[1] The soldiers drank alcohol and carried liquor in their water bottles. They did not bat an eye while beating and stabbing citizens and did not attempt to hide the amusement on their faces.[2] They were enjoying "human hunting." If some colleagues were wounded or dead, the paratroopers inflicted merciless violence on anyone in sight as revenge, believing it was a justifiable reason for violence.[3] In addition, there are numerous testimonies of soldiers and sergeants beating those they had arrested, taking away money and goods or demanding money for drinks (ICKHD 1990a, 3047: 637; 7058: 1308 etc). There was even an officer who ordered his subordinates to kill a person because he was "too much trouble."[4]

The device of discourse that tacitly approved or recognized the paratroopers' private violence at an official level was none other than the word "communists." For example, Heo Hyeon, a 35-year-old mother-of-pearl craftsman, told how he was caught and beaten by paratroopers.

> A paratrooper sat on the back of a person next to me and said. "You bastard, what's this riot, not studying as you're supposed to do?" The man answered, "I'm not a student. I was arrested while I was on my way back after running an errand." The trooper beat him up for a long spell. Now he sat on my back and said, "This bastard is a student." It was farfetched because I was 35 years old. The paratroopers kicked my bottom with their booted feet and made a fuss, saying, "We should kill this son-of-a-bitch." . . . Soon five or six paratroopers got

on the car and they started kicking with their booted feet and wielding clubs. They shouted, "You communist bastards! We should kill you all. You sons-of-bitches don't study as you're supposed to. We can't sleep and we're going through all this because of you bastards." They were filled with a murderous spirit (ICKHD 1990a, 7141: 1463).

The word "communists" was a figure of speech, meaning that they were "no different from communists." It was a justification for inhuman violence, the kind that was not supposed to be directed even to enemies, and it was a joke as well. The theory of "impure elements" had a close relationship with inhuman violence in downtown Gwangju and other areas. Although the Martial Law Command officially branded the Gwangju citizens' action as agitation by fixed spies and impure elements, it was not actually what the military believed. It was a discourse to justify the exercise of violence throughout the county. It is likely that most soldiers did not take seriously that communists were manipulating the demonstrations, but regarded this assertion as a usual ploy. At the same time, the soldiers had no qualms about using as much violence as they pleased, shouting that they would kill the communists. Preparations to open fire on the crowd in front of the Provincial Hall were under way when the Gwangju uprising was officially explained as an act of impure elements.

More than anything else, however, the worst factor of inhuman violence was a competition in brutality practiced among paratroopers. In particular, the cruel acts that have become legendary "malevolent rumors" must have stemmed from individual competitiveness. These actions took place all over the city, and were vividly revealed in the testimonies of those who were arrested by the airborne unit. Some soldiers told the victims their names, experience, and background; in such cases, they beat and tortured the victims severely, boasting of their cruelty and viciousness.[5] Some soldiers personally explained and showed off their techniques and cruelty. Gang Gil-jo, who has been quoted earlier, testified as follows:

A considerable number of paratroopers would talk about what they did during the Vietnam War. One of them pulled out a bayonet and boasted, "This bayonet is a souvenir sword. It cut off more than 40 breasts of Vietnamese women." He then swooshed it over the head of a man in front of him. His long hair was cut off and he now sported a cropped haircut" (ICKHD 1990a, 7134:1451).

Kim Yeon-tae, who was captured by paratroopers on May 21 and dragged to Chonnam National University, left the following testimony:

There seemed to be more than 200 people; some were bloody and moaning and others had cracks in their heads. A person who looked about 30 with a split skull looked so horrible that I couldn't bring myself to look at him. A trooper was sewing him up with a boot string. How can I describe that terrible scene with words? That appalling and mad scene. . . . They were animals (ICKHD 1990a, 3119: 814).

In this case, had it not been an account using a real name, we would have doubted the story. The interpretation of this scene is no easy matter. The soldier displayed tongue-in-cheek cruelty. He was showing off brutality that was beyond human comprehension. He made his captives tremble in fear, and showed off his brutality as well as his "sense of humor." At this point, we can say for sure that violence reached a realm of art—rather, counter-art that pursued fear of death and ugliness, not beauty.

Such a competition took place not only between individuals but also among different units. Soldiers of the 3rd Airborne Brigade, which arrived later than the 7th and the 11th brigades, regretted that they had been unable to beat up demonstrators as much as the other units had done. Probably concerned that their unit would look weaker than the others, its members committed indescribably brutal acts on citizens who had been arrested and taken to Chonnam National University, and according to testimonies, they did not hesitate to kill people. In fact, some soldiers openly expressed how they felt. The soldiers of the 20th Division, who replaced the 3rd Airborne Brigade in guarding the correctional facility after the prisoners were moved from Chonnam National University, tried to prove to the jailed people that they were not inferior to the previous troops in cruelty.[6] Each unit competitively attempted to prove to the prisoners its superiority in violence and brutality. The soldiers in the regional division and at Sangmudae, who had been stationed in Gwangju for a long time, did not refrain from joining the competition.

The paratroopers handled the arrested citizens with a total lack of respect, beating them at will and tormenting them with various methods. They made the captives play games to supply excuses to beat them. The most common game was to order prisoners to stand or sit immobile, and if they wavered a little, they were thrashed relentlessly. More inhuman games included "cooking chicken feet," which entailed stabbing toes with a bayonet, and "making an ashtray," in which the captives who shifted their eyes were burned in the face or in the eye with lit cigarettes (ICKHD 1990a, 7145: 1476). The soldiers of the 20th Division, upon their arrival at the correctional facility, had the prisoners kneel, and at night ordered them to sleep with the toes joined together. Of course, it was impossible to do so. Many were pummeled and could not resume their sleep throughout the night (ICKHD 1990a, 7147: 1479). The troopers enjoyed a double measure of violence by devising games that were impossible to win. When the arrested citizens were moved from Chonnam National University to the correctional facility, the 3rd Airborne Brigade soldiers filled trucks chock-full with them. They sprinkled tear gas powder inside the vehicles and amused themselves as they watched the citizens writhe in agony. Upon arriving at the correctional facility, the soldiers ordered the citizens to get off the trucks and aimed their guns at them, saying that everyone would be executed. They enjoyed themselves at the sight of human beings who thought they were going to die soon.

Needless to say, this was a game.[7] The soldiers came up with all sorts of games and enjoyed themselves as they inflicted violence.[8] All such violence, with its various applications and highly twisted perversity, ended up defiling the human character and trampling on human dignity.[9]

Such public and private exercises of violence, which government power guaranteed and provided with various methods, were oddly linked with the military's official command system. To begin with, this type of violence did not seem to be order-following actions. The commanders above the battalion chiefs kept their distance from such violence.[10] Rather than commit violence behind the commander's back, the soldiers stopped beating, albeit briefly, when the battalion commander arrived, in order to pay respect to him in a solemn atmosphere. On the other hand, low-level commanders had a completely different attitude. They joined the privates in beating the arrested people and sometimes adjusted the level of violence. From time to time, officers deterred their sergeants and privates from beating, but in the manner of giving advice, not issuing an order.[11] The soldiers of course lived and died by orders. This was confirmed by the fact that they maintained an immobile posture in confrontation with a huge crowd on the morning of May 21 in front of the Provincial Hall. All understood that beating and stabbing citizens were beyond the officers' command. At the same time, the superiors concealed the outcome of the soldiers' violence. The airborne unit's official command system provided enough room for the soldiers' public and private violence and the officers' infrequent advice. When people were wounded or killed as a result, the commanders thoroughly concealed the accidents.

The boundary of the space where such violence took place was secured by the new military junta's official ascent. Fundamentally, demonstrative violence was established as an official doctrine by the paratroopers' crackdown during the Busan-Masan incident. When a quelling operation was delayed during the Gwangju uprising, the junta officially ordered a bold strike. The introduction of lethal riot police clubs in the early 1980s amounted to an official order that stronger violence than the Busan-Masan incident should be used. The frenzy of the soldiers' violence—inflicted as they saw fit, seizing that opportunity, under their superiors' protection—was a shameful picture of the Korean governmental power in May 1980.

To list all the incidents of the martial law troops' cruelty during the Gwangju uprising would be endless. We have no choice but to understand that the troops gave up representing state power. In a word, they went back to barbarity and enjoyed a carnival of brutality. These issues end up being a matter of human character. Hwang Nam-yeol, who used to be a teacher, recollected his feelings at the time:

> After the Gwangju uprising, I was in agony. The soldiers who went around shooting had been produced while I was a teacher. I felt a strong sense of responsibility as an educator. I wondered whether it was possible to take human dignity so lightly. The soldiers who opened fire on citizens were members of the general public and the same ethnic people, before they were soldiers. Good soldiers do not obey an order to shoot the same ethnic people, even if their superiors order them to do so. I kept asking myself whether our national characteristic was so cruel (ICKHD 1990a, 5035: 997).

Needless to say, this question is a matter of being human, rather than having to do with human nature. Involved, however, are all types of overlapping social and political issues. Various factors came into play: old problems in the organization of the South Korean military, hostile relations between the military and society that had been building up for a long time, antipathy between classes that had come to the fore since the 1970s, and the character of the regime that mobilized paratroopers to crack down on demonstrators in a large city despite being aware of all these problems. After displaying the kind of violence that is impossible to use by people in their right minds, the military at last opened fire.

The new military leaders were not surprised by the actions of their soldiers, at least officially. What is notable is that the soldiers who were not core members of the new military authorities were shocked at the time, but the officers in airborne units and the key members of the new military junta, who had served in paratroop units, were not appalled. It appears, however, that at least the military authorities realized that there were problems; they controlled the media thoroughly, banned talk of what had happened in Gwangju with the mobilization of state power, made it an offense to spread malevolent rumors, received a pledge from all those arrested at the time of their release that they would never talk about what had happened, and mobilized even generals to threaten the lives of the detainees if they talked about their experience.

There is no ground to view this type of state violence as arising from the structure of a modern state or of the world capitalist system. Although there are numerous capitalist societies and modern states, there are few examples of this degree of violence inflicted on the general public. Yet, state violence cannot be understood as a universal attribute of undemocratic dictatorship. The state's violence during the Gwangju uprising must be understood as a unique case. Understanding the particularity of this violence may be a matter of analyzing why and how public power in a modern state joined forces with private violence to carry out a crazy carnival targeting citizens. In addition, this issue may be related with the emergence of twisted human beings, or monsters, who appeared during the period of rapid economic growth in the 1960s and the 1970s.

When the Park Chung-hee regime began to feel a sense of crisis about its own legitimacy after revising the constitution for a third presidential term in 1969, it began to take on a strong private or patrimonial character.[12] Such a trend peaked in the mid-1970s when the economy and national defense were promoted by the state power's direct protection of private interests with policies favoring conglomerates. During the 1970s, the re-emergence of some figures who had played a leading role in the 1961 military coup was a step back for a modern state. State authority was under the control of a regime that represented private and collective interests, with prejudices that changed the principle of operating the institutions of state power. Discrimination against the Honam region, which became controversial during the Gwangju uprising, had become official in government organizations during this period. In conclusion, state authority expressed not only the interests of various private groups—the regime's key groups and the bourgeoisie—but also their class prejudices and arrogance, expressed in the various individual resentments, competitiveness, and class and regional hostilities existing in society and the army. As a result, prejudices, arrogance, interest, and resentment of various classes were blessed with an official status.

The Hana Society was a core group for the new military junta; it was a typical private group cultivated during Park's Yusin regime. The members of this society seized control of state power in a mutiny against the army on December 12, 1979, and were looking for a chance to exercise power. The paratroopers' violence on May 18 was based on the order of a private group that controlled state organizations, but the content of this violence was beyond the group's control. As long as the members of this private group unleashed ferocious beasts, they must have expected that it would be impossible to keep them under control, but the atrocities committed by these savages, who had tasted deviant pleasures during the Busan-Masan incident, went beyond the new military junta's wildest imagination.

Theoretical analysis of the particularity of state violence during the May 18 Gwangju Uprising confirms that national division was a structural cause of the uprising; and all Gwangju citizens agree. The possession of immense military power and the logic of security that justified every step of change were used directly or indirectly, and sometimes in distortion, in the reality of the nation's division. However, it is clearly an important theoretical issue to determine how the state's public authority and society's private interest and resentment were intertwined to create the specific case of state violence during the Gwangju uprising.

2. Logic of Resistance

There are no grounds to suppose that the paratroopers' violence was intended to trigger a larger-scale revolt by provoking the Gwangju citizens; they could not put up with the atrocities. The citizens felt that the paratroopers' violence destroyed the dignity of both the victims and witnesses. The first standard of human dignity, although impossible to put in words, was the type of act inflicted on human bodies.

After human dignity, the next standard was courage, which has been a universal value by which human beings in all times and places have judged others. The validity of this standard was clearly revealed during the Gwangju uprising. When citizens witnessed the destruction of their fellow citizens' physical dignity, they felt miserable and furious over their own lack of courage. As soon as they realized how wretched they felt, the bitterness and resentment they had felt in poverty and discrimination were awakened, fueling their sense of misery and rage. The underlying social structural factors throughout the society were mobilized.

At a certain point, citizens could no longer tolerate the rage, and they embarked on a rebellion with their lives on the line by taking action with rational courage in order to find a modicum of value as human beings. Therefore, the Gwangju citizens' resistance during the uprising was a mixture of unreason and reason. Courage manifests itself as an active standard that makes human beings dignified. Courage leads people to overcome the instinct of self-preservation, enabling them to risk their own lives for a certain lofty value. In so doing, human beings are reborn as beings carrying divine attributes, going beyond death and temporal limitations.

In the next stage, citizens met other great fellow citizens who bravely fought in the streets and formed an absolute community made of great human beings. In this absolute community, citizens confirmed their greatness, blessed each other, and experienced an absolute liberation from all social bondages and constraints. At this moment, many citizens were plunged into such an extreme ecstasy that they would not have minded dying right then and there, and the struggle changed into a festival. The absolute community was the product of the struggle waged by Gwangju citizens against paratroopers. Individuals tasted the first liberation from the meshes of long-time social bondages and were melded into the community of absolute equality. The citizens' individual identities were absorbed into the absolute community, and all fought as brave nameless warriors. The nameless warriors became a legend characteristic of the Gwangju uprising, as can be seen in Gwangju's Mangwol-dong cemetery, where 11 unnamed warriors' graves exist. Although the experience of the absolute community has rarely been expressed other than by the words "fervor" and "fervent struggle," it is an important part of the legend of the Gwangju uprising.

At its birth, the absolute community was a process in which a state as a political community was being born for human beings. With the realization of the absolute community, citizens began to wage a war against the enemy with the conviction that their own intention was absolutely correct. 800,000 Gwangju citizens emerged as a single absolute entity, and as a result, they were convinced that the actions that deviated from routine standards were doubtlessly just. They conscripted all types of materials and people's lives, demanded each other's sacrifice, mobilized dead bodies, and attempted negotiations with devils. With the assumption of state authority, the smell of revolution began to appear in the absolute community. The classes that had been on the fringes of the existing society occupied the center stage in the absolute community where absolute equality existed, while the classes that had believed themselves rulers were pushed to the edge of the absolute community and slowly began to feel threatened. In a word, the world was turned upside down. The natural logic that all citizens should come forward to defend the existing Gwangju community from the enemy gave rise to a contradiction in which the existing ruling classes degenerated into betrayers.

The emergence of the minjung was a product of the absolute community. The theoretical difficulty of the minjung as a concept of social science is to grasp that they maintained an independent character in the society prior to the Gwangju uprising. Although the minjung were a phenomenon that appeared in the process of struggle, it would be troublesome to understand them as a driving force of struggle before the actual revolt. Of course, it would be possible to reveal the composition of the minjung in the community prior to the uprising by tracing their class positions, but it is far from easy to prove that these classes had a unified, consistent understanding or that they played a leading role. The pronouncement that the minjung were none other than those who were the final victims of dictatorship and who looked forward to democracy more than anybody else is merely a post-facto interpretation of the minjung theory in the early days after its genesis amid the ascent of the democratization theory. Furthermore, it is not easy to confirm whether the bourgeoisie, who did not appear as part of the minjung, supported the new military authorities, the enemy of the minjung. Many people who constituted the core of the minjung did not know at the time who Chun Doo-hwan was. In a sense, it is possible to describe the bourgeoisie as merely "disloyal" individualists.

The emergence of the minjung was not a specific phenomenon that appeared only during the Gwangju uprising. It is a phenomenon that has appeared in the history of many countries' social and political struggles. In many other countries, the failure of populism as a political doctrine came from the error of trying to understand the minjung as a driving force, not as a phenomenon. The idea of artificially putting together the minjung, who appeared in the process of struggle, as one big class is bound to fail. Class cannot be created by politicians.

What has been problematic in revolutionary theory and its application was the narrow view in the 1980s of the minjung as those at the very bottom of the social hierarchy. Karl Marx and Friedrich Engels once said that when the classless proletariat took power, society would become classless (Marx & Engels 1973). Contrary to their expectations, it turned out that the classless have-nots could not become vanguards of a revolution. They were ghosts who appeared out of the blue in the process of a revolution but disappeared without a trace, like the "sans-culottes" of the French Revolution. The word "déclassés," which is talked about by the social democratic intellectuals who pursue stabilized democracy in modern Western societies, also refers to similar types of the downtrodden. The so-called minjung, whether in a narrow or a broad sense, are certainly a group that frequently appears in a sociopolitical struggle, but it is unrealistic to regard them as a driving force that leads social change or transformation.

In discussing the Gwangju uprising, Professor Kim Seong-guk wrote the following regarding the issue of "the driving force," the name that has been continuously imposed on the minjung since the 1980s.

> I think that establishing a driving force of the Gwangju uprising is a misguided heritage of the revolutionary theory by the leftist elite, which in some sense has an "anti-minjung" nuance. I believe that the determinism of the theory of class revolution—which assumes the leadership of the so-called professional revolutionaries or revolutionary experts, and postulates the proletariat's historical mission as the vanguards and the main force of the revolution—has been reapplied to the Gwangju

uprising against all evidence in history. In the process of unfolding a revolution, numerous people join or they are mobilized. Each individual, however, plays his or her own role, and
each stratum and class also plays a role of its own. The historical practice of classifying those who fought most passionately
and actively as a privileged group is used by the rulers of power
or as a discourse at the time, whether they are rightists or left-
ists, as part of the strategy to dole out unequal merits in a bid
to maintain the system or as part of the "divide and conquer"
policy. (Korean Sociological Association ed. 1998, 122)

The driving force may be merely a repetition of the revolutionary theory's dogma. More than anything else, at issue in the empirical dimension is the fact that the answer to the question, "Why
am I fighting?" asked by the driving force—the fighting citizens—evolved in the course of the uprising. This question was
asked after the event; when the citizens fought in the streets, they
didn't have the luxury of entertaining such a thought. When the
Gwangju citizens participated in the protest with their lives on
the line, most of them did not try to justify the decision. At the
level of consciousness, it was because they couldn't tolerate what
they saw. Bak Nam-seon, head of the civilian militia's Situation
Room, ended his testimony with the following words:

> I reject everything that takes advantage of the uprising politi-
> cally, disparages Gwangju, and looks down on Gwangju citi-
> zens. We did not fight simply with regional sentiment or indi-
> vidual emotion. When the amazing power poured out of us,
> the situation calling for it was already in place. Who can speak
> critically of us or blame us? This colossal event in which we
> learned through a single act, rather than one hundred hours of
> studying. I respect it. This is life to me (Bak Nam-seon 1988,
> 223).

In the first stage, the Gwangju citizens participated in the rally
and waged a struggle as human beings. In other words, they

wanted to do what human beings were supposed to do. If we have to discuss the driving force of the struggle, it is none other than human beings. Of course, this assertion does not mean that the struggle of the Gwangju uprising must be understood by the logic of the situation. The Gwangju citizens came forward to resist for the value of human dignity, which we do not frequently put in words. To repeat, the Gwangju uprising is a great history for South Koreans because it was a struggle of human beings, a pure protest that lacked ideology.

With the emergence of the absolute community, however, people began to become conscious of the community's boundary. Individual resentment, which had worked as a constraint in the citizens' internal process, found a new common meaning. It appears that as a result, narrower and more concrete identities, such as the Jeolla people and the Gwangju citizens, came to the fore. For the formation of such secondary identities, the rumor about the Gyeongsang Province soldiers had a big impact. In the third stage where absolute equality existed in the absolute community and the world turned upside down, it appears that people became conscious of class identity. The driving force as a class seemed to be formed from the outside as the bourgeoisie and petit-bourgeoisie were fearful of those who were at the bottom of the social hierarchy and working classes, rather than hostilities of the downtrodden toward the bourgeoisie. It was mostly in liberated Gwangju that the civilian militia, composed of working people, began to be conscious of their hostility toward the bourgeoisie; rather than resentment felt during the existing community, it seemed to be a question of loyalty in terms of a joint struggle atop a sense of alienation they felt vis-à-vis the haves in the existing community. With the start of full-fledged weapons collection on May 23, the civilian militia made up of workers and those at the bottom of society began to express considerable hostility toward influential figures.

Empirically speaking, the view regarding the motives and the driving force as socially accumulated interest and resentment from a perspective of the usual social movement does not work. Social structural problems were limiting factors that came into play in the second stage. It must be questioned whether Gwangju citizens believed that discontent and resentment based on such structural conditions could be resolved with a struggle like the Gwangju uprising. With regard to discrimination against the Honam region, the military authorities at the time pronounced that the Gwangju citizens were guilty of regionalism, and in terms of class discrimination, many participants had to go through more pain. Although it is true that resentment over discrimination against the Honam region played a large role in the Gwangju uprising, even the victims of discrimination could not have thought that the uprising was a reasonable solution to the problem. Regarding the attempt to explain the Gwangju uprising as expressing resentment by a social class, it is difficult to conclude that the working classes fought to enhance their status; it may easily be refuted with the explanation that they fought until the end because they had nothing to lose.[13] The issues of regional and class discrimination may be viewed as secondary factors that appeared in the wake of primary reactions, which were shown in the uprising's development.

The so-called "liberated Gwangju," the period in which paratroopers withdrew to the outskirts of town and citizens seized control of the city, consisted of the inevitable hours of agony when the citizens slowly returned to reality from the intoxication of the absolute community. As mentioned earlier, liberated Gwangju was not where a revolution was under way. At no time did the civilian militia or the activist youths completely deny the status of the existing ruling class and intellectuals. It has been pointed out from various angles that some militiamen, in particular the masked troops, cried for radical struggle. We must understand, however, that the masked troops did so because they were liminal entities briefly placed at the threshold of change between the absolute community and the existing Gwangju community, not because they were the revolutionary working classes or the stooges of the Martial Law Command.[14] The fight against the Martial Law Command had no revolutionary meaning at the time.

In liberated Gwangju, there was no concept of "public sovereignty," although sovereignty was evident in the absolute community when the Gwangju citizens were born as independent entities with a clear will, participants in a war. In liberated Gwangju, the remnants and atmosphere of the absolute community were still evident, but these independent entities were officially dismantled. In liberated Gwangju, there was no political system that allowed citizens to decide on the issues of the community's life. With the disappearance of such a concept, we cannot say that public sovereignty existed.[15] No entity of authority determined how the citizen's everyday life should be. Also, no one conceived or exercised the authority of conscripting citizens for the civilian militia. Although the war against the military authorities was the community's issue in the absolute community, in liberated Gwangju it was thoroughly a matter of individual choice.

In liberated Gwangju, the leaders of the existing community and the militants, the sons of struggle, wanted coexistence and cooperation, and at the same time, they wanted both their lives and the truthfulness of struggle through co-existence. The only way to maintain the two values was to get help from the outside world, and a majority of the Gwangju citizens knew that revolts in other areas or the United States' help would make it possible for them to achieve their two simultaneous desires. Gwangju was completely cut off and the United States officially refused to play the role of defending the Gwangju citizens. Under military pressure, the Gwangju citizens had to make a "Sophie's choice" between life and truthfulness. With the forced choice, unless the new military authorities were overthrown with the help of outside forces, the citizens were going to carry pain in their hearts to their graves.

On the one hand, Gwangju citizens had to protect the lives of their own and others to avoid the enforcement of the open threat by the martial law commander after encircling and isolating Gwangju on May 21 that "your hometown will be devastated" and "your livelihoods and homes will be destroyed." On the other hand, the Gwangju citizens had to defend their honor as innocent citizens, never rioters. Unless they defended it, Gwangju would become the city of rioters, the city of treason, and their children would never be free of severe discrimination. This was a choice between two deaths, and the act of choosing was to make themselves accomplices in murder. Although it was not a path they willingly opted for, the memory of warm hearts in the absolute community, felt with blood and tears in the course of the struggle, was precious, and they were determined not to forget it. The truthfulness of the absolute community's wish was impossible for those who had not experienced the community in the Gwangju streets to understand, and it could never be conveyed in any length of words.

The final choice made in liberated Gwangju was to secure slivers of life and truthfulness, without discarding them all. Instead of dedicating hundreds of youths on the altar of sacrifice to the devils, citizens earned physical life and decided to keep the truth to which the youths had borne witness with the pledge of permanent revenge. It was a third choice that traversed reality and history, rejecting a choice between the two; it stole victory from the military authorities that intended to obliterate the Gwangju citizens' souls and hide their own shameful deeds forever.

The experience of the absolute community and the truthfulness of the wish, which the youths intended to defend beyond the recovery of the Gwangju citizens' honor, complicated South Korean thoughts on, and history of, political practice. Some fighters of the uprising who joined activist circles must have seen the truth of political human beings, as was the case with Carl Schmitt, a legal and political theorist of Nazi Germany.

274

Telling the enemy from our side is the nature of politics. A political community has homogeneity as a condition, and the leader must guide the nation's destiny after making a hard decision. The usual practice of activist circles in the 1980s—supporting and obeying the organization's absolutism and an absolute leader—could have been the first lesson obtained from the Gwangju uprising. It was a distortion of the Gwangju uprising, however. In the absolute community, there was neither organization nor leader. All citizens participated in the absolute community voluntarily, and they never yielded their freedom within it. The activist organizations in the 1980s did not reproduce the Gwangju uprising; rather, they sacrificed something in order to make a certain aspect of the absolute community permanent—in other words, it is routinization (Veralltäglichung) in Max Weber's sense (Weber 1978, 1121-1148). We cannot deny the reality that the Gwangju citizens had to keep fighting after the Gwangju uprising. With the paratroopers' disappearance, it was difficult to organize everyday life for a continued struggle.

The absolute community was a short period of absolute liberation that was destined to end shortly; this is a community in which everyday life was suspended and a pure human community existed, before it was destined to return to an oppressive reality. In this community, there was no peace and no productive activities could take place. The experience of the absolute struggle in the Gwangju uprising and the continued struggle pushed South Koreans to become as violent as the paratroopers, their enemy, and to pay for the price of mistaking facts for the truth. Carl Schmitt mistook facts for the truth, mistook the obligation and reward of the struggle for a community for the human race's permanent truth, and these errors drove him to indulge in idealistic fascism. This danger exists for the descendants of the Gwangju uprising as well.

The memory of the fervent absolute community itself cannot be viewed as a blueprint of a new society. This experience was an inspiration that is opposite to our routine social reality.

South Koreans began a new history with this inspiration, along-side the pledge for revenge. From this point on, South Korean history was a matter of putting goals into practice, and it was perceived as footsteps of a pilgrimage. Since the 1980s, the destination and the name of the pilgrimage have belonged to the ideological struggle. The desire of the fervent absolute community was called the "community of the nation" at one point, followed by the expressions, "the world with no highs and lows" or "socialism." These two concepts were in conflict, but were regarded as precious partners in struggle. The destination of the pilgrimage for these two models was the Westerners' holy place. The destination was not what South Koreans found in Western history to remember what happened during the Gwangju uprising; it was already known to them. It was only after the uprising that South Koreans felt the holiness of this place. In the West, a holy place has never existed in reality, and it is now forgotten and no longer pursued.

At first glance, the word "community of the nation" seems to refer to South Koreans, but it is a Western thought, and the nation is no more than an imagined community (Anderson 1991). Unless Koreans fill it with the details of the Korean nation's life, the word "nation" is merely an empty shell. South Koreans are well aware that the word, at different times, referred to the theory of remodeling the Korean nation, nationalism, national security, and economic development. Unless Koreans fill this word with clear pictures of the Korean nation's lives and culture, it has the danger of leading to the politics of hatred, such as fascism and totalitarianism. Socialism was a utopia pursued by Western intellectuals, but now everyone knows that its reality has been negated, and it was merely a dream of intellectuals under capitalism, those who had lost their ruling stature to capitalists. Now, socialism is not a holy place in the West, but the name of an inspiration that helps to turn capitalist society into a more human place to live through piecemeal reform.

Despite it all, it will never do if the pilgrimage leading to this fervent inspiration comes to an end. It will not do if we mistake a place for a sacred destination and abruptly stop our journey. On the other hand, it will be dangerous to hasten our steps in the pilgrimage. Our pilgrimage might be reminiscent of the destiny of Sisyphus, as we slowly proceed with slow steps, though we know that there may be no holy place. If so, rather than rushing toward the sacred destination, we might as well go on a wise pilgrimage, taking a step at a time with a grateful heart. The ideological struggle, then, should not end as a one-time event, but must be repeated at every step.

South Korean history was rewritten with the expectations of revenge and salvation and the memory of the struggle period. The descendants of the uprising have a burden they must carry for a long time when it comes to how to interpret the memory, how to name it, and what path to take. The "citizens of Calais" might have embraced the memory in order to teach the rest of South Koreans to be appreciative of what they did. It must be remembered that the struggle remains as a precious memory because its core was love. Recently Korean history was complicated with the rule that the will to love is bound to lead to hatred. Probably it is time to seek a clever way, instead of repeatedly searching for love.

3. After the Uprising

The Martial Law Command arrested the surrendered militiamen and took them to the military jail in Sangmudae in four buses. While they were being dragged and also during their stay in jail, the Martial Law Command beat, tortured, and starved them to deprive them of their human dignity, which they had found as civilian fighters, and turned them into lowly animals begging for survival. They gave them tiny portions of food to make them believe that they were mere animals looking for fodder. Their murderous beating forced the prisoners to betray everything to extend their lives. Some young men tried to maintain their dignity by killing themselves, while others survived and waited for a day of revenge. Although they endured like animals under the severe beating and hunger, no one could ever take away the dignity they had once tasted.

In addition, what troubled the survivors jailed at Sangmudae was the conflict between students and the civilian militiamen of working-class background. After a bout of being beaten, the students and militiamen felt they were different from each other. The first experience of conflict was food. As for the students and bourgeois intellectuals, their families and friends mobilized social networks to send in food and arrange secret meetings with their families; workers had no one to rely on but themselves. While workers tended to help each other to survive, students and intellectuals did not pay any attention to the workers; intellectuals shared food among themselves, never offering it to workers. Students and working-class militiamen often sat apart, and their tastes were different, as were the methods they used to survive the hell. The students and workers stayed together in such close quarters for the first time in their lives. Of course, the two groups had experienced frictions in liberated Gwangju, but now they were thrown into a tiny place and were able to closely observe each other. When many returned to reality, they did so with disappointment in the other group, resentment, and hostility.

Bak Ok-jae, who once headed the Association of Wounded Comrades, explained the difficulties:

> The members of the Association of Wounded Comrades are diverse, from minors to people in their 80s, and their backgrounds are varied, from education to upbringing. It is hard to lead them, and they are opinionated because they have lived in bitter resentment for more than nine years. It is difficult to lead them in single file, but as the main characters who personally participated in the Gwangju uprising, after wrapping up the fact-finding and the consequent issue of dealing with those

who were responsible, they have become members who make efforts for democratization and the fatherland's reunification following the intention of the souls who cried for democratization, and . . . (ICKHD 1990a, 7073: 1343).

The warriors found themselves on opposite poles overnight, although they had shared a high sense of homogeneity at one point. Those who felt they were part of a single entity on Geumnam Avenue suddenly discovered that they were markedly different, and they fought among themselves.[16] The brave warriors who had forgotten the fear of death seemed helpless as they wallowed in defeatism and guilt. The gap between the memory of the absolute homogeneity and the conflict in reality could have been filled with the hatred of the United States by some and a limited political unity centered on Kim Dae-jung by others.

The conflict in the aftermath of the Gwangju uprising, deplored by many, may be a subjective perception rather than an objective phenomenon. People may have been shocked by small disappointments in real life after loving each other and expecting too much. We may have to consider that a new alliance was formed after the uprising, based on the realization that the two groups led completely different lives. What happened in the jail at Sangmudae does not seem to be entirely a conflict between students and workers. People who were jailed there until October or November 1980 had a more complex experience. Yi Jae-chun, who stayed in the Sangmudae jail as a member of the civilian militia's mobile strike unit, testified as follows:

> The most detestable people in the jail were students. Their individual backgrounds were better than ours, so they ate much better than we did. All we could hope for was a small amount of rice in a bowl that had to be shared with another person and low-quality side dishes. For this reason, we were obsessed with food, but students didn't share their food when their families sent it to them, which gave rise to a lot of conflict. Such

conflict, however, dissipated gradually as we lived side by side. Most students were arrested during a preliminary roundup, so their investigations ended easily. They sometimes helped us with filing our reports. While we were together with the students, our consciousness was raised as we talked a lot with them. We were able to see with enhanced consciousness the social aspects that we had accepted naively. At first, the students thought it was frustrating to talk with us and we believed we didn't need to listen to them, but dialogues were gradually possible after many conversations (ICKHD 1990a, 2038: 499).

It took a considerable time to begin a dialogue between the workers and the intellectuals. It appears that the intellectuals initiated conversations most of the time, conscious of the workers' acute discontent and criticism. The first stage was direct dialogue with the workers, followed by a lecture. Professor Yi Sang-sik described his lecture as follows:

In lectures on history, I talked about Manjeok's Uprising, the Donghak Uprising, and the March 1 Independence Movement. I emphasized, "We were not arrested for the sake of individual wellbeing. Rather, we fought risking our lives to realize the country's democratization. Therefore we should not cut an ugly picture by putting forth trifling matters. Although we are being persecuted now, we will become victors in the near future." After some time, mutual hatred disappeared and a sense of community and alliance were formed (ICKHD 1990a, 3013: 554).

The working-class civilian militiamen began to change, in part because Professor Yi's lectures were interesting and he taught them many historical facts. More importantly, through his lectures, the workers, who did not know who Chun Doo-hwan was and exactly why they fought, began to understand the reasons, purposes, and historical meanings of their fight in South Korean history. He also taught them why they were starving and beaten in the hellish jail. In other words, the civilian militiamen began to feel proud of themselves through such lectures and dialogues. This was a process in which the bourgeois-intellectual class took the initiative in engaging the militiamen. Although those who fought and sacrificed themselves were mostly the downtrodden and working classes, they learned from the intellectual class the reason and meaning of their fight and sacrifice. Through exchanges with university students and intellectuals, working-class militiamen realized how they were different from university students, why they had to carry out an individual struggle, and why they were qualified to do so.

In the next stage, intellectuals displayed strength, though they looked pale and weak. It was no easy feat to show off the prisoners' strength in a jail where military policemen frequently administered beatings. Professor Yi's testimony regarding a hunger strike in the Sangmudae jail needs to be quoted in length:

It was mostly university students and people who had held important executive positions at the Provincial Hall who were of the opinion that we should carry out a hunger strike. The dominant opinion was to put up a fight in the jail as well. When we rejected food, the military police, suddenly changing their attitude, began to beat us. They exuded a menacing air, saying that they would ferret out the leaders and kill them. Sergeant Hong, a military policeman, beat us so severely that I couldn't tolerate it any longer. I called him and said, "You may act as you please in the military police jail, but you cannot keep doing it forever. A man like you cannot live in Jeolla Province." He didn't reply. I continued, "I know that you are from Do Island, and your wife gave birth to a daughter this morning. Do you think you can live comfortably in the future?" He said, "I am very sorry. Please forgive me." I said, "We will forgive you if you're really repentant. But you can never be salvaged if you beat us or commit atrocities again." That afternoon, Sergeant Hong came again and politely expressed apologies. He seemed genuinely remorseful, so I responded warmly, saying that it was all right. He suggested that I give lectures to all prisoners to create an atmosphere of unity. I readily agreed and gave

281

lectures to all prisoners. When we skipped breakfast and rejected lunch, the jailers ferreted out the leaders and while beating them shouted that they would kill them. The hunger strike in the jail ended with our missing two meals. I don't remember that we were better treated as a result, but it proved to be an occasion that firmed up the unity among the prisoners (ICKHD 1990a, 3013: 554).

Organization was the bourgeois intellectuals' traditional stronghold. Language was a medium to organize, and language was a weapon for them. For the organization to display power, it is necessary to have a broad view of society—in other words, the entirety of the social relations that support Sergeant Hong and his weaknesses. Such perspective and intelligence were the intellectuals' monopoly. Working-class militiamen had to admit that they had lacked organizational power in liberated Gwangju, and they could not imagine putting up an organized resistance in the Sangmudae jail. Through a hunger strike, the intellectuals displayed their unique strength and organizational power, their secret weapon, to the workers. Life in the jail did not simply end as a conflict between the intellectuals and the working classes, but provided an opportunity for the genesis of a new relationship between the two classes, the formation of the bourgeois hegemony.

The above case was merely one example, but after the uprising, intellectuals and university students carried out such activities in a continued struggle. Their hegemony over the working-class militiamen could not be understood simply as a dominant relationship. The emergence of the working classes as the mainstay of the struggle in the late 1980s might have been the result of intellectuals' seizing of hegemony in the wake of the Gwangju uprising. After the uprising, Gwangju went through an internal conflict, but at the same time it created a community of struggle. Each class perceived itself as unique, and although it understood the limitations of the other classes and was jealous of them, in the face of a common problem, it had the capability to recognize that it was in the same boat with the other classes. Such a community of struggle with inherent individuality appeared in Gwangju after the uprising. Jeong Mun-yeong describes a street struggle during a May event in Gwangju around 1987:

> However, demonstrations and rallies were no longer the monopolies of university students. The crowds sat or stood around at the center of town, waiting for university students to make their appearance. When students emerged, the citizens spilled out to the streets and partly copied students' demonstrations that they had watched all along, but in their own style. When there was news that a popular rally was planned to address a political issue, the organizing group's phones kept ringing, to inquire about the details. Many complained that rallies addressing particular issues were not staged (Jeong Mun-yeong 1999, 50-51).

This narrative indicates that in 1987 a giant community of struggle involving the entire citizenry was formed, centered on university students. The so-called "labor-student alliance" in the 1980s was born in the wake of the Gwangju uprising and subsequent experiences. Only after the Gwangju uprising did intellectuals understand the importance of physical action, while workers and citizens learned language, organization, and social analysis. Their outward conflict and alliance of struggle were key factors in the struggle against the military authorities in the days following the Gwangju uprising. This was the very picture of the minjung that existed in the 1980s.

After the Gwangju uprising, the Gwangju citizens and the intellectuals advocated the Korean nation's reunification, but they harbored an instinctive sense of clique and hostility against people from other regions. During the Gwangju uprising, those who had Seoul accents, or worse, Gyeongsang accents, were cowed by the sharp eyes upon them. In actual actions, the Gwangju citizens seemed to put the hatred of outsiders and foreign powers on the fore, rather than love of the nation. As mentioned above, such contradictions could have resulted from the fact that the Gwangju citizens' identity shifted in a certain direction through the uprising. In the course of the uprising, the Gwangju citizens' identity narrowed down, starting from human beings to the Jeolla people, to the Gwangju citizens, and to the working classes. The Gwangju uprising was cut off from the rest of the world under the martial law troops' siege. Although the Gwangju uprising was an important event in human history, it ended up being a history of Gwangju alone. In addition to the military authorities' policy of oppression, it seemed to come from the fact that the Gwangju citizens went through the course of change in their identity. Although they shouted that the meaning of the uprising was democratization, what they kept deep in their hearts was a vow of revenge.

Before the uprising, it was a matter of course that the university students' demonstrations would come to an end when martial law was declared and troops entered. Leaders of student associations and dissident activists would give up everything and flee, thinking they would resurface later with another demonstration. This also happened on May 18 in Gwangju. Such a custom could never repeat itself after the Gwangju uprising, however. Even if stronger and more brutal troops entered, students, the downtrodden, and workers would fight them, risking their lives, and at least they would not allow the troops an easy victory. This expectation worked as a decisive factor in leading South Korea's democratization movement in June 1987. It was generally judged that handling the citizens with a show of armed might was out of the question, and that it was impossible to wage battles with citizens all over the country with the size of the troops that could be arbitrarily mobilized by the military authorities. After the Gwangju uprising, the harsh reality that violence in any form could no longer solve political conflict proved to be a decisive factor in South Korea's democratization process.

However, political democracy was merely the bottom line of the spirit of the Gwangju uprising. In other words, through democracy, it was possible to prevent the government from inflicting cruel violence on the general public, but it was impossible to realize the truth of the desire—the spirit of the absolute community of the Gwangju uprising—that all citizens be liberated from all bonds and born again as dignified beings. The experience of such human dignity could be reproduced partly through a desperate struggle with the military, which continued after the Gwangju uprising. The Gwangju citizens could not rely on violence alone for the struggle to recover their honor.

Even during the uprising, the Gwangju citizens began to look for other means of struggle, and an essential method they found was art that reproduced the scenes of their fight. The bloody experience of the uprising triggered artistic and cultural movements and social science researches. I dare say that until then Korean art, culture, and scholarship merely copied Western models. The Gwangju citizens and South Korean intellectuals and artists began to think seriously about their identity through the desperate struggle. Primarily, to the Gwangju intellectuals and artists, culture and art were means of struggle and revenge. Paintings, songs, and traditional plays were no more than paper tigers, however. The artwork intended to reproduce a picture of great human beings during the uprising, which could not be expressed in logic and words, in hopes of re-creating the absolute community and the height of human dignity felt there. Such efforts did not stop at reproducing the past; they naturally created new warriors and a new South Korean identity. Literary and art movements after the Gwangju uprising were developed in integrated forms, rather than in fragmented and specialized forms.

The involvement in art and culture was an attempt to achieve greatness as creators, departing from having been creatures. Friedrich Nietzsche maintained that art provides an opportunity by which human beings bring the "will to power" from the stage of dominating and harassing other people to the birth of supermen by overcoming themselves (Nietzsche, 1954: 1966; 1974). Literature and art may not be the tasks left behind as the dying words of the warriors of the uprising. Just as they died like flower petals, their descendants who watched them may have found the path that allowed the community to exist beautifully and greatly, going beyond the government's apology, revenge for those responsible, compensation for losses, and democratization. Only through such activities was the shell of the community of the nation filled, and was a true community of love formed from the community of hatred.

Not all literary and art movements with their roots in the Gwangju uprising were successful. In particular, considerable imbalance is noticeable in the language arts and academic areas. Poetry showed rapid development. The Gwangju uprising could not be explained with rational language. It was not easy to convey the frightening, concrete experience in logical language with the medium of universal abstraction. It was natural to first express the experience of the uprising in poetry. The political language conveying their experience during the uprising was centered on the symbol and imagery of blood. "The dirty blood," "the clean blood," "must receive the price of blood," and "it will not do to sell blood" were representative political language that could not be resolved with a debate at the time. Pools of blood in the streets and hospitals, the blood that stuck to the soles of the shoes, the blood that soaked their hands as they slipped and fell, the blood whose remembered smell made it impossible to eat red strawberries, and the blood with which people shared their lives—these were all too vivid. For vivid, frightening experience robbed of universality, poetry was the only means of communication, but even with this form of language it was difficult to convey the event's meaning to those who had not shared the experience.

In the prose and social science fields—areas of universal, logical language, which enables communication of the experience to those who did not share it—development was relatively slow compared with poetry, and also it is difficult to evaluate whether the achievements were artistically and commercially successful. This is a decisive issue in evaluating the heritage of the Gwangju uprising. Democracy as the heritage of the Gwangju uprising was achieved in return for the undemocratic organization of the physical battles waged by student activists, working classes, Gwangju citizens, and Jeolla Province voters. We need to recognize that due to this fact, even now the leading forces of South Korean democracy lack the capabilities of participating in the democratic political system. A true democracy can be achieved only through the development of communications throughout society centered on the representative system, going beyond the current politics of gangster-like fighting between ruling circles and the opposition. In the act of communication, logical prose has to be the central means of mediation, with which communications can take place between those who have no common experience. In other words, without the development of prose and academic writing, it is impossible to achieve democracy that can practically prevent the recurrence of tragedies like the Gwangju uprising.

"Our social science," which seemed to put a closure to the resurrection of the Gwangju uprising, flourished in 1989 and 1990, but since the mid-1990s, it went down the path of rapid decline. The reason lay in hastily packaging the Gwangju uprising with the imported discourse of struggle from the West. This issue was not merely the problem of the social science that directly handled the Gwangju uprising, but the entirety of "our social science" that was born with the resurrection of the Gwangju uprising. At the time, "our" was put in front of social science because it squarely challenged the dominant view of the social science field, which was in harmony with the existing ruling system. The problem was that this new stance was merely a hasty import of a minority approach from Western academia, and its logical structure was extremely crude. Such social science was no more than language expressing hatred, humorless abusive remarks disguised in highbrow words. It was impossible to produce original works and achievements with it. The current question is how faithfully we should study and show South Korean lives and experience, rather than what form to employ, such as whether we should find the base of "our social science" in Western philosophy or Eastern philosophy. "Our social science," which emerged toward the end of the 1980s, was rejected by the vested rights, but it was forgotten in the boredom of reiterating the already established stance. In hindsight, such social science was a product of anti-intellectualism, which regards intellect as merely a tool for struggle and does not recognize its own beauty and unique meaning. This was the revival of the barbarism that appeared during the period of high economic development in the 1960s and 1970s. Social scientists may have felt rage over the Gwangju uprising, but they failed to learn anything from it.

It is also difficult to say that of the language-art genre, fiction and essay were successful. Many young artists devoted their creative energy, but no commercial or artistic success appeared among the works that directly deal with the Gwangju uprising. The primary reason may be found in the experience of the uprising itself. The uprising was like fiction, with a clear beginning and end, teeming with unimaginable incidents. In other words, it would be difficult to write fiction based on a bizarre story.

In the aftermath of the uprising, many short writings were produced to explain the event and circulated underground, but the first reproduction of the Gwangju uprising as history with the use of logical language was Hwang Seog-yeong's *Over Death, Over the Darkness of the Era*. Written by one of the foremost writers, the standard of writing and reputation were guaranteed. In some ways, Hwang was able to attempt a logical narrative because he was not a concerned party. Writing the history of the Gwangju uprising was an instinctive affair. Some young men in the Sangmudae jail gathered together and started recording what had happened after obtaining a pencil stub. Kim Hui-gyu remembered the scene:

> Still, there was something that pleased me. A guy, holding a pencil stub, asked me what I had gone through and wrote it down. Watching him, I thought, "Some guys are doing what they have to do for the sake of history behind the scenes" (ICKHD 1990a, 6020: 1091).

I do not know what happened to the history written behind the backs of the military police. Many of the jailed men must have started writing in consideration of their own history and that of their fellow warriors. After the June democratization movement in 1987, a number of testimonies of the Gwangju uprising were published. Of them, I would like to mention *Flag of Mt. Mudeung: Testimonies of the May 18 Gwangju Minjung Protest*, published in 1987 by the Young Comrades Society of May 18 Gwangju Righteous Uprising. This volume deserves attention. People commonly believe that a book of testimonies simply conveys facts, but the true value of the testimony of the concerned party can be found when internal experience is used as the theme of testimony. This particular volume may be the first work that revealed a simple, frank, living history. In this sense, there may be no inherent difference between history, social science, and literature.

In writing the history and social science of the Gwangju uprising, we focused on the so-called facts, asking questions such as, "How many people were killed and wounded?" "Who issued the order to open fire on the citizens?" "Whose order prompted the paratroopers to engage in an operation?" We felt frustrated because these facts have not come to light. These types of facts consist of outward appearance with legal meaning and importance. That we have clung to them indicates that we regarded the fact-finding of the uprising as a means of revenge, as an offering to solicit a third party for revenge. The truth of the

Gwangju uprising is clear to all Gwangju citizens and all South Koreans who were part of the miserable spirit of the times. If we rely on the military for that truth, it is a tragedy. The military authorities' lies cannot deprive us of the truth. The truth of the Gwangju uprising is already ingrained in the general public, and the parts being concealed by the military constitute only a small part of the truth.

The purpose of this book was to write about the Gwangju uprising with only the truth in our possession, and re-attempt "our social science." Approaching the uprising from a perspective of social science was impossible before the publication of the *Collection of Historical Data on the Gwangju Minjung Uprising* by the Institute of Contemporary Korean Historical Data in 1990. Only through real-name testimonies by numerous people could the entire picture of the uprising be turned into a debatable form on the basis of firm evidence. Numerous books of testimonies were published prior to this tome, but given the character of the uprising, it was difficult to recompose the entire tableau of the event with just a handful of people's testimonies. The serious problem is that no social scientific achievements have come out using the valuable data in this particular volume. *Study of the Gwangju Minjung Uprising* (1990) by Jeong Hae-gu et al. is definitely a serious social scientific attempt, but the book was written before the publication of the *Collection of Historical Data on the Gwangju Minjung Uprising*. Since 1990, many social scientists and historians have lost interest for some reason. The vast *Library of Data for May 18 Gwangju Democratization Movement*, which has been recently published up to Book 15, will be another fertile ground for scholars.

Lessons learned from the Gwangju uprising are expressed in art and culture. This path toward art and culture was taken by academics and artists, but it was paved with a bloody struggle by numerous Gwangju citizens and the minjung. A balanced development of art and intellect is an essential condition to establish sound democracy and the community of the nation. Although it will not do to forget the experience and fury of the Gwangju uprising, it must be transcended, and fury must be cherished along with transcended intellect. If we lack the capability and interest to write our own history, we are not qualified to enjoy the democracy left behind by the warriors of the Gwangju uprising.

ENDNOTES

[1] A sergeant in the 11th Brigade at the time testified as follows: "After some time passed (2-4 minutes), the order was issued that we should get off. To our ears, this order sounded like an instruction to 'beat up young men mercilessly.' The tragedy of the Geumnam Avenue began on 10:30 on May 18, 1980 [actually it was May 19]. When we got off, demonstrators had already dispersed, and we had to vent this hatred on someone, but there were no demonstrators, so all of us began to search the buildings nearby, a tourist hotel, tea rooms, and barber shops. . . . After 2-3 minutes, four employees lolled on the cement floor, with their white dress shirts and bow ties gone. We made them stand up with their backs against the wall. At the time, a major who was the head of the region entered. There was no difference between officers and enlisted men when it came to beating. The major had the captured men kneel and kicked their faces one by one with his boot, using all his might" (Jeong Sang-yong et al. 1990, 179). Jang Gil-jo testified about his experience of being beaten by paratroopers: "In the meantime, I was beaten beyond description. I was beaten hundreds of times every day. When officers beat for a hundred strokes or more and left, the sergeants entered and did the same, and then came enlisted men. While being beaten that way, it was difficult to know how the 24 hours of a day passed" (ICKHD 1990a, 7134: 1451).

[2] Go Seok-nam, who was 40 years old at the time, recalled being rounded up and beaten: "I was upset about my arrest because of my innocence. While being beaten, I stupidly tormented myself trying to find an excuse to get released. I pleaded with them, 'I work in a construction site and I was on my way home to Seoseokdong after my work was over.' It didn't work. As was the case at the first checkpoint, they didn't seem to pay any attention to what I had to say. Instead, they enjoyed my suffering. They took a break after a long beating, for it was probably hard labor for them, and

then they resumed. A satisfied smile flitted across the faces of the martial law troops" (ICKHD 1990a, 7110: 1409).

[3] There are many testimonies by those who experienced such a situation after their arrest. Here is an example: "When the members of the unit died or were wounded while they were out on an operation, they brought the bodies over and said, 'They were killed by people like you bastards. You guys should die like them.' They beat the detainees to death one by one as if they were animals" (ICKHD 1990a, 7134, 1452).

[4] In the case of murdering bus passengers at Junam Village on the afternoon of May 23, an officer of an airborne unit said about a wounded student, "Why did you bring him over? He's too much trouble. Shoot him" (ICKHD 1990a, 5122: 971).

[5] Some of the martial law troops and the military police revealed, "I'm from Jeolla Province" or "My hometown is such and such in Jeolla Province." In most such cases, they committed more brutal acts (ICKHD 1990a, 7110: 1409; 7120: 1426; 7158: 1514 etc). They seemed to show off that they could be as brutal as Gyeongsang Province soldiers.

[6] Gang Gil-jo testified the following about the time when the 20th Division came to replace the previous unit in the correctional facility: "After the 20th Division replaced the paratroopers, we expected that the brutality would lessen, but our expectations proved to be completely wrong. As if they were in competition with the paratroopers, a first lieutenant named Yi said, 'We came from the Demilitarized Zone, where we cut off North Korean puppet soldiers' necks and they chop off our necks. We are qualitatively different from those weaklings of paratroopers.' He slapped our shins with a steel pipe, and indiscriminately beat us on the back, knees, and head. A thread of hope that we might be able to sleep was shattered again" (ICKHD 1990a, 7134: 1453).

[7] A citizen testified about what happened after he got off the truck: "An armored vehicle was targeting us and paratroopers had their loaded guns trained on us. I thought it was the end for all of us. Chaos ensued; some people wept here and there, and others called out their friends' names. A gray-haired man appeared and went to

the man standing in the middle of the three commanders and said something. Then the paratroopers assumed the position of 'port arms!' Only then did I heave a sigh of relief, thinking, 'Now, I don't have to die'" (ICKHD 1990a, 7145: 1475).

[8] Kim Ok-hwan testified: "There, people were classified into two categories. Those who were categorized as heavyweights (Class A and Class B) were ordered to hit others in the chest. Although infuriating and regrettable, there was no choice but to follow their directions, because a paratrooper, as he handed over a stick, threatened, 'If you hit gently, you'll get beaten.' People beat the fellow citizens with all their might. It was a sight that was difficult to watch. It was an act to make us mistrust human beings and turn human beings into animals. Those who had been classified as lightweights (Class C and Class D) were forced to watch the scene" (ICKHD 1990a, 7143: 1470).

[9] Gang Gil-jo testified: "We clamored for water, for we were exhausted after having no water for several days. A paratrooper said, 'Give them piss.' A soldier relieved himself into a glass and handed it over to us. One of the citizens grabbed it and drank as if he were drinking cold water. I still remember the gurgling sound as it went down his throat. We were no longer human beings; we were animals. I still can't forget the sense of humiliation I felt at the time. . . . We ate and went to the bathroom amidst corpses. Since it was difficult for us to urinate or move our bowels, we were often beaten while we were doing our business. Only when I gave up being human could I do bathroom business in front of others" (ICKHD 1990a, 7134: 1452). "The military police doled out dehumanizing punishment even when they disciplined the imprisoned. At one time, as a disciplinary measure at Sangmudae we had to crawl to the toilet one by one and come back with excrement on our tongues. All crawled to the toilet and returned with feces at the tips of their tongues" (ICKHD 1990a, 7145: 1476).

[10] Kim Seung-cheol testified: "What we wanted most while being there was the arrival of field-grade-level officers. This was a time when we didn't get beaten. A general came to see us once while

we were at Chonnam National University, and it was a really great break for us" (ICKHD 1990a, 3057: 657).

[11] For example, there is a scene described in the following testimony: "We were beaten with riot sticks for some time before our hands were gathered together behind our backs and bound by our belts. Since our pants fell down, they stuck a stretch of the fabric into the gap between our hands. We were taken to an alley between Kookmin Bank and the Korean Housing Bank and were made to kneel for 2-3 hours. With my legs bent for a long time, my feet ached, blood didn't circulate, and grew numb. There was the constant noise of soldiers kicking with their booted feet, beatings, and screams. Then a man who looked like a commander said, 'Hey, all right. That's enough'" (ICKHD 1990a, 7133, 1448).

[12] Please refer to Weber (1978, 1006-1069) about patrimonialism.

[13] It is necessary to bring to attention the dialogue in a short story mentioned before: "Students have their knowledge, so they can fill their stomachs even if they didn't do it. So they ran away. The body-scrubbers are resentful because they have no education. Body-scrubbers are body-scrubbers and factory hands are factory hands whether they demonstrate or not, so they fight. More than anything else, to them loyalty is everything" (Jeong Do-sang, "Tale of Fifteen People," Han Seung-won, et al. 1987, 316-317).

[14] As mentioned above, the fact that masked troops were the specters of the absolute community and also, those who were afraid of the exposure of their identities, explains that they were people expecting to return to the existing community. Therefore, they were of a special free status between the two communities, rather than belonging to any responsible position in them. They were beings who could act freely or irresponsibly, occupying no position on either side. Although the concept of liminality is used in the way Victor Turner analyzes and discusses religious rites from an anthropological viewpoint, it may be limitedly applied to the situation of the Gwangju uprising, for the absolute community was where citizens' everyday life and routine social structure were completely on hold, and where another reality, resembling some ritual or drama, was in place (Turner 1969, 1974).

[15] In analyzing liberated Gwangju, Han Sang-jin put forth public sovereignty as a keyword (Han Sang-jin, "Public Sovereignty and Struggle for Recognition in the Gwangju Democratization Movement" Korean Sociological Association ed., 1998, 60). Han Sang-jin explains the Gwangju Uprising as a struggle for recognition (Der Kampf um Anerkennnung), recently developed by Axel Honneth from Hegel's suggestion in his book *Phenomenology of Spirit* (Honneth 1995). The struggle for recognition is a very comprehensive concept, and therefore there are some aspects that are quite awkward to apply to a specific incident. Of course, factors of a struggle for recognition are widely found in the Gwangju uprising. I think it is wise to avoid the issue of interpreting the uprising as a struggle for recognition, and along with criticism of this approach, in this book; I shall deal with it in a different study.

[16] For a recent study on the conflict between classes after the Gwangju uprising, refer to Kim Du-sik's "The Process of Change in Composing the Meaning Regarding the Gwangju Uprising and Change in Regional Society" (Korea Sociological Association ed. 1998).

References

Domestic Sources

Dailies and monthlies

Donga Ilbo

Kyunghyang Sinmun

Jeonnam Ilbo (Gwangju)

Chosun Ilbo

Joongang Ilbo

Maeil Sinmun (Daegu)

Sindonga

Wolgan Chosun

Independent volumes and theses

5 Wol Yeoseong Undonghoe (Women's Movement Society for May). 1991. *Gwangju minjung hangjaenggwa yeoseong* (Gwangju Minjung Uprising and Women). Seoul: Hanguk Gidokgyo Sahoe Munje Yeonguwon, Minjungsa.

5.18 Gwangju Minjung Hangjaeng Yujokhoe (Yujokhoe) (Association of Surviving Family Members of Victims of the May 18 Gwangju Minjung Uprising), ed. 1989. *Gwangju minjung hangjaeng bimangnok: mangwoldong myobimyeong* (A Memorandum: Names of Graves in Mangwol-dong of the Gwangju Minjung Uprising). Gwangju: Nampung Publishing Company.

5.18 Gwangju Uigeo Cheongnyeon Dongjihoe (Ocheongdong) (Young Comrades Society of May 18 Gwangju Righteous Uprising), ed. 1987. *5.18 Gwangju minjung hangjaeng jeungeorok I: Mudeungsan Gitbal* (Testimonies of the Gwangju Minjung Uprising I: Flag of Mt. Mudeung). Gwangju: Doseochulpan Gwangju.

Bak, Il-mun. 1992. *Saranameunjaui seulpeum* (The Sadness of Survivors). Seoul: Mineumsa.

Bak, Nam-seon. 1988. *Owol geunal: simingun sanghwang siljang Gwangju sanghwang bogoseo* (That Day in May: Report on Gwangju Situation by the Civilian Militia's Situation Room Chief). Gwangju: Doseochulpan Saemmul.

Bak, No-hae. 1989. "Gwangju mujang bonggiui jidoja Yun Sang-won pyeongjeon" (A Critical Biography of the Gwangju Armed Revolt Leader Yun Sang-won). In *Nodong Haebang Munhak*, 2.

Cheonjugyeo Gwangju Daegyogu Jeongui Pyeonghwa Wiwonhoe (Catholic Justice and Peace Committee of the Archdiocese of Gwangju). 1988. *Gwangju simin sahoe uisik josa: Gwangju uigeo jaryojip* (Study of Gwangju Citizens' Social Consciousness: Collection of Data on Gwangju Righteous Uprising) 4. Gwangju: Bitgoeul Publishing Company.

Choe, Hyeop. 1994. "Honam munhwaronui mosaek" (Searching for Honam Cultural Theories). *Hanguk Munhwa Illyuhak* 25.

———. 1995. *Jeonnam imiji siltae yeongu* (Study on the Actual Condition of South Jeolla Image). Chonnam National University Social Science Research Institute.

———, ed. 1996. *Honam sahoeui ihae* (Understanding Honam Society). Seoul: Pulbit Publishing Company.

Choe, Jang-jip. 1989. *Hanguk hyeondae jeongchiui gujowa byeonhwa* (The Structure and Change of Contemporary Korean Politics). Seoul: Kkachi Geulbang.

———, et al. 1989. "Gwangju hangjaengui minjoksajeok uimi: baljewa toron" (National Historical Meaning of the Gwangju Uprising: Presentation of Topics and Discussion). *Yeoksa Bipyeong*, 5 (Summer).

———. 1996. *Hanguk minjujuuiui jogeongwa jeonmang* (Conditions and Prospects of Korean Democracy). Seoul: Nanam.

Choe, Jung-woon. 1996. "Saeroun bureujuaui tansaeng: robinseun keurusoui godogui geundae sasangjeok uimi" (Birth of a New Bourgeoisie: The Modern Ideological Meaning of Robinson Crusoe's Solitude). In *Modernity, Modern Man,*

Modern State (collection of papers presented at the Korean Political Ideology Research Society's first annual academic seminar), December 13.

———. 1997. "Pongnyeokgwa eoneoui jeongchi: 5.18 damronui jeongchi sahoehak" (Politics of Violence and Language: Political Sociology of May 18 Discourse). A collection of papers presented at the symposium held by the Korean Political Science Association, May 8.

———. 1998. "Pongnyeokgwa sarangui byeonjeungbeop: 5.18 minjung hangjaenggwa jeoldae gongdongcheui deungjang" (Dialectics of Violence and Love: May 18 Minjung Uprising and the Emergence of the Absolute Community). In *Human Rights and Social Movements of the Globalized Times: Refocusing on the 5.18 Gwangju Democratization Movement.* Edited by Korean Sociological Association, Seoul: Nanam.

Donga Ilbosa. 1994. *5 gonghwaguk pyeongga daetoron* (Debate on Evaluation of the Fifth Republic). Donga Ilbosa.

Gang, Jun-man. 1995. *Jeollado Jugigi* (Killing Jeolla Province). Seoul: Gaemagowon.

Gang, Sin-cheol, et al. 1988. *80 nyeondae haksaeng undongsa: sasang irongwa jojik noseoneul jungsimeuro 80-87* (History of Student Protests of the 1980s: The Focus on Ideological Theories and Organizational Lines in 1980-1987). Seoul: Hyeongseongsa.

Gwangju Gwangyeoksi 5.18 Saryo Pyeonchan Wiwonhoe (Gwangju City Committee for the Compilation of Historical Data for May18), ed. 1997. *5.18 Gwangju minjuhwa undong jaryo chongseo* (Library of Data for May 18 Gwangju Democratization Movement) (1-10). Gwangju: Gwangju City Committee for the Compilation of Historical Data for May 18.

———. 1998. *5.18 Gwangju minjung hangjaeng yaksa* (Brief History of the Gwangju Minjung Uprising). Gwangju: Doseochulpan Goryeong.

———. 1999. *5.18 Gwangju minjuhwa undong jaryo chongseo* (Library of Data for May 18 Gwangju Democratic Movement) (11-

15). Gwangju: Gwangju City Committee for the compilation of Historical Data for May 18 .

Gwangju Maeil "Jeongsa 5.18" Teukbyeol Chwijaeban (Gwangju Maeil) (Gwangju Maeil "Authentic Records of May18" Special Investigation Unit (Gwangju Maeil)). 1995. *Authentic Records of May 18*. Sahoe Pyeongnon.

Gwangju Sahoe Josa Yeonguso (Gwangju Social Research Center). 1998. *Gungmini Boneun 5.18* (May18 As Seen by Citizens). Gwangju: Gwangju Social Research Center.

Han, Seung-won, et al. 1987. *Ileoseoneun ttang: 80 nyeon 5 wol Gwangju hangjaeng soseoljip* (Rising Land: Collection of Stories of Gwangju Uprising in May 1980). Seoul: Doseochulpan Indong.

———. 1990. *Buhwalui dosi: Gwangju minjung hangjaeng 10 junyeon ginyeom jakpumjip* (City of Resurrection: Collection of Works on the Gwangju Minjung Uprising in Commemoration of 10th Anniversary). Seoul: Doseochulpan Indong.

Han, Yong, et al. 1989. *80 nyeondae hanguk sahoewa haksaeng undong* (Korean Society and Student Movements of the 1980s). Seoul: Cheongnyeonsa.

Hangminsa Editorial Office, ed. 1989. *1980 nyeonui jinsil: Gwangju teugwi jeungeollok* (Truth of 1980: Testimonies in the Special Commission on Gwangju Uprising). Seoul: Hangminsa.

Hanguk Gidokgyo Gyohoe Hyeobuihoe Ingwon Wiwonhoe (Korean National Council of Churches' Human Rights Committee), ed. 1987. *1970 nyeondae minjuhwa undong* (Democratic Movements of the 1970s) Vol. 1-4. Korean National Council of Churches.

———. *1980 yeondae minjuhwa undong* (Democratic Movements of the 1980s) Vol. 6-8. Korean National Council of churches.

Korean National Council of Churches. Mudeung Ilbo. Coalition of Citizens' Organizations compiled. 1997. *5.18 teukpawon ripoteu* (Reports by May 18 Correspondents). Seoul: Pulbit Publishing Company.

Hanguk Hyeondaesa Saryo Yeonguso (Hyeonsayeon) (Institute of Contemporary Korean Historical Data [ICKHD]), ed.

1990a. *Gwangju owol minjung hangjaeng saryo jeonjip* (Collection of Historical Data on the Gwangju Minjung Uprising). Seoul: Pulbit Publishing Company.

———. 1990b. "5.18 Gwangju minjung hangjaeng 9 junyeon haksul toronhoe" (Academic Seminar on the Gwangju Minjung Uprising for the 9th Anniversary). In *Yeoksawa Hyeonjang*1 (May).

———. 1990c. *Gwangju 5 wol minjung hangjaeng: Gwangju 5 wol minjung hangjaeng 10 junyeon ginyeomhoe jeonguk haksul toronhoe* (May 18 Gwangju Minjung Uprising: National Academic Seminar in Commemoration of the 10th Anniversary of the May Gwangju Minjung Uprising). Seoul: Pulbit Publishing Company.

Hanguk Sahoehakhoe (Korean Sociologcial Association), ed. 1998. *Segyehwa sidaeui ingwongwa sahoe undong: 5.18 Gwangju minjuhwa undongui jaejomyeong* (Human Rights and Social Movements of the Globalized Times: Refocusing on the May 18 Gwangju Democratization Movement). Seoul: Nanam.

Hong, Seong-dam. 1990. *Tongil hwaga Hong Seong-dam munjip: owoleseo tongillo* (Anthology of Reunification Artist Hong Seong-dam: From May to Reunification). Edited by Hong Hui-dang and Yun Jeong-mo. Seoul: Cheongnyeonsa.

Hwang, Seog-yeong. 1985. *Jeugeumeul neomeo sidaeui eodumeul neomeo* (Over Death, Over the Darkness of the Era). Edited by Jeonnam Sahoe Undong Hyeobuihoe. Seoul: Pulbit Publishing Company.

———, et al. 1996. *5.18 geu samgwa jugeumui girok* (May 18, The Record of Life and Death). Seoul: Pulbit Publishing Company.

Hwang, Tae-yeon. 1997. *Jiyeok paegwonui nara* (The Country of Regional Hegemonism). Seoul: Mudang Media.

Jeon, Yong-ho. 1985. "Jiyeok undongnon" (Theories of Regional Movements). In *Jiyeok Munhwa*, 1. Gwangju: Doseochulpan Gwangju.

Jeong, Geun-sik. 1996. "Jiyeok jeongcheseonggwa sangjing jeongchi" (Regional Identity and Politics of Symbols). In *Gyeonjewa Sahoe*, 30 (Summer).

———. 1997a. "Jiyeok jeongcheseonggwa dosi sangjing yeongureul wihayeo" (For the Study of Regional Identity and Urban Symbols). In *Jiyeok sahoe yeongu bangbeobui mosaek* (Searching for Regional Society Research Methods). Edited by Chonnam National University Institute of Social Science. Chonnam National University Press.

Jeong, Hae-gu, et al. 1990. *Gwangju minjung hangjaeng yeongu* (Study of Gwangju Minjung Uprising). Seoul: Sagyejeol.

Jeong, Ho-gi. 1996. "Jibaewa jeohang, geurigo dosi gongganui sahoesa—Chungjangno, Geumnamnoreul jungsimeuro" (Reign and Resistance, and the Social History of the Cityscape—Focusing on Chungjang Avenue and Geumnam Avenue). In *Hyeondae Sahoe gwahak Yeongu*, 7. Chonnam National University Institute of Social Science.

Jeong, Mun-yeong. 1999. "Gwangju '5wol haengsa'ui sahoejeok giwon: uiryereul tonghan jibangui yeoksa ikgi" (The Social Origins of the Gwangju 'May Event': Reading the Region's History Through Rites). Seoul National University Anthropology Department masters thesis.

Jeong, Sang-yong, et al. 1990. *Gwangju minjung hangjaeng: Dakyumentari 1980* (Gwangju Minjung Uprising: Documentary 1980). Seoul: Dolbaegae.

Jeonnam Sahoe Munje Yeonguso (Jeonsayeon) (Jeonnam Social Research Institute (JSRI)), ed. 1988. *5.18 Gwangju minjung hangjaeng jaryojip* (Collection of Data on May 18 Gwangju Minjung Uprising). Gwangju: Doseochulpan Gwangju.

———, ed. 1991. *Deulburui chosang: Yun Sang-won pyeongjeon* (A Portrait of Wild Fire: A Critical Biography of Yun Sang-won). Compiled by Bak Ho-jae and Yim, Nak-pyeong. Seoul: Pulbit Publishing Company.

Jo, Bi-o. 1994. *Sajeui jeungun* (Testimony of a Priest). Gwangju: Bitgoeul Publishing Company.

Jo Gab-je. 1988. "Gongsu budaeui Gwangju satae" (Airborne Troops' Gwangju Incident). *Wolgan Chosun*, July.

Jo, Hui-yeon, ed. 1990. *Hanguk sahoe undongsa: hanguk byeonhyeok undongui yeoksawa 80 nyeondaeui jeongae gwajeong* (History of Korean Social Movements: The History of Korean Transformation Movement and the Development of the 1980s). Seoul: Juksan.

Jo, Myeong-rae. 1994. "Yeonghonam galdeungui sajeol yumullonjeok gochal" (Historical Materialistic Examination of the Yeongnam and Honam Conflict). In *Jiyeok bulgyunhyeong yeongu* (Research of Regional Imbalance). Edited by Hanguk Gonggan Hwangyeong Yeonguhoe. Seoul: Hanul.

Kim, Dae-jung. 1987. "Gwangju sataeui jinsang: gija hoegyeon balpyomun" (The Truth of the Gwangju Incident: Press Conference Statement). December 14.

Kim, Jong-cheol, Choi, Jang-jip, et al. 1991. *Jiyeok gamjeong yeongu* (Study of Regional Sentiment). Seoul: Hangminsa.

Kim, Jun-tae, Hong, Seong-dam. 1989. *Owoleseo tongillo* (From May to Reunification). Gwangju: Nampung Publishing Company.

Kim, Mun. 1989. *Jjijeojin gipok: 5.18 tujaeng cheheomgi* (Torn Flag: My Experience of the May 18 Struggle). Gwangju: Nampung Publishing Company.

Kim, Sam-ung, ed. 1987. *Seoului bom: minju seoneon* (Spring in Seoul: Declaration of Democracy). Seoul: Ilwolseogak.

Kim, Won-hui. 1988. "Jeonnam daehakgyo haksaenghoeui yeoksa" (The History of Chonnam National University Student Council). In *Yongbong*, 20. Chonnam National University.

Kim, Yang-jin. 1989. *Chungjeong jakjeongwa Gwangju hangjaeng: cheongmunhoereul tonghae bon yeoksajeok jinsilgwa geu uiui* (Suppression Operation and the Gwangju Uprising: The Historical Truth and its Meaning Seen Through a Hearing) Volumes 1 & 2. Seoul: Donggwang chulpansa.

Kim, Yang-o. 1988. *Gwangju bogoseo* (Report on Gwangju). Seoul: Doseochulpan Cheongeum.

Kim, Yeong-taek. 1988. *10 ilganui chwijae sucheop* (Notes on News-Gathering for 10 Days). Seoul: Sagyejeol.

———. 1996. *Sillok 5.18 Gwangju minjung hangjaeng: jayuui bulkkochiyeo, minjuuibulkkochiyeo* (An Authentic Record of the May 18 Gwangju Minjung Uprising: Flames of Freedom, Flames of Democracy). Seoul: Changjaksidaesa.

Kim, Yong-gi, and Bak, Seung-ok. 1989. *Hanguk nodong undong nonjaengsa: 80 nyeondaereul jungsimeuro* (History of Disputes in the Korean Labor Movement: Focusing on the 1980s). Seoul: Hyeonjang munhaksa.

Minjok Minju Yeonguseo (Minminyeon) (National Democratic Research Institute), ed. 1989. *Mintongnyeon—Minju tongil minjung undong yeonhap pyeonggaseo* (Assessment of the Alliance for Democratic Reunification and Minjung Movement).

Minjung Munhwa Undong Hyeobuihoe (Minmunhyeop) (Minjung Culture Movement Council, ed. 1985. *80 nyeondae minjung minju undong jaryojip* (Data on the Minjung Democratization Movement of the 1980s). Seoul: Minjung Culture Movement Council.

Mun, Byeong-ran, Lee, Yeong-jin, eds. 1987. *Nuga geudae keun ireum jiurya: 5 wol Gwangju hangjaeng siseonjip* (Who Would Erase Your Grand Name: Selected Poems of the May Gwangju Uprising). Seoul: Doseochulpan Indong.

Mun, Seok-nam, Jeong, Geun-sik, Ji, Byeong-mun. 1994. *Jiyeok sahoewa jiyeokjuui: Gwangju, Jeonnam jiyeok yeongu* (Regional Society and Regionalism: A Study of the Gwangju, South Jeolla Region). Seoul: Munhakgwajiseongsa.

Na, Gan-chae, Jeong, Tae-sin. 1996. "Hangjaeng ihu Gwangju jiyeogui 5.18 undong: undong danchereul jungsimeuro" (Gwangju Area's May 18 Movement After the Uprising: Focusing on Activist Organizations). In *5.18 undongui pyeonggawa gyeseung: simpojium* (Evaluation and Succession of the May 18 Movement: A Symposium). Professors' Council for Democratization in Gwangju and Soueth Jeolla

Province, Jeonnam Social Research Institute, Gwangju Maeil, May 16.

Seo, Jung-seok, et al. 1989. "Gwangju hangjaengui minjoksajeok uimi" (National Historical Meaning of the Gwangju Uprising). In *Yeoksa Bipyeong* 5 (Summer).

Son, Ho-cheol. 1995. *Haebang 50 nyeonui hanguk jeongchi* (Korean Politics for 50 Years After Independence). Seoul: Saegil.

Song, Haeng-hui. 1991. "Jeonnamdae haksaeng undongsa—80 nyeon Gwangju minjung hangjaeng ihu 83 nyeon malkkaji" (History of the Chonnam National University Student Movement—From the Gwangju Minjung Uprising of 1980 to the End of 1983). In *Yongbong*, 23. Chonnam National University.

Wolgan Chosun. 1999. *Chongguwa gwollyeok: 12.12, 5.18 susa girok 14 man peijiui jeungeon* (Gun Muzzle and Power: Testimonies of 140,000- Page Investigation Records for December 12 and May 18). Supplementary Volume for January.

Yi, Gyu-hyeon. 1985. "Jeonnamui madanggut undong" (Traditional Open Theater Movement in South Jeolla Province). In *Yongbong*, 16. Chonnam National University.

Yi, I-hwa. 1988. "Jeollado jeongsiniran mueosinga" (What Is Jeolla Province Spirit). In *Yehyang*, October.

Yi, Jeong-no. 1989. "Gwangju bonggie daehan hyeokmyeongjeok sigak jeonhwan" (Revolutionary Change of Viewpoint on the Gwangju Uprising). In *Nodong haebang munhak*, No. 2, enlarged special issue in commemoration of Labor Day: 14-57.

Yi, Jong-beom. 1988. "5.18 ui yeonghyang, hangye, gyeseung" (Influences, Limitations, and Succession of May18). Chonnam National University Newspaper, May 19.

Yi, Sam-seong. 1989. "Gwangju minjung bonggiwa miguk" (Gwangju Minjung Uprising and USA). In *Sahoewa Sasang*, February.

Yim, Cheol-u. 1997-98. *Bomnal* (Spring Day). 5 Volumes. Seoul: Munhakgwajiseongsa.

Yim, Cheol-u, Hwang, Jong-yeon. 1998. "Yeoksajeok akmonggwa inganui sinhwa" (Historical Nightmares and Human Mythologies). In *Munhakgwa Sahoe*, 42.

Yim, Hyeok-baek. 1994. *Sijang, gukga, minjujuui: Hanguk minjuhwawa jeongchi gyeongje iron* (Market, Country, Democracy: Korean Democratization and Theories of Political Economy). Seoul: Nanam.

Yim, Nak-pyeong. 1987. *Gwangjuui neok: Bak Gwan-hyeon* (The Soul of Gwangju: Bak Gwan-hyeon). Edited by the Association To Memorialize the Late Martyr Bak Gwan-hyeon. Seoul: Sagyejeol.

Yu, Gwi-suk. 1992. "87 nyeon 6 wol Hangjaengeseo Jajujeok Haksaenghoe Geonseollo" (From the June 1987 Struggle to Constructing an Independent Student Councils). In *Yongbong*, 24. Chonnam National University.

Yun, Gong-hui, et al. 1989. *Jeohanggwa myeongsang: Yun Gong-hui daejugyowa sajedeului owol hangjaeng cheheomdam* (Resistance and Meditation: Stories of Experience by Archbishop Yun Gong-hui and His Priests During the May Uprising). Gwangju: Bitgoeul Publishing Company.

Yun Han-bong. 1996. *Undonghwawa ttonggabang: 5.18 choehuui subaeja, Yun Han-bong miguk jeongchi mangmyeonggi* (Sneakers and Shit Bag: Chronicle of Political Asylum in America by Yun Han-bong, the Last Wanted Man For May18). Seoul: Hanmadang.

Yun, Jae-geol. 1984. "80 nyeondaeui minjung munhwa yesul undong" (Minjung Culture and Art Movement in the 1980s). *Sindonga*. October.

———, ed. 1988a. *Gwangju, geu bigeugui 10ilgan* (Gwangju, Those 10 Days of Tragedy). Seoul: Geulbang Mungo.

———. 1988b. *Jakjeon myeongryeong hwaryeohan hyuga* (Operational Order: Glorious Vacation). Seoul: Silcheon Munhaksa.

Foreign Sources

Abelmann, Nancy. 1993. "Minjung Theory and Practice." Harumi Befu (ed.), *Cultural Nationalism in East Asia: Representation and Identity*. Institute of East Asian Studies, University of California.

Anderson, Benedict. 1991. *Imagined Communities*. Revised edition. London: Verso.

Arendt, Hannah. 1958. *The Human Condition*. Chicago: University of Chicago Press.

———. 1963. *On Revolution*. New York: The Viking Press.

———. 1969. *On Violence*. New York: Harcourt, Brace & World.

Aron, Raymond. 1967. *Peace and War: A Theory of International Relations*. Translated by Richard Howard and Annette Baker Fox. New York: Frederick A. Praeger.

Bakhtin, Mikhail M. 1984. *Rabelais and His World*. Translated by H. Iswolsky. Bloomington: Indiana University Press.

Ball, Terence. 1988. *Transforming Political Discourse: Political Theory and Critical Conceptual History*. Oxford: Basil Blackwell.

Bourdieu, Pierre. 1985. *Distinction: A Social Critique of the Judgment of Taste*. Translated by Richard Nice. Cambridge: Harvard University Press.

Chartier, Roger. 1998. *The Cultural Origins of the French Revolution*. Translated by Baek In-ho. Seoul: Ilwol seogak.

Clausewitz, Carl von. 1976. *On War*. Indexed Edition, Edited and Translated by Michael Howard and Peter Paret. Princeton: Princeton University Press.

Comaroff, Jean. 1985. *Body of Power, Spirit of Resistance: The Culture and History of a South African People*. Chicago: University of Chicago Press.

Dirks, Nicholas B., Geoff Eley and Sherry B. Ortner, eds. 1994. *Cultural Power / History*. Princeton: Princeton University Press.

Dunn, John. 1972. *Modern Revolutions: An Introduction to the Analysis of a Political Phenomenon.* Cambridge: Cambridge University Press.

Finer, S. E. 1988. *The Man on Horseback: The Role of the Military in Politics.* Second Enlarged Edition. Boulder, Colorado: Westview Press.

Foucault, Michel. 1976. *Discipline and Punish: The Birth of Prison.* Translated by Sheridan Smith. New York: Pantheon Books.

———. 1980. *History of Sexuality Vol.1: An Introduction.* Translated by Robert Hurley. New York: Vintage Books.

Girard, René. 1977. *Violence and the Sacred.* Baltimore: Johns Hopkins University Press.

———. 1987. *Things Hidden Since the Foundation of the World.* Translated by Stephen Bann and Michael Metteer. Stanford: Stanford University Press.

Gurr, Ted Robert. 1970. *Why Men Rebel.* Princeton: Princeton University Press.

Haffner, Sebastian. 1967. *Failure of a Revolution: Germany 1918-1919.* Translated by Georg Rapp. Chicago: Banner Press, 1986.

Honneth, Axel. 1995. *The Struggle for Recognition: The Moral Grammar of Social Conflicts.* Translated by Joel Anderson. Cambridge: The Policy Press.

Lacan, Jacques. 1977. *Ecrits: A Selection.* Translated by Alan Scheridan. New York: W. W. Norton & Company.

Lukes, Steven, ed. 1986. *Power.* New York: New York University Press.

Marshall, Peter. 1993. *Demanding the Impossible: A History of Anarchism.* London: Fontana.

Marx, Karl. 1963. *The Eighteenth Brumaire of Louis Bonaparte.* New York: International Publishers.

——— & Frederick Engels. 1973. *Manifesto of the Communist Party.* 2nd Edition. Peking: Foreign Languages Press.

Michaud, Yves. 1990. *Violence and Politics.* Translated by Na Jeong-won. Seoul: Ingan sarang.

Nietzsche, Friedrich. 1954. *Thus Spoke Zarathustra.* Translated and with a Preface by Walter Kaufmann. Harmondsworth: Penguin Books.

———. 1966. *Beyond Good and Evil: Prelude to a Philosophy of the Future.* Translated, with commentary, by Walter Kaufmann. New York: Vintage Books.

———. 1974. *The Gay Science, with a Prelude in Rhymes and an Appendix of Songs.* Translated, with commentary, by Walter Kaufmann. New York: Vintage Books.

O'Donnell, Guilermo, et al., eds. 1986. *Transitions from Authoritarian Rule: Comparative Perspectives.* Baltimore: Johns Hopkins University Press.

Ortega y Gasset, José, 1985. *The Revolt of the Masses.* Translated, Annotated, and with an Introduction by Anthony Kerrigan, Edited by Kenneth Moore, With a Foreword by Saul Bellow. Notre Dame: University of Notre Dame Press.

Peterson, Arnold A. 1995. *5.18 Gwangju Incident.* Translated by Jeong Dong-seop. Seoul: Pulbit.

Rajchman, John, ed. 1995. *The Identity in Question.* London: Routledge.

Rousseau, Jean-Jacques. 1964. *Oeuvres complètes, III: Du Contrats social, Écrits politiques.* Édition publiée sous la direction de Bernard Gagnebin et Marcel Raymond. Paris: Gallimard.

———. 1969. *Oeuvres completes, IV: Émile, Éducation-Morale-Botanique.* Edition publiée sous la direction de Bernard Gagnebin et Marcel Raymond. Paris: Gallimard.

Rudé, George. 1988. *The Face of the Crowd: Studies in Revolution Ideology and Popular Protest.* Selected Essays of George Rudé, Edited by Harvey J. Kaye. Atlantic Highlands, NJ: Humanities Press.

Sartori, Giovanni. 1987. *The Theory of Democracy Revisited.* Chatham, NJ: Chatham House Publishers.

Schmitt, Carl. 1976. *The Concept of the Political.* Translation, Introduction and Notes by George Schwab, With Comments on Schmitt's Essay by Leo Strauss. New Brunswick, NJ: Rutgers University Press.

Scott, James C. 1990. *Domination and the Arts of Resistance: Hidden Transcripts.* New Haven: Yale University Press.

Shapiro, Michael J., ed. 1984. *Language and Politics.* New York: New York University Press.

Sorel, Georges. 1961. *Reflections on Violence.* Translated by T. E. Hulme, Introduction by Edward A. Shils. New York: Collier Books.

Tönnies, Ferdinand. 1957. *Community and Society.* Translated and Edited by Charles P. Loomis. East Lansing: The Michigan State University Press.

——. 1971. *On Sociology: Pure, Applied, and Empirical.* Edited with an Introduction by Werner J. Cahnman & Rudolf Heberle, Chicago: University of Chicago Press.

Touraine, Alain. 1981. *The Voice and the Eye: An Analysis of Social Movements.* Translated by Alan Duff, with a Foreword by Richard Sennett. Cambridge: Cambridge University Press.

Turner, Victor. 1969. *The Ritual Process: Structure and Anti-Structure.* Ithaca: Cornell University Press, 1977.

——. 1974. *Dramas, Fields, and Metaphors: Symbolic Action in Human Society.* Ithaca and London: Cornell University Press.

Violence et Dialogue. 1981-83. *Comprendre: Revue de Politique de la culture 47-48.* Venise: Société européene de culture.

Weber, Max. 1978. *Economy and Society. 2 vols.* Edited by Guenther Roth & Claus Wittich. Berkeley: University of California Press.

——. 1988. *Gesammelte Aufsätze zur Wissenschaftslehre.* Tübingen: J.C.B. Mohr.

Williams, Roger L. 1969. *The French Revolution of 1870-1871.* New York: W. W. Norton & Company.

INDEX

Capitalism
    capitalist, 35, 264, 276
    world capitalist system, 264
    monopolistic capitalist, 35, 37
Carnival, 211, 246, 254, 263-64
Casualties, vii, x, xvii, 1, 6, 25,
    111, 143, 146
Catholic Church
    Catholic Center, xiii, xiv, 75,
        98, 110, 154
    Catholic Justice and Peace
        Committee of the
        Archdiocese of Gwangju,
        78, 298
    Catholic priest, xviii, 23, 144,
        168, 229, 232
    Roman Catholic priests in the
        Gwangju Archdiocese, 23,
        144
Charismatic leader, 164, 215
Choe Han-yeong, 243
Choe Jang-jip, 73
Choe Ung, 42
Choe Ye-seop, 138
Choi Kyu-hah, 20, 72, 199
Chonnam National University
    Chonnam National University
        professors' meeting, 170
    Chonnam National University
        Student Association, 178
    Chonnam National University
        students, xiii, 96, 139
    Chonnam University Hospital,
        111
Chosun Ilbo, The, 19, 138, 153, 297
Chosun University
    Chosun University students,
        177
Chun Doo-hwan, 10, 27, 48, 68,
    72, 79-80, 92, 95, 115, 138,

148, 150, 200, 211-12, 223,
    268, 280
    burning an effigy of Chun
        Doo-hwan, 199
Chungjang Avenue, xiii, 136, 139,
    302
Citizens
    citizens' rally, 15, 74, 175, 177,
        188,
    citizens' uprising (righteous
        rebellion), 16, 26, 144
    civic spirit, 23, 38, 39, 166
    civil militia, 220
    general citizens, 95, 129, 163,
        166, 186, 188-89, 209, 210-
        11, 213-14, 225, 239
    transportation (of citizens), 152
City Hall, x, 121, 137, 226, 240
Civil war, 30
Civilians, 22, 59, 258
Class (social class)
    class consciousness, 53
    class structure, 101
    class struggle, 33, 36
    class weaknesses, 194
    classes, 25-26, 37-38, 50-54,
        108-9, 118, 126-27, 132,
        138, 179-80, 187, 213-14,
        263, 265, 267-68, 282-84,
        287, 296
    déclassés, 269
Clausewitz, Carl von, 56, 92
Cleary, Cornelius, 242
Clown (team), 54, 139, 172, 185
Collect money, 115, 235
Combat Training and Doctrine
    Command
    Armor Academy (head), 138
    Artillery School (head), 199

chief of the staff of the
Combat Training and
Doctrine Command, 44,
137, 144
Deputy commander of the
Combat Training and
Doctrine Command, 14, 43,
76, 170, 199
infantry school (head), 199
Commando Unit
civilian militia, 148, 163, 186,
218, 246
martial law troops, 208
Committee for Democracy and
Reconciliation, 4
Communists
communist sympathizers, 143
leftist prisoners, 22
reds, 74
Communitarianism, 182
Community
absolute community, viii, xi, 85,
96, 99, 116-21, 124-28, 131-
35, 157-58, 161-63, 165-66,
168-69, 179-82, 187-89,
191, 197-98, 205, 210-13,
217-18, 221, 223, 225, 247,
267-68, 271-76, 295
agrarian community, 102
imagined community, 276
sense of community, 105, 280
traditional community, 94, 116,
127, 132-34, 190
Compensation, 17, 52, 72, 286
Congress for National Unity, 77
Conscript (citizens), 152
Conspiracy
conspiracy theory, 84, 86-87,
92-93
conspiring group, 8-9

military authorities'
involvement, 86
North Korea's involvement, 85
theory of Kim Dae-jung's
conspiracy, 60
Contradiction, 268
Corpse (body), xiv, 120, 174, 182,
215, 228, 244, 246, 294
Council of Artists for Free
Gwangju, 188
Coup d'état, 5, 48, 72, 104-5, 197
Courage, vii, 52, 117, 123, 133,
178, 191, 210, 266
Crackdown, Suppression
(demonstration, rally)
armed suppression, 20, 82, 91-
92, 239
Crime, 18, 104, 186-87
Culture (cultural)
cultural movement, 285
Current Affairs Research Institute,
75
Daein-dong
Daein Market, 101, 113, 149
Death, vii-viii, xi, 1, 10, 18, 23, 26,
32, 46, 48, 55-58, 63, 84, 114,
117-120, 123, 125, 128, 135,
152, 154, 162, 166, 181-82,
184, 187, 189, 196, 198, 202,
205-7, 213, 215-16, 245, 260,
267, 279, 293
Democracy (democratization)
bourgeois democracy, 29, 144
democratic capabilities, 24
democratic revolution (theory
of), 48
democratization movement
(struggle), 4, 24, 36, 47, 73,
78, 168, 284, 289
free democracy, 34

313

315

Molotov cocktail, 54, 66, 88, 95-
96, 112, 139, 143, 147-48, 152,
157, 171
Monopoly Bureau, 151
Mt. Mudeung, 23, 112, 224, 289,
297
Mun Jang-u, 111, 164-65, 216,
218, 238
Mun Sun-tae, 166, 227
Mudeung Gymnasium, xv
Myeong No-geun, 76, 177
Naju, 12, 124, 238
Naktong River battle, 45
Nam Jae-hui, 238
Namdo Arts Hall, 177
Nam-dong Catholic Church
Nam-dong Catholic Church
group, 201
Nampyeong, 156
Nation
(nation's) reunification, 28-29,
72, 279, 283
community of the nation, 276,
290
nation's right to survive, 29
national division, 265
theory of remodeling the
Korean nation, 276
National Alliance (National
Alliance for Democracy and
National Reunification), 40, 75
National Assembly
Defense Committee, 32
National Assembly hearing, 2,
42, 69, 76-77, 145-47, 228,
231, 239, 246
parliamentary resolution, 31
National Democratic Research
Institute, 73
National Democratic Students
Alliance, 29

National Police Headquarters, 6
Negotiation, xvi, 13, 58, 69-70,
76, 120-22, 152-53, 164, 170-
71, 174, 178, 184-85, 202, 232-
34
Neighborhood associations, 122
Neo-colonialism and state-
monopoly capitalism, 35
New Democratic Party, 31
New Korea, 36
New York Times, The, 82, 136
Nietzsche, Friedrich, 132, 158,
285-86, 309
Nokdu Bookstore
Nokdu Bookstore team, 171,
188, 230
North Korea (North Korean
puppet government), 12, 15,
41, 78, 85, 145
Numun-dong, 112
O Byeong-mun, 228
Open fire. See Guns
Order, xvi, 12, 14, 19-20, 26, 49,
55, 57, 58, 61, 71-72, 89-90,
107, 118, 143-44, 165, 169,
178, 181, 185-86, 188, 192-93,
196-98, 204-5, 212, 233-37,
240-41, 243, 252-53, 256, 261-
63, 265-66, 275, 277, 289, 292
Organization
organizational power, 179,
215, 282
Parade of death, 199, 234
Paratroopers (Airborne Unit,
Special Warfare Command)
11th airborne brigade, 88, 143,
199
7th airborne brigade, 88, 103,
147
airborne brigade head, 67

189-90, 197-98, 210, 220, 242, 258, 266, 279, 281, 287-88, 290

Rebellion, x, 16, 23, 36, 77-79, 98, 103, 139, 144, 198, 236, 266

Recovery of honor, 17-18, 64

Regional defense
regional defense unit, 194, 218, 238

Regional sentiment
regional discrimination (discrimination against Honam, 98-99, 105, 108

Religious people, 28, 214

Requisition, 119, 121

Resentment, 38, 42, 56, 94, 98, 100, 103, 106, 108-9, 126-27, 130, 141, 147, 212, 239, 246, 256-57, 265-66, 271-72, 278

Reserve Army, 165

Resistance (movement), 4, 11, 15-16, 36, 45, 47, 54, 69-70, 73, 84, 86-87, 92, 94, 100-101, 107, 110, 112, 129, 146, 171-72, 179, 186, 188, 193, 195-97, 199-204, 208-9, 222, 230, 233, 240, 252, 266, 282

Resistance leadership, 195-96, 202, 204, 233, 240

Revenge, viii, xi, 36, 56, 208, 223, 258, 274, 276-78, 284-86, 289

Revision of the constitution to allow a president's third term, 252

Revolution
communist revolution, 125
revolutionary (revolutionaries), 14, 29, 30, 33-35, 49, 52-53, 62, 127-28, 133, 135, 168, 180, 209, 269-70, 272-73, 305

revolutionary consciousness, 53
revolutionary line, 29
revolutionary situation (smell of revolution), 127, 180, 267
revolutionary struggle, 34
socialist revolution, 58
theory of revolution, 49, 53, 58
violent revolution, 79

Riot, 19, 22, 26, 44, 74, 76, 81, 83, 86-88, 90, 95, 103-5, 112, 121, 128, 130, 141, 144-45, 150, 152, 219, 221, 251, 254, 258, 263, 295

Rioters, 9, 14-15, 18-19, 22-25, 27, 32, 37-39, 59-60, 62-64, 183-84, 186, 223, 239, 241, 274. *See also* Disturbers

Rogues
theory of rioters, 39

Roh Tae-woo, 4, 36, 43

ROK-US Combined Command, 199

Rousseau, Jean-Jacques, 133, 309

Routinization, 275

Rule
ruling class, 28, 169, 179-80, 239, 268, 272

Sabuk miners' uprising, 128

Sangmu Gymnasium, 66, 182, 240

Sangmudae
Sangmudae jail, 279, 281-82, 288
(Sangmudae) military police, 248, 281, 289, 293-94
Sangmudae jail, 279, 281-82, 288

Sansu-dong, 109, 153, 236

Scarce good, 132

Homa & Sekey Books Titles on Korea (1)

East and West: Fusion of Horizons
By Kwang-Sae Lee, Kent State University
ISBN 1931907269, Order No 1030, 6 x 9, Hardcover, $59.95, £35.00
ISBN 1931907331, Order No 1041, 6 x 9, Paperback, $34.95, £22.00
Philosophy/Culture/Comparative Studies, 2006, xii, 522pp

**A Topography of Confucian Discourse: Politico-philosophical
Reflections on Confucian Discourse since Modernity**
By Lee Seung-hwan, Korea University
ISBN 1931907277, Order No 1031, 6 x 9, Hardcover, $49.95, £30.00
ISBN 193190734X, Order No 1042, 6 x 9, Paperback, $29.95, £19.00
History/Culture/Philosophy, 2006, xii, 260pp

**Developmental Dictatorship and the Park Chung-hee Era:
The Shaping of Modernity in the Republic of Korea**
Edited by Lee Byeong-Cheon, Kangwon National University
ISBN 1931907285, Order No 1032, 6 x 9, Hardcover, $54.95, £32.00
ISBN 1931907358, Order No 1043, 6 x 9, Paperback, $32.95, £20.00
History/Politics, 2006, xviii, 384pp

**The Gwangju Uprising: The Pivotal Democratic Movement
That Changed the History of Modern Korea**
By Choi Jung-woon, Seoul National University
ISBN 1931907293, Order No 1033, 6 x 9, Hardcover, $49.95, £31.00
ISBN 1931907366, Order No 1044, 6 x 9, Paperback, $29.95, £19.00
History/Politics, 2006, xx, 326pp

**The Land of Scholars:
Two Thousand Years of Korean Confucianism**
By Kang Jae-Un
ISBN 1931907307, Order No 1034, 6 x 9, Hardcover, $59.95, £35.00
ISBN 1931907374, Order No 1045, 6 x 9, Paperback, $34.95, £22.00
History/Culture/Philosophy, 2006, xxx, 516pp

Korea's Pastimes and Customs: A Social History
By Lee E-Wha. 16 pages of color photos. B&W illustrations throughout.
ISBN 1931907382, Order No 1035, 6 x 9, Paperback, $29.95, £21.00
History/Culture, 2006, x, 264pp

Homa & Sekey Books Titles on Korea (2)

A Love Song for the Earnest: Selected Poems of Shin Kyungrim
ISBN: 1931907390, Order No 1037, 5 ½ x 8 ½, Paperback
Poetry, $11.95, 2006

Cracking the Shell: Three Korean Ecopoets
By Seungho Choi, Chiha Kim, and Hyonjong Chong
ISBN: 1931907404, Order No 1038, 5 ½ x 8 ½, Paperback
Poetry, $12.95, 2006

Sunrise over the East Sea: Selected Poems of Park Hi-jin
ISBN: 1931907412, Order No 1039, 5 ½ x 8 ½, Paperback
Poetry, $10.95, 2006

Fragrance of Poetry: Korean-American Literature.
Ed. by Yearn Hong Choi, Ph.D., 5 ½ x 8 ½, Paperback, 108pp
ISBN: 1931907226, Order No. 1027, **Poetry**, $13.95, 2005

A Floating City on the Water: A Novel by Jang-Soon Sohn
ISBN: 1931907188, Order No: 1025, 5½ x 8½, Paperback, 178pp
Fiction, $14.95, 2005

Korean Drama Under Japanese Occupation:
Plays by Ch'i-jin Yu & Man-sik Ch'ae, 5½ x 8½, Paperback, 178pp
ISBN: 193190717X, Order No: 1026, **Drama**, $16.95, 2004

The Curse of Kim's Daughters: A Novel By Park Kyong-ni
ISBN: 1931907102, Order No: 1018, 5½ x 8½, Paperback, 299pp
Fiction, $18.95, 2004

I Want to Hijack an Airplane: Selected Poems of Kim Seung-Hee
ISBN: 1931907137, Order No: 1021, 5½ x 8½, Paperback, 208pp
Poetry, $15.95, 2004

Flowers in the Toilet Bowl: Selected Poems of Choi Seungho
ISBN: 1931907110, Order No: 1022, 5½ x 8½, Paperback, 112pp
Poetry, $12.95, 2004

Drawing Lines: Selected Poems of Moon Dok-su
ISBN: 1931907129, Order No: 1023, 5½ x 8½, Paperback, 112pp
Poetry, $11.95, 2004

Homa & Sekey Books Titles on Korea (3)

What the Spider Said: Poems of Chang Soo Ko
ISBN: 1931907145, Order No: 1024, 5½ x 8½, Paperback, 96pp
Poetry, $10.95, 2004

Surfacing Sadness:
A Centennial of Korean-American Literature 1903-2003
Ed. by Yearn Hong Choi, Ph.D & Haeng Ja Kim
ISBN: 1931907099, Order No: 1017, 6 x 9, Hardcover, 224pp
Asian-American Studies/Literature, $25.00, 2003

Father and Son: A Novel by Han Sung-won,
ISBN: 1931907048, Order No: 1010, 5½ x 8½, Paperback, 285pp, 2002,
Fiction, $17.95

Reflections on a Mask: Two Novellas by Ch'oe In-hun.
ISBN: 1931907056, Order No: 1011, 5½ x 8½, Paperback, 258pp, 2002,
Fiction, $16.95

Unspoken Voices: Selected Short Stories by Korean Women Writers
By Park Kyong-ni, et al.
ISBN: 1931907064, Order No: 1012, 5½ x 8½, Paperback, 266pp, 2002,
Fiction, $16.95

The General's Beard: Two Novellas by Lee Oyoung,
ISBN: 1931907072, Order No: 1013, 5½ x 8½, Paperback, 182pp, 2002,
Fiction, $14.95

Farmers: A Novel by Lee Mu-young,
ISBN: 1931907080, Order No: 1014, 5½ x 8½, Paperback, 216pp, 2002,
Fiction, $15.95

www.homabooks.com

Ordering Information: Within U.S.: $5.00 for the first item, $1.50 for each additional item. **Outside U.S.:** $10.00 for the first item, $5.00 for each additional item. All major credit cards accepted. You may also send a check or money order in U.S. fund (payable to Homa & Sekey Books) to: Orders Department, Homa & Sekey Books, 138 Veterans Plaza, P. O. Box 103, Dumont, NJ 07628 U.S.A. Tel: 800-870-HOMA, 201-261-8810; Fax: 201-261-8890, 201-384-6055; Email: info@homabooks.com

CPSIA information can be obtained
at www.ICGtesting.com
Printed in the USA
BVHW070126140620
581354BV00001B/35